BILLY, ALFRED, AND GENERAL MOTORS

BILLY, ALFRED, AND GENERAL MOTORS

THE STORY OF TWO UNIQUE MEN, A LEGENDARY COMPANY, AND A REMARKABLE TIME IN AMERICAN HISTORY

William Pelfrey

AMACOM AMERICAN MANAGEMENT ASSOCIATION

New York ■ Atlanta ■ Brussels ■ Chicago ■ Mexico City ■ San Francisco
Shanghai ■ Tokyo ■ Toronto ■ Washington, D.C.

Special discounts on bulk quantities of AMACOM books are
available to corporations, professional associations, and other
organizations. For details, contact Special Sales Department,
AMACOM, a division of American Management Association,
1601 Broadway, New York, NY 10019.
Tel.: 212-903-8316. Fax: 212-903-8083.
Website: www.amacombooks.org

This publication is designed to provide accurate and authoritative
information in regard to the subject matter covered. It is sold with the
understanding that the publisher is not engaged in rendering legal,
accounting, or other professional service. If legal advice or other
expert assistance is required, the services of a competent professional
person should be sought.

Rolls Royce is a registered trademark exclusively licensed to Rolls-
Royce Motor Cars Ltd.

Library of Congress Cataloging-in-Publication Data

Pelfrey, William.
    Billy, Alfred, and General Motors: the story of two unique men, a
legendary company, and a remarkable time in American history /
William Pelfrey.
        p.   cm.
    Includes bibliographical references and index.
    ISBN 0-8144-0869-9
    1. General Motors Corporation—History.   2. Automobile industry and
trade—United States—History.   3. Businesspeople—United States—
Biography.   4. Durant, William Crapo, 1861–1947.   5. Sloan, Alfred P.
(Alfred Pritchard), 1875–1966.   I. Title.

    HD9710.U54G47544   2006
    338.7'6292'—dc22   2005024657

Printing number

10   9   8   7   6   5   4   3   2   1

For Lilia, my Believer

CONTENTS

ACKNOWLEDGMENTS

I WANT TO THANK Deirdre Crowley and Tallulah Crowley, for their visionary prodding and confidence as well as their keen editorial eyes; Lt. Col. Terence Doherty (ret.), for his friendship and support, going back to our days in the Pearl of Punjab; CSM Ron Soden (ret.), for his living example of the leadership creed of "Deeds, Not Words" at a best-forgotten place called LZ Jude; and John Roach, for his insightful comments on the proposal that led to the writing of this book. Special gratitude goes to my agent, Nina Graybill, who saw potential in the story where others didn't, and to my editor, Adrienne Hickey, at AMACOM Books, whose enthusiasm, hard work, and patient nurturing made the book a reality. Above all else, I thank my wife Lilia for her love and faith during a most bizarre and unpredictable career.

A NOTE ON SOURCES AND PERMISSIONS

IN ADDITION TO works cited in the bibliography, *Billy, Alfred, and General Motors* draws heavily on company documents kept at General Motors Corporation's Detroit headquarters and personal papers left by Billy Durant that are now in Kettering University's Scharchburg Archives in Flint, Michigan. The author was given generous and gracious access to both sources. Special thanks go to General Motors research librarian Suzanne Petre and her colleague Joanne Rutkowski in Detroit and to Scharchburg archivist David White and his teammate Carolyn Phillips in Flint.

The first five photographs (three Billy Durant portraits, Raymere estate, and Catherine Lederer Durant) are from the Scharchburg Archives at Kettering University and are used with its permission. All other photographs are from the GM Media Archives, General Motors Corporation, and used with its permission. Special thanks go to David White at the Scharchburg Archives and Larry Kinsel at the GM Media Archives.

Passages from Alfred Sloan's *My Years with General Motors* are quoted with permission from the Harold Matson Literary Agency, Inc.

INTRODUCTION

WHAT THEY WROUGHT

They were opposites in all respects. William C. (Billy) Durant, the high school dropout, was the flamboyant dreamer and gambler, focused on personal relationships and risk. Alfred P. Sloan, Jr., the MIT engineer, was the stern organizer and manager, focused on data and logic (not to mention profit). Billy managed to create General Motors in bold defiance of the industrial and financial powers of his day. Alfred went on to transform it into the largest and most successful enterprise the world had ever seen. Today, for better or worse, executives and employees all over the globe, in all kinds of businesses, are dealing with the effects of precedents set in motion by what these two men wrought in the first half of the twentieth century.

Their business legacies, like their lives, are studies in contrast. Billy was done in by his own wizardry in expanding his empire through financial manipulation and speculation. Alfred mastered both the art of corporate vision and the science of nuts-and-bolts management; yet his tragic failure to understand the changing nature of the relationships between employee, company, and government left a legacy of resentment and mistrust that remains unresolved today.

The contrasting character, struggles, and triumphs of the two men show clearly, hauntingly, in their last official oil portraits. Billy Durant, GM's founder, is seated, wearing a wrinkled black suit that looks too big for him. He is gazing slightly off to the side with a squint rather than directly at the artist. His thin, tense smile is that of a man who knows the meaning of adversity firsthand; a man who still has pride but is no longer quite sure how far to trust those looking upon him. Alfred Sloan, the successor, is standing ramrod straight, wearing a bluish-gray suit that is perfectly tailored and buttoned. He is neither smiling nor frowning but looking directly (slightly down) at the artist, unashamed to be in command and at ease with himself and the world, holding a memo in his left hand.

In the year 1904, when Billy Durant ventured into the automobile business at the urging of friends, the average life expectancy in the United States was forty-seven years; only 14 percent of households had bathtubs; the average wage was twenty-two cents an hour; and there were only 8,000 motor vehicles in the country, with a total of just 144 miles of paved road to drive them on. New York City's streets were polluted with the manure of more than a hundred thousand horse-drawn hacks. Some fifty years later, when Alfred Sloan was putting together a team to write his story, wages had risen by a factor of close to thirty; most working Americans looked forward to retirement with a pension after the age of sixty-five; a nationwide interstate highway system was about to bring new meaning to mobility; and the juggernaut called General Motors was dominating every market it entered, influencing American manufacturing and marketing like no other company ever had or would again. Billy and Alfred had wrought not only the largest but one of the most misunderstood enterprises in the annals of business.

Billy died quietly in New York City on March 18, 1947, five years after suffering a stroke in a hotel room in Flint, Michigan, the town he had put on the map. Eighty-five years old, he had been reduced to living off the secret charity of Alfred and three other former business associates (all of whom had been brought onto the General's board of directors by Durant) in a Gramercy Park apartment. Apart from creating General Motors and losing control of it not once but twice, he had amassed and lost several personal fortunes. When he finally declared bankruptcy, after losing all in the stock market crash of 1929 and the Great Depression, he listed his total assets at $250, the value of the clothes on his back.

Billy's obituaries, not surprisingly, focused on his spectacular fall rather than what he had contributed to the auto industry and the art of management. The *New York Times* mentioned only that he had been responsible for "the building up of General Motors." In fact, he had created the company single-handedly. Also unmentioned was Billy's role in revitalizing and transforming Flint, Michigan, a former lumber center and modest agricultural community, into one of the nation's key industrial cities. One of the local Flint jokes the year he died was:

Q. How many states does the United States have now?
A. Forty-seven. Tennessee has moved to Flint.

In contrast, Alfred Sloan's name remained synonymous with success and big business for more than four decades. By the 1950s, with Alfred still serving as chairman of the General Motors board of directors, television host Dinah Shore was striking a chord in every American household when she sang, "See the USA in your Chevrolet." Thanks to the Sloan team's mastery of the annual model change, retail finance, and mass marketing, everyone yearned to buy next year's model and was embarrassed to drive last year's; and the world would never be the same.

When Alfred died in 1966, at the age of ninety, all of the obituaries focused on how he had led General Motors to such heights. Under his leadership, the company's share of the U.S. automobile market had risen from 12 percent to 52 percent. Its organizational structure and product strategy were emulated by corporations around the world. Its annual revenues surpassed the annual gross national product of half the world's countries.

Unlike Alfred, who had amassed a wealth of corporate documents, press clippings, and official correspondence for his private twenty-person research team to draw upon in compiling his own version of his contributions to management in the bestselling (ghostwritten) *My Years with General Motors,* Billy left only scattered and sketchy reminiscences of all his successes and disappointments. Most of his recollections are in an often-incoherent, incomplete, forty-five-page typed monograph entitled "The True Story of General Motors." It was clearly intended to defend his legacy from the charges and assumptions of his legions of critics and enemies, including Alfred Sloan, but was never finished or published. Durant's other papers are randomly collected letters, memoranda, and news clippings.

In December 1941, when Billy Durant was eighty years old, he sent part of the manuscript to his daughter Margery for review. In his cover letter, he told her, "Most of the stories now for public consumption lean to the sensational and do not favor the factual. While I cannot be accused of being a brilliant writer, the True Story will be based entirely on facts. I still am unable to thank you for what you have done for me."[1]

His emphasis on the "factual" was, ironically, right in line with Alfred Sloan's own public philosophy. Sloan's most constant criticism of Durant was that he acted on instinct and whim rather than facts. Yet the achievements and decisions of Durant the dreamer were what made Sloan the manager's spectacular career possible.

This book is neither an expose nor a company-sanctioned "official" history. Rather, it is an attempt to provide a fresh look at the possibilities and the obstacles the two men dealt with: how they viewed events through very different lenses, and how their conflicting yet groundbreaking definitions of what a corporation should be have influenced the way all large companies today deal with employees, investors, and governments. It was researched primarily from three sources: papers left by Durant and now stored at Kettering University's Scharchburg Archives in Flint, Michigan; policy edicts, speeches, and pamphlets left by Alfred Sloan and now stored in General Motors' corporate archives in Detroit; and dozens of little-known and long out-of-print articles, memoirs, and biographies of the two men and their contemporaries (including Henry Ford) published in the 1920s and 1930s.

Today, the corporate world is typified more than ever by acquisitions, integration, and constant consolidation, a process that Billy Durant mastered with the creation of General Motors in 1908. At the same time, business theorists, executives, and investors alike are questioning whether the structures and policies established by Alfred Sloan have become barriers rather than enablers of speed and innovation in the twenty-first century. Leaders in all kinds and sizes of companies are attempting to redefine their enterprises in a world far more complex, interdependent, and uncertain than either Billy or Alfred could have envisioned. They are also still struggling to resolve (or at least balance) many of the same core issues Billy and Alfred faced. As the drama continues, and as those leaders and companies look for new insight about what works and what doesn't, the story of the ascendance of Billy, Alfred, and their General is more relevant (and more filled with lessons) than ever.

How had it all come about, and how could their individual fates have been so different even as their beloved General Motors soared?

The answers remain as complex as they are worth pondering. As Sloan himself observed, "The perpetuation of an unusual success or the maintenance of an unusually high standard of leadership in any industry is sometimes more difficult than the attainment of that success or leadership in the first place. That is the greatest challenge to be met by the leader in any industry."[2]

BILLY, ALFRED, AND GENERAL MOTORS

CHAPTER | **ONE**

1920: The Fateful Year

IT WAS THE YEAR of decision for Alfred Pritchard Sloan, Jr., the gangly, introverted executive with a Brooklyn accent who was on his way to becoming one of the greatest business legends of all time. Within the next three years, Alfred would be credited with the salvation and turnaround of General Motors. From there, he would go on to be hailed as the father of the modern corporation, the master of consumer mass marketing, and the most effective chief executive officer ever.

All of that lay far ahead in the unknown future that fateful summer of 1920, when Sloan had had enough of his former mentor Billy Durant and was contemplating quitting the company that was to become the definition of his own life.

On the surface, things could not have been going better for Alfred that summer. Wealthy beyond his own dreams, he was a General Motors vice president and a member of its board of directors. General Motors itself was the company everyone was watching on Wall Street. Sloan was also universally regarded as one of the most

astute and capable up-and-coming executives in the entire automobile industry, which had become a crucial force in America's economy and seemed poised for even more unprecedented growth.

The General Motors annual report to stockholders for 1920 included a succinct but bullish assessment of the automobile's growth
and its importance:

> Records show that the first garage for the storage and repair of motor
> cars was opened in Boston, Massachusetts, in the spring of 1899. In
> that year the investment in the industry was $5,768,000, with a produc-
> tion of 3,700 cars, while in 1919 the investment was estimated at
> $1,800,000,000 and car production at 1,974,300, a three hundred fold
> growth in capital during the twenty years and a five hundred fold in-
> crease in cars manufactured.

The report went on to note that employment in the industry had
grown from a little over 13,000 people in 1904 (the year General
Motors' founder Billy Durant turned his full attention to the automobile) to more than 651,000 in 1919. That was a 5,000 percent
increase. During the same period, annual wages in the industry
had grown from less than $8.5 million to more than $2 billion. Automotive production ranked number one among the nation's top-ten
industries. Men's and women's clothing was a distant second, followed by coal, hay (yes, hay!), construction, mining for metals,
wheat, cotton, pig iron, and petroleum.

In short, the automobile had become the place to be, and Sloan
was close to the driver's seat.

Yet Alfred Sloan was more uncertain about his future than he
had ever been. Despite his own success and the sunny horizons that
appeared to be ahead, he saw growing problems where others seemingly failed to see anything beyond a constant flow of black ink and
revenue growth. While he felt a moral obligation to stick with and
help the enterprise that had given him his greatest opportunity, he
also believed the enterprise was threatened by the leadership fail-
ings of its visionary founder, who also happened to be the man who
had hired him.

In Sloan's mind, high-flying Billy Durant had fallen victim to
the news media's glowing headlines and his own boundless dreams
(as would dozens of other founders of even higher-flying start-ups
many years later). Sloan was convinced that too much of General

Motors' growth had been financed through the issuance of stock and Billy's personal charm, rather than through cash and hard assets. He was also convinced that the dozens of separate business units within the company were out of control. He saw duplication and lack of accountability in all product lines, staffs, and plants; and he blamed it on the lack of clear and firm policies from the central office.

Although Sloan was aware that fellow executives and employees viewed Billy as a genius, he was certain that none of them really knew just how each business unit within General Motors fit with the others, let alone how much each was spending and borrowing or how much total debt was on the books. Each of the company's five largest automobile divisions (Buick, Oldsmobile, Cadillac, Chevrolet, and Oakland) would have been a fully integrated manufacturer and marketer in its own right if split off from General Motors. Yet, rather than leverage each unit's strengths to create distinctive brands and enhance the marketing and manufacturing efficiency and effectiveness of the entire enterprise, Durant was letting each division run largely on its own, with internal competition ignored if not encouraged.

What was Alfred to do? Voice his concerns to the founder and risk losing his influence and ability to affect change from within the company? Quit? Or bide his time and hope that if the crisis did come, the company would be able to survive long enough for a new management to right the course?

His answer would make him a legend and forever change the structure and direction of American business, for better or worse.

AMERICA AND THE GENERAL ON A ROLL

While Alfred gnashed his teeth, Billy Durant and the rest of America remained confident in what that year's Republican Party presidential candidate, Warren G. Harding, called the return to "normalcy," the word he invented accidentally when stumbling over *normality.* In his famous campaign stump speech, Harding nailed the mood of the country, proclaiming, "America's need is not heroics but healing, not nostrums but normalcy, not revolution but restoration . . . not surgery but serenity."

There was little outcry when the Ku Klux Klan launched an unprecedented (and successful) nationwide recruitment drive the year Harding was elected. Nor was there much concern that the mercurial Henry Ford, universally regarded as the most innovative and savvy industrialist of the day, was using his own wholly owned weekly newspaper, the *Dearborn Independent,* to spread his belief that all the nation's ills were caused by Jews.

Progressivism on all fronts—political, social, and economic—was a far more resonant theme with most Americans than were the Klan and Ford's hatred and paranoia. For the first time ever, more people in the United States were living in cities than on farms. Despite the passage of the Eighteenth Amendment to the U.S. Constitution the previous year, banning the sale and drinking of alcohol, women's skirts were getting shorter and bootleg liquor was ubiquitous. A new term, "the Jazz Age," was in vogue to describe the hedonistic tastes of a generation determined to put memories of war and doing-without behind it. Women had just been given the right to vote, and the sky had failed to fall as a result.

The faults that Alfred Sloan saw in Billy Durant's loose management style and his lack of consistent policies and controls were both unseen and irrelevant to the country in general and General Motors' investors in particular. Thanks to the unprecedented mobilization required by America's entry into World War I, the country's annual investment in new manufacturing plants and equipment had soared from $600 million in 1915 to $2.5 billion in 1918. At war's end, both business and consumers were eager to refocus production on consumer goods.

The automobile industry, which had diverted only a fraction of its production to the war effort, was especially eager to meet Americans' apparently insatiable demand for the machine that gave mobility to their daily lives and their dreams. Detroit, Michigan, where General Motors was building a new headquarters that was to be the largest office building in the world, was the fastest-growing city in the nation. Its population had more than doubled in ten years, from under 467,000 people in 1910 to nearly 994,000 people in 1920. More significant for the future (but little noted at the time), the percentage of Detroit's African-American population nearly quadrupled during that period, growing from 1.2 percent in 1910 to 4 percent in 1920.[1]

There seemed to be even more reason for confidence and optimism in General Motors' own performance. Durant proudly referred to the company as "my baby," and its numbers seemed to justify the pride. The General's fixed assets in plants and equipment had grown from $19 million in 1912 to $179 million in 1919. Total car and truck sales for 1919 were nearly double the previous year's. More impressive, profits for that same twelve-month period were up more than 500 percent. And things were looking even better for the current year, with car and truck sales up 45 percent over the first quarter of 1919.[2]

Although General Motors was still a distant second to Ford Motor Company, which had a market share of 42 percent compared to the General's 11 percent, Durant was widely seen as the only competitor with even a chance of catching Henry Ford. On Wall Street even more than in Detroit, Billy and his General Motors were the names to watch in the automotive race. During the years 1914–1920, the market value of the General's stock had more than quadrupled.

Most remarkable of all was an increase in employment from 49,118 people at the end of 1918 to 85,980 at the end of 1919. The vast majority of these new employees were migrating from the rural South of the United States or Europe to the General's key plants in Michigan. Billy explained in his letter to stockholders that the company had initiated an unprecedented program of building new housing to help the affected local communities as well as the employees and their families. A grand total of $2.5 million was allocated for new employee housing in 1919, making it the company's fifth-largest capital expenditure. Arthur Pound, son-in-law of an early General Motors executive, described the motive in the company's first and only officially sanctioned history, *The Turning Wheel,* a book completely sympathetic to the company's view on all events and issues, published at the height of the Great Depression:

A new spirit of brotherhood was abroad in the land, and General Motors was one of the first to respond to it. Owing to the uncertainties attendant upon the change from war activities to peacetime pursuits, the Corporation considered it necessary to have the basic needs and living standards of its employees studied, to the end that wage rates would be fair and living conditions acceptable to thousands of families likely to move into cities where General Motors was rapidly expanding its operations. Accordingly, the Executive Committee, consisting of Messrs Durant, Haskell, and Chrysler [Walter P. Chrysler, a General

Motors vice president at the time], was directed to investigate industrial conditions affecting the plants of the Corporation.[3]

That same year, 1919, saw the birth of a company-matched employee investment plan covering all units of General Motors: a precursor of today's 401(k) plans, with employees investing up to 20 percent of their wages or salary and the company matching every penny invested by the employee.

To cap it all off, General Motors had also made several key acquisitions in 1919, guided by Billy's vision of even more uninterrupted growth and consolidation in the industry. These purchases included controlling interest in a company called Fisher Body, which would become crucial to the corporation's future production volume and efficiency, and complete ownership of Dayton, Ohio–based Frigidaire, which had originally been called Guardian Frigerator. Intrigued with the latter company's attempt to develop an electric refrigerator, Billy had purchased it with $100,000 of his own money, renamed it Frigidaire, and sold it to General Motors, his baby, for the same amount. Under the General's umbrella, Frigidaire dominated the growing refrigerator business within a year of the purchase and would soon also dominate the air-conditioning business.

Billy's baby had also established a new business unit in 1919 called General Motors Acceptance Corporation (GMAC), whose initial purpose was to "assist dealers in financing their purchase of General Motors' products, and also to finance, to some extent, retail sales." GMAC would soon revolutionize the way Americans bought and paid for all big-ticket purchases with what came to be known as installment buying, the precursor of revolving credit and today's credit card.

Billy concluded his letter to stockholders with a typically succinct and optimistic assessment of the future, noting that the first quarter of 1920 had also been a good one:

There is no diminution in the demand for your product, the number of passenger cars, trucks, and tractors sold for the first quarter of 1920 to March 31 being 119,779, as compared with 82,456 for the corresponding period of the previous year, an increase of 45.2 percent. The net profits for this period, before deducting federal taxes, are estimated upwards of $26,500,000.00. Your directors take pleasure in acknowledging their appreciation of the loyalty and efficiency of your officers and employees.

Why, then, should Alfred Sloan worry?

LOSING A MAN NAMED CHRYSLER

Sloan's doubts about Durant's leadership had begun surfacing in the spring of 1919, when General Motors was gaining momentum on what appeared to be an unstoppable roll. The catalyst was the abrupt resignation of one of Durant's most able lieutenants and Sloan's best friend, Walter P. Chrysler.

Chrysler had been brought to General Motors in 1911 by then-president Charles Nash, who had been hired by Durant as a blacksmith in his carriage factory in 1890, long before anyone had foreseen a General Motors. By 1916, Chrysler was in charge of all General Motors' manufacturing and was the highest-paid man in the entire auto industry, with annual salary and bonus exceeding $600,000. By 1919, Chrysler and Sloan were widely viewed as the two most capable of all the "new" generation of automobile executives born after the Civil War.

In Chrysler's autobiography, *Life of an American Workman,* published in 1937 and cowritten with Boyden Sparkes (the same ghostwriter Sloan was to use for his first memoir four years later), there is great warmth and respect for Durant as a person:

> I cannot hope to find words to express the charm of the man. He has the most winning personality of anyone I've ever known. He could coax a bird right down out of a tree, I think. I remember the first time my wife and I entered his home. The walls were hung with magnificent tapestries. I had never experienced luxury to compare with Billy Durant's house. In five minutes he had me feeling as if I owned the place.[4]

Yet there is also disdain for Billy's leadership style. More than once, Chrysler had been summoned by "the Man" only to be kept cooling his heels and then to discover that the urgent matter that needed to be discussed was nothing that couldn't have been resolved quickly at the plant level rather than wasting top management's time and brainpower. Chrysler's description of one meeting in particular summarized both his admiration and his frustration:

> Once I had gone to New York in obedience to a call from him [Durant]; he wished to see me about some matter. For several days in succession I waited at his office, but he was so busy he could not take the time to talk with me. It seemed to me he was trying to keep in communication with half the continent; eight or ten telephones were lined up on his desk. He was inhuman in his capacity for work. He had tremendous courage too. He might be risking everything he had, but he never faltered in his course. He was striving to make completely real his vision of a great corporation. Men, big men, came and went at his command. "Durant is buying" was a potent phrase in Wall Street then. . . . I waited four days before I went back to Flint; and to this day I do not know why Billy had required my presence in New York. Compared with what I had to worry me in Flint, I know that he had vastly greater worries.[5]

When Chrysler finally threw in the towel in a burst of anger and frustration in 1919, Alfred Sloan was one of two people other than Durant himself who tried to get him to change his mind. After Chrysler had already submitted his resignation, he was asked by the vice president in charge of personnel and administration, J. A. Haskell, to accompany Sloan on a fact-finding trip to Europe at General Motors' expense. The official purpose of the trip was to analyze the facilities and management of the French automaker Citroen, which Billy was eager to acquire for General Motors, but it was also timed as an opportunity to lure Walter Chrysler back into the fold. Chrysler agreed to go as an unofficial adviser after Haskell agreed that General Motors would foot the bill for Chrysler's wife Della and Sloan's wife Irene to accompany the delegation.

In the end, Sloan and Chrysler both concurred that acquiring Citroen would be a disaster. Not only did General Motors lack the depth of management talent to run the operation, but the Citroen plant complex was old and antiquated, and updating it would cost more than the construction of an entirely new facility. A disappointed Billy went along with the recommendation not to make a run at Citroen, but the greater failure of the trip was Sloan's inability to woo back Chrysler.

In fact, Alfred Sloan returned home with his own doubts about Billy reinforced. Alfred and Walter Chrysler remained lifelong friends, even when Chrysler went on to create a rival car company under his own name. Describing Chrysler's actual resignation more than twenty years later, Sloan placed all the blame at the feet of Billy Durant and his caprice:

> Often when he [Durant] called an executive meeting in Detroit, the ten or fifteen of us who gathered there would wait all day for the Chief. I would have traveled there from New York or elsewhere. Others would come from their posts in different towns. Walter Chrysler would have driven sixty-five miles from Flint. Often he arose before six to snatch a few precious minutes at his office desk. Sometimes he came without breakfast, because Mr. Durant always planned an early beginning. But whenever Mr. Durant appeared in Detroit, old friends could not easily be denied, and so we had to wait. One caller after another would delay him. There would be urgent telephone calls. We scarcely felt like doing anything else until he rang the bell, so tempers soured.
>
> "Shall we go to lunch?"
>
> "No, no! Mr. Durant regrets the delay. He'll return to you gentlemen in just a minute."
>
> Sometimes it was four o'clock before we got started. Frequently, when he did get an earlier start, Mr. Durant kept the conference going without regard to appetites. Walter Chrysler used to chafe as he waited. . . . However, the day came when Walter Chrysler quit. Twice in our meetings the two had exchanged words with a flaring of tempers. Actually they were devoted friends, but on an empty stomach, and worried about his huge stake in General Motors, Walter Chrysler resigned.
>
> There was never a minute after Chrysler's decision when we would have been less than happily grateful if he had changed his mind. We wanted him for his own sake; for his strength, his wisdom, his fine understanding of men.[6]

THE EVE OF SHOWDOWN

In August 1919, after Walter Chrysler's departure, Sloan wrote a remarkably candid personal letter to General Motors' founder that has been preserved among Durant's papers. The immediate issue was the impact of the new employee savings plan on field operations and central office administration. Alfred viewed the plan itself as an ingenious way to retain employees at a time when turnover was high. What he vehemently objected to was Billy's decision to administer the plan through the treasurer's office rather than at the local operating level.

In his letter, Alfred voiced what later became a concern of all kinds of field and plant managers in all kinds of companies: namely, the fear that two separate fiefdoms would develop, neither of which would trust the other. The operations side would end up viewing itself as a stepchild to the financial side and the chief executive officer would be helpless to bridge the gap. Sloan's letter was three pages, single-spaced, and often rambling (uncharacteristic of the scores of letters and memos later reprised in his 1963 classic management tome, *My Years with General Motors*), but the issues raised in the section on plan administration remain relevant to all large organizations today:

> In view of the fact that all financial, accounting, and cost work is primarily in the Treasurer's department and directed by the Finance Committee as compared with purely operating matters, there is necessarily going to be a feeling on the part of our operating people that they are not responsible for anything pertaining to that division of the work. No matter what their disposition may be, there is bound to be a feeling of that kind. In other words, there will result in the organization, as prescribed, two divisions of the Corporation's activities—one operating and one financial.
>
> The Savings and Investment Fund, we all believe, is going to be a big factor in stabilizing our labor and reducing our turnover. The hardest problem before our operating staff at the present time is satisfying and increasing the effectiveness of our labor. Therefore, it seems to me that putting the thing across, that is, selling the Savings and Investment Plan to our operating force, is more an operating matter than it is a treasury matter, and being transferred to the treasury division under the Finance Committee, our operating side is bound to lose, and I know will lose, in many instances under my supervision, the interest in the development of the matter which now exists.
>
> I feel that the development of the Savings and Investment Fund, in not only increasing the percentage but maintaining it, requires [a] considerable sales effort, and I feel that that is a matter which, although [it] might be handled by the treasury staff, could be better handled by the operating staff.[7]

Sloan concluded his letter with a guarded criticism of Billy Durant:

> Understand, Mr. Durant, in calling your attention to the above I am not in any way finding fault with the organization as it stands. I am absolutely supporting same as it reads, but I do not think that it is the right thing to do nor in the interest of the situation as a whole. I may say that this letter is written very hurriedly—just as I am leaving, and simply roughly presents to you my ideas on the subject.[8]

It is not known whether the two men ever discussed the letter, but the fact that Billy held onto it for the rest of his life is itself testimony to how personally he took such criticism. In his letter to stockholders in the 1919 annual report, Durant offered no more than a concise nuts-and-bolts summary of the employee savings plan:

> During the year the Corporation established an Employee Savings Plan under which employees have the privilege of paying into an interest-bearing Savings Fund a limited portion of their wage or salary. The amount so paid in by employees is duplicated by the Corporation paying a like amount into an Employees Investment Fund [that] is invested in securities selected by the Board of Directors. . . . Out of 62,297 employees eligible to participate in this plan, 33,641 have already taken advantage of its provisions.

Also in 1919, Alfred drafted a lengthy personal analysis of what he saw as the failures of General Motors' lack of clear organizational structure. He included an organizational chart and laid out a plan that drew little notice at the time but was eventually copied by all corporations and even governmental and nonprofit organizations. The concept was "decentralized operations with coordinated control," and it forever changed the way large enterprises and institutions were administered. Alfred submitted the plan to Billy, who never took action. Both men filed it away as the drama of 1920 played out.

With the company progressing and with Durant clearly not in a mood to accept suggestions, Sloan continued to keep his doubts largely to himself, at least inside the company. He put up the front of a team player throughout the spring of 1920. His August 1919 letter and his organizational plan remain the only recorded instances where he expressed doubt directly to the founder.

Outside of General Motors, however, Alfred Sloan was letting his dissatisfaction be known to trusted potential new employers. The investment bank Lee, Higginson and Company, which had played a key role in propping up General Motors' finances and temporarily ousting Durant ten years earlier (and whose leaders all still mistrusted Durant), made Sloan a firm offer of a partnership.

With the course of action appearing clearer and almost inevitable, Alfred decided to take an unprecedented vacation to escape the pressures and weigh the options. He and his wife Irene took another excursion to Europe, this time alone. He even ordered a Rolls Royce®, to be delivered to him in England, where he and Irene would begin a driving tour of the continent.

Sloan recalled his dilemma and Durant's response to the request for the time off in a little-known and often sentimental memoir entitled *Adventures of a White Collar Man.* The book was published in 1941, when Sloan was at the peak of his career and when industrialists as a group were still on the defensive in the wake of the Great Depression of the thirties. Although cowritten with Boyden Sparkes, the same writer who wrote Walter Chrysler's biography, it is far more revealing of Sloan the man than the later *My Years with General Motors.* The latter book was also ghostwritten (by one lead writer and a team of twenty researchers and collaborators hired by Sloan himself) and reveals little of Alfred's life and character, yet it became an instant bestseller when published in 1963. In *Adventures of a White Collar Man,* Sloan described the 1920 predicament as follows:

> Everything, if we kept on our course, added up to just one way: ruin. I could not protect myself and sell my stock without being disloyal to Durant. That was impossible. I wanted to think this matter out.
>
> "I'd like a month's leave of absence, Mr. Durant."
>
> He was telephoning. Sometimes I used to feel as if he were always holding a telephone in his hand. I think there were twenty telephones in his private office, and a switchboard. He had private wires to brokers' offices across the continent. In the same minute he would buy in San Francisco, sell in Boston.
>
> My fingers were drumming on his desk. It did not seem to me that the operating head of a corporation had any right to devote himself to

the market, even if the stock of the corporation was involved. He looked up.

"What is it?" There was a fleeting smile. He was never too tired to be kind.

"I wish to go away. Not feeling well." This was no exaggeration.

"Certainly," he said. "That will be perfectly all right with me. Get some rest."

I went to Europe. In London I made up my mind. I'd return to New York and resign. . . . But on the day I got back and walked into the New York office I sensed something unusual.

"Where's W. C.?"

"Gone away. A month's vacation."

Queer indeed. He'd never done anything of the sort before. I decided to postpone my resignation. I was a manufacturer, and this could be made the grandest manufacturing enterprise the world had ever seen. I did not want to leave. So I said to myself, "I'll ride along awhile and see what happens."[9]

And so the stage was set for a final showdown when the postwar boom in demand for all types of consumer goods abruptly stalled in the late summer of 1920. General Motors' growth strategy ran head-on into a vehicle market that was suddenly shriveling rather than expanding.

The ambitious expansion program of 1919 had doubled General Motors' production capacity, but it had all been predicated on the assumption of continued steady sales growth: an assumption that has since been the downfall of hundreds of high-flying start-ups and conglomerates in all kinds of industries. Total cost of the program was estimated at the time at $52.8 million, and the bulk of it was to come from the issuance of new stock. By the end of 1919, after all the different issues of debentures and different classes of stock were tallied, General Motors had become the second company in U.S. history to be capitalized at $1 billion (U.S. Steel being the first).

Billy and most of the members of his board of directors saw little risk in this approach of financing growth through the sale of new shares of stock and dilution of existing shares: The auto industry had had to weather only one brief disruption since its birth (the so-called Panic of 1907), and General Motors' common stock price had steadily outpaced the market. Alfred, however, saw dark clouds of overexpansion, overproduction, unsustainable debt, and a lack of accountability and control looming on the horizon.

The crisis faced by Alfred Sloan, Billy Durant, and General Motors in 1920 set the stage for one of the most dramatic and unprecedented boardroom coups in the annals of business. It was the defining moment for not only Billy and Alfred, but for their company as well. It also brought into public play all the issues of corporate governance and leadership accountability that dominate the business headlines to this day. The way most companies and executives perceive those issues is still in many ways a reflection of how these two men perceived them and dealt with them.

The crisis at General Motors in 1920 was also a watershed event in the way American corporations were organized and held accountable for results. The way in which General Motors dealt with the issues of organizational structure, production control and forecasting, brand management, finance, leadership development, and communications became the paradigm for all large companies during the following fifty years, until a handful of Japanese manufacturers established a new manufacturing and marketing paradigm and forced the General to again deal with the same problems that had almost sunk it in 1920.

How had the problems and the crisis developed, and why did the ensuing responses have so much success and so much impact on the rest of the world?

The answers and the lessons have their roots in the contrasting backgrounds and values of the two men at the center of General Motors, and in the long and twisting way the auto industry itself evolved in the first three decades of the twentieth century. The two men's lives and characters are in fact a looking glass into what works and what doesn't in building and preserving a business empire. And the lessons remain as relevant today as they were when Billy Durant and Alfred Sloan were testing and living them.

With Sloan watching closely, Durant was about to face a reckoning throughout the fall of 1920 that would have ended the careers of most business people, then and now. Yet Billy faced this crisis, as he did all others, with resolute and incorrigible optimism. That optimism had already taken him on one of the most incredible journeys of anyone of his generation.

Where did the optimism come from? What was it in Billy's genes and character that had led the high school dropout from rural

Michigan to even dream of building an empire that would change the world? What made him so different from Sloan? What led them to take such opposite approaches to leadership and management? Or, in the end, were they actually more alike than either would ever imagine, let alone admit?

Both the questions and the answers go back to before the automobile itself was ever heard of in America, to a rural town called Flint, sixty-five miles due north of Detroit.

CHAPTER | **TWO**

A Precocious Dropout Forges His First Empire

IN THE END, William Crapo Durant was perhaps not only the most forgotten but the most enigmatic of the twentieth century's great entrepreneurs and innovators. He was:

- The son of an alcoholic father who abandoned his family

- Raised by a socialite divorcee in an era when single mothers were shunned

- A high school dropout

- A devoted son but distant father

- The romantic suitor of a teenage girl younger than his own daughter

- A teetotaler who passionately supported the Eighteenth Amendment to the U.S. Constitution and its prohibition of the sale and consumption of alcoholic beverages, right up until its repeal in 1933

- A constant dreamer, never content to hold one job or stay focused on just one enterprise or endeavor

- The creator of what was to become the world's largest and most effective enterprise, only to lose control of it not once but twice

- The Warren Buffett of his day, at one time leading an investment syndicate with more than $4 billion in paper assets

When Billy Durant died in New York City on March 18, 1947, five years after suffering a stroke, The *New York Times* summarized his career and legacy as follows:

> At one time, Mr. Durant's wealth was placed at $120,000,000. When he filed a petition in bankruptcy in 1936, he listed his assets at $250 in clothing. At the height of his activity on Wall Street, his broker's annual commission was $6,000,000. Someone with a flair for figures once estimated that in the year of his most turbulent speculations he traded in securities at the rate of 5,000 shares every hour the Exchange was open. A genius at manipulation, perpetrator of one of the historic bluffs of financial history, Mr. Durant was also responsible for the building up of General Motors, one of America's dominant industries.

General Motors was almost a footnote. Yet what the *Times* referred to as a bluff had actually been the largest stock buyback ever recorded up to that time, and Billy had pulled it off with hardly anyone noticing. Not only had he been responsible for "the building up of General Motors," as the *Times* put it, he also happened to have created the company single-handedly and in bold defiance of both the auto barons and the bankers of the day.

People who claimed to know him well (even his enemies) always put integrity at the top of the list of his character traits. In Flint, Michigan, where he was best known, there were never any negatives to describe him, although many people knew the dark side was there. There are no remaining anecdotes to show close boyhood or adolescent friendships. Nor are there any details of how he met his first wife. If there ever were such stories and memories, they have all disappeared. By his early twenties, however, Durant was known and recognized by all as a young man whose drive and potential matched his charm.

As a child, he was called Willie; as a boy and man, Billy, never the formal, standoffish William. Standing five-feet-eight inches tall and never weighing more than 135 pounds, with brown eyes and a constant smile, he was said to win people over instantly with his energy and his modest voice.

His daughter Margery, who was to battle personal demons far worse than her father's during her own tragic life, wrote a little-noticed biography in his defense in the late 1920s, when he was trying to make a comeback in the automobile business and on Wall Street after his humiliation and downfall during the crisis of 1920. Published in 1929, *My Father* was ghostwritten by Commander Fitzhugh Green, who also wrote Charles Lindbergh's bestselling autobiography. Margery's husband at the time (her third) died before the book was finished. Shortly afterward, Margery went on to marry Fitzhugh Green and attempt to live the life of a globe-trotting socialite, at least on the surface.

Margery recalled a friend once asking her father, "Do you ever worry?"

"Never," Billy answered, with his usual smile. "In the daytime I'm too busy. At night I'm too sleepy."[1]

A HANDS-ON EDUCATION

In high school, Billy played baseball and the cornet. He was also an excellent student but was eager to apply his talents in the real world rather than the classroom. Like most Americans of his generation, he saw little advantage in formal education. Hard work and ambition, not education and intellect, were the popular keys to success in the America of Billy's youth. Confidence and optimism were sweeping America in the wake of the Civil War, driven by restless inventors and dreamers rather than students or sages. Despite the drudgeries of the day (with indoor plumbing and running water still the exception in homes and public buildings alike; with furnaces not yet replacing fireplaces or wood stoves as the primary heating source; and with commercially feasible electric power still years away), the western frontier was being pushed back daily and new inventions abounded. There seemed to be no excuse for any young man with spirit and ambition not to have a better life than his parents had. And the keys to that better life were hard work and inventiveness, not school. Young college graduates entering the business world would often actually hide their degrees, lest they be teased as spoiled and not knowing what it meant to do "real" work.

Thus it came as no great surprise or shock to proud Rebecca Durant, whose New England roots included a pilgrim descendant of the *Mayflower* and who herself served as a vice regent of the Daughters of the American Revolution, when her sixteen-year-old son Billy announced in the winter of 1877 that he had had enough of the classroom and was ready to take on the world. Daughter Margery described the scene in her book:

> . . . [H]e came home from school one afternoon, threw his books on the library table, and announced:
> "Mother, I'm not going back to school any more."
> His reasons weren't very good. They aren't when a boy is sixteen and the world is still a mystery. He didn't respect his Principal. In short, the same impatience at fettering routine and roundabout convention so needful for the mediocre, which was to goad him all his life, was beginning to emerge.
> "But what are you going to do?" she asked, well knowing the answer.
> "Work, mother."[2]

At the time, Billy was just six months away from his scheduled graduation from high school. A few days later, he appeared at the Crapo Lumberyard, which had been founded by his grandfather, expecting to be put to work in the front office. Instead, he got a rude awakening. As Billy recalled it to Margery:

> Being the grandson of the [lumberyard's] President I felt I had obligations a little beyond the average applicant. I rose early; I had laid out my best suit the night before. After I had put it on, carefully brushed my hair, and shined my shoes I got a new pair of brown gloves out of my bureau drawer. . . .
> I suppose I figured they would give me some sort of desk work, befitting the dignity of my blood-relationship to the company's owner. But I was painfully mistaken.

Without delay I was sent out into the yard to report to the foreman. He was a big burly Irishman with heavy shoulders and a heavier voice.

"What's your name?" he shouted at me, though I was only a few feet from him.

"Durant."

I seem to remember that he hesitated a second before he went on. But his Irish wit promptly came to his rescue. I might be grandson of the Boss, but so far as he was concerned I was just a young man going to work.

I could see he was sizing me up. His eyes lit on my hands. They gave him his cue. "Take off them gloves!" he yelled. "What do you think you came here for, anyway?" I obeyed while he stood over me. "Now take off your coat and pile up that lumber there in the corner!"[3]

Billy accepted the manual labor without argument, but immediately set out to supplement his daily wage of seventy-five cents with other work more suited to what he saw as his talents: namely, sales.

First came a job as night clerk at the neighborhood drugstore. Then he persuaded the store owner to let him try his hand at selling patent medicines door-to-door on his own time. From there, he talked his way into cigar sales, working on commission for the largest distributor in the western half of the state. Before his twenty-first birthday, he had sold more cigars in a single day than the owner's other three agents combined: The owner let the three go and gave Billy their territories.

During these traveling salesman days, Billy developed his two most famous passions: cigar smoking and playing checkers. Later, in his industrial mogul period, he would chastise and even fire men who smoked cigarettes rather than cigars, and he would delay a business meeting if need be to finish a game of checkers with the doorman or elevator operator. The cigar smoking would end in his fifties, but the checkers and other games would continue throughout his life.

As his success as a salesman grew in Flint, so did his reputation as a young man who was unafraid of difficult challenges that more experienced businessmen would decline. Each new job brought more money and, more important, more self-confidence and more respect throughout the community. When a delegation of local citizens approached him with an offer to help turn around the city's privately held waterworks, he couldn't refuse.

The waterworks was losing money and receiving regular complaints: Many customers had simply stopped paying their bills. Less than eight months after Billy accepted the job, the operation was not only making a profit, it was receiving compliments rather than complaints and adding new customers rather than losing them. Billy was now in charge.

In her book, daughter Margery attributed his success in turning the waterworks around to the same formula that countless chief executive officers have since learned the hard way: taking the time to listen to what the disgruntled customers had to say and then, most difficult, getting the organization focused on what needed fixing rather than following their former routines. As Margery summed it up:

> Young Willie hadn't been a cigar and insurance salesman for nothing. Like every born salesman, he had quickly learned that salesmanship is the key to all successful business operations. He had discovered that one had to sell many more things than manufactured articles in order to get along. Instinctively he had learned to sell himself; to sell ideas; to sell quality of operation and supply, as well as quality of goods.
>
> Almost the first thing he did, after a good look at the water pumps, was to make a round of the customers. He went from house to house talking to the wives as well as the husbands. He got the other fellow's point of view. He matched complaint against availability, demand against supply, citizen against government, justice against politics. He sold both sides to each other. And he won concessions from both.
>
> In eight months the Flint City Waterworks was on its feet, the users were happy and the bankers satisfied.[4]

While managing the waterworks, Billy also established a local insurance agency with a friend. It, too, was soon growing and adding to Billy's own reputation. At the age of twenty-two, he purchased his own house, near his mother's.

Prosperous beyond any level his father had ever approached, Durant was high on the list of Flint's most eligible bachelors. He married Clara Pitt, daughter of the Flint and Pere Marquette Railroad's local ticket master, on June 17, 1885, in a ceremony conducted at his new house. Although no known photos of the bride and groom together remain, Clara was by all accounts one of the town's most attractive girls, and there were no intimations even among Flint's elite that Billy Durant, the young man on the rise, might be marrying beneath his station.

Billy's mother and older sister were in attendance at the wedding, but his father's name was not mentioned. Nor would his daughter mention her paternal grandfather a single time in her book. Billy had put that part of his past behind him—or so he thought.

SINS OF THE FATHERS

What had driven young Billy so far, so hard, so fast?

Everyone chose to see in him the best qualities of his maternal grandfather rather than the worst of his father, who was described as a ne'er-do-well when people were kind and far worse when they were frank. Yet both the values of the grandfather and the demons of the father would characterize Billy's often contradictory optimism and restlessness throughout his life.

Billy's father, William Clark Durant, was born in 1827 in rural New Hampshire, son of an innkeeper who died penniless when the boy was five years old. Raised by his mother and various relatives, he was to become a schemer and a dreamer rather than a hard worker or good provider. He met the prosperous Crapo family and began courting third daughter Rebecca when he was twenty-six, while working as a collection clerk at the National Webster Bank of Boston, the only steady job he ever held. After a short romance while Rebecca's father was away in Michigan on business, he married her on November 29, 1855, a week after Thanksgiving. He left the bank soon afterward, but the couple stayed in Boston. Unemployed, he was soon known far and near as a drunk more bent on avoiding work than anything else. Fascinated and obsessed with the stock market, he was never shy to approach anyone for a loan or to decline any offer of a job.

At the opposite end of the value scale, Billy's maternal grandfather, Henry Howland Crapo, was living testimony to Puritan ethics and success. Born on a farm near Dartmouth, Massachusetts, on May 24, 1804, he spent his boyhood working the fields by day and writing his own dictionary by candlelight when finished with his chores. At the age of twenty-one, he married Dartmouth native Mary Ann Slocum, whose family tree went back to the *Mayflower* and beyond. Moving to nearby New Bedford and proceeding to father ten children, the self-educated Henry was employed as a school-teacher, land surveyor, and auctioneer—all at the same time. Elected town clerk, treasurer, and tax collector, he filled out his free time as a renowned horticulturist, cultivating 150 varieties of pears and 120 varieties of roses and contributing regularly to the *New England Horticultural Journal,* all while in his thirties.

Less than three years after daughter Rebecca's marriage, Henry Howland Crapo uprooted the rest of the family and moved to the booming frontier of a former fur-trading post called Flint, Michigan. On the banks of the Flint River, just sixty-five miles due north of Detroit, Flint was perfectly located to become the focal transportation and milling point for Michigan's coming lumber boom, and Henry was following it closely. By the time Michigan became a state in 1837, a thousand people were landing at the port of Detroit every day. Many ventured north to Flint, where they quickly broadened the local economy to agriculture (wheat and potatoes, in particular) as well as timber. By 1847, the Genesee Ironworks was producing mowing machines and other agricultural machinery in Flint. In 1848, the town's first steam-generated power plants appeared. Soon, steam-powered saw mills were making Flint the focal point of a booming logging industry for the entire lower peninsula of Michigan.

Studying this growth from afar, Henry Howland Crapo began purchasing land near Flint in 1850. In 1854, he made his largest purchase: 14,000 acres of prime timber land for $150,000. Soon, he was buying and upgrading sawmills in Flint to process not only his own timber but that of others.

Henry's rise in Flint was no less spectacular than his career in New Bedford. At the time he uprooted his brood in 1858, he was fifty-four years old. He again immediately immersed himself in local politics and soon expanded his timber and lumber interests to railroads, building the Flint and Holly line in 1863 to connect Flint to cities to the south, including Detroit. In 1860, just two years after the move, he was elected mayor of Flint. One of the largest timber barons and wealthiest citizens in Michigan, he was elected to the State Senate in 1862 on the Republican ticket and then elected governor in 1864 and 1866.

Rebecca watched her father and the rest of her family flourish from afar as her husband William Clark Durant dabbled unsuccessfully in a series of land and stock speculation schemes. Soon, she was making frequent trips from their home in Boston to Flint, to be in the comfort of her sisters and parents. On November 24, 1857, with her husband now struggling to build his own stock brokerage firm, she gave birth to a daughter, Rebecca, who would be "Rosy" to all who knew her. Four years later, on December 8, 1861, son William Crapo Durant was born, also in Boston.

During those more-and-more frequent trips to Flint, grandfather Henry would dote on Willie, to Rosy's chagrin. Rosy would always feel (perhaps rightly) that she received less attention than her baby brother. When the boy was three years old, right after the bloodiest phase of the Civil War, Governor Crapo had a local printer and uniform maker create an elaborate certificate and elegant military uniform to commission grandson William Crapo Durant as a major in the Fifty-seventh Regiment of the Michigan Cavalry Volunteers (a fictitious unit).

Grandfather Henry revealed his own unfailing New England values, as well as his concern for Willie's future, in correspondence to son William Wallace Crapo (Willie's uncle) back in Massachusetts. On August 13, 1863, after one of those tense visits from Rebecca and her husband, he wrote:

> When Durant was here I thought he was too much imbued with a mania for stock speculation and my advice to him was to go back into the bank and hold on to his place there and be careful about committing himself solely and entirely to the troubled and uncertain sea of stock speculation, which I regard like every other system of gambling whether personal or professional. I hope he has done so, [for] it is well enough to make something out of stocks if one keeps within their means and has a legitimate business to rely on.[5]

Alas, the governor's advice went unheeded. In 1868, with Willie just seven years old, push finally came to shove during another visit to the Crapo home in Flint. After a drunken outburst by his son-in-law, Henry gave Rebecca a hundred dollars so that she could return home with the children but *without* her husband. On the day they left, July 30, 1868, Henry again wrote to his son:

> Since Rebecca and the children were here Durant has been "drifting about"—up to Lake Superior, down to Detroit, and anywhere else that

he could find a pretext to drift. I have seen enough to satisfy me that
he must change his course at once, or a short time will land him in the
gutter. There is nothing of him. He has a peculiar kind of smartness,
but it is without judgment, principle, or even common sense, at least in
his present state of mind. . . .

He has been so intoxicated here as to have regular drunken jabs
with Rebecca at the table before us all, so that we felt the best course
to leave the table one by one to avoid a scene. Poor Rebecca! Her visit
was not half out, and has been spoiled by him, and she has gone home
almost broken-hearted.

His mind now seems to run to going into some saloon, where he
thinks that he can make piles of money.[6]

Shortly after that, Henry changed his will to make sure that his
daughter Rebecca and her children would be provided for and that
her husband would get nothing. Almost exactly a year later, on July
23, 1869, the recently retired governor died at his home in Flint,
attended by his son-in-law Dr. James Willson, after a severe attack
of gallstones. The *Detroit Tribune* wrote in his obituary:

He was not a man of brilliant or show qualities, but he possessed sharp
and remarkably well-developed business talents, a clear and practical
understanding, sound judgment, and unfailing integrity. In all the walks
of life there was not a purer man in the state. So faithful, so laborious,
so conscientious a man in office is a blessing beyond computation in
the healthful influence which he exerted in the midst of the too preva-
lent corruptions that so lamentably abound in the public service. We
have often thought that in his broad and sterling good sense, Governor
Crapo closely resembled a lamented Lincoln.

Within months, Rebecca finally left her husband and moved to
Flint with the children. They lived with her sister Rhoda and her
husband until her mother died in 1875, when she claimed her inheritance and bought her own home across the street.

During these formative years, Billy watched and felt his mother
enduring all the stigmas of a single mother in a society where divorce and infidelity were rare and never discussed openly. The
home Rebecca bought was within walking distance of her father's
former residence. Just two years after moving to the new house,
Billy made his fateful announcement that school was not for him.

Despite his constant precociousness and optimism, the effects of his father's restlessness, failure, and alcoholism would stick with Billy throughout his own journey. He would be an outspoken proponent of Prohibition and the Eighteenth Amendment banning the sale and consumption of alcoholic beverages. He would remain absolutely devoted to his mother but aloof from first wife Clara.

While Billy was building his first business empire, he and Clara had two children: Margery, born in 1887, and Cliff, born in 1890. Billy would be distant from his son yet far closer to his daughter than he had ever been to her mother. He would later express regret that the challenges and responsibilities of business kept him on the road and away from his children during their crucial childhood years: a regret no doubt made all the more painful by memories of Billy's own absent father.

Like so many self-made successes, Billy never mentioned his father and never discussed his own family life. Yet he never lost touch with his mother, who actually wrote him every day until her death in 1925. As daughter Margery recalled:

> On her seventieth birthday father gave her a wonderful dinner at the Waldorf Astoria, a "surprise dinner." Because she had "always been a great soldier," as my father put it in a little speech before the guests, he gave her on that occasion a big hand-made silk American flag. This flag he had draped on her casket when she died.
>
> "My Willie" she called him; and she was always waiting at the door for him with a smile on her lips and a kiss of devotion. To witness the love of that mother and son has been one of the most beautiful things in my life.[7]

He had few close friends but hundreds of business associates, all of whom claimed to know him well but few of whom had an inkling of the demons behind his drive. On the surface, he was a role model of success and the same virtues his grandfather, the governor, had lived by and his father had failed to grasp. Like his father, however, Billy would eventually become obsessed with speculation in the stock market, thrilled by its risks and ignoring its dangers. Yet all of that still lay ahead when young Billy Durant took a ride in a newfangled, flimsy-looking horse-drawn cart: a ride that was to change his outlook on the world and its possibilities.

JUST A SHORT RIDE ACROSS TOWN

Billy took his ride on a dare and a whim on a September day in 1886. By the time he set foot back on terra firma, he already had a vision of a new business empire.

In 1854, just before Henry Howland Crapo had entered the local picture, Flint had been home to only five hand-assembly carriage shops, none of them producing in volume or on a full-time basis. By the turn of the century, when Billy's name had become familiar far beyond Flint, there were more than thirty carriage manufacturers in Flint, which was by now known as "the Vehicle City," its main thoroughfare graced with a cast-iron arch bearing those words. (The restored arch is still there today.) One of these operations, the William A. Paterson Company, founded in 1869, was, at its height, building thirty different varieties of carriages.

Although the details of the story have been embellished or downplayed according to the memory and bias of whoever has told it or written it down, all agree that Billy was walking across town, on his way to a board of directors meeting at the Flint City Water-works, and worried that he would be late. He paused to say hello to his good friend Dallas Dort, ten months older than Billy and part owner of the local hardware store. As they were talking, another friend, John Alger, approached in a bizarre horse-drawn cart whose two wheels were four feet in diameter and whose seat and axle looked too frail to take a bump or a sharp turn without tipping over.

Alger offered Billy a ride, but Billy doubted they could both fit on the seat or that the cart could make it across town. Half-teasing, Alger proceeded to defend the vehicle, bragging about a new and unique set of springs located under the seat and also integrated with the base of the seat in one piece, to minimize the bouncing caused by the horse's movement. More worried than ever that he would be late, Billy climbed in.

A smooth ride despite a fast horse and a rough road made Billy an immediate believer in the new cart. Billy saw that the odd-looking contraption was perfect for a market niche that no one else had focused on—short trips involving little cargo and needing less power than the traditional wagon or carriage, but requiring more than just a horse and saddle; in essence, the first commuter vehicle. He asked Alger where he could buy one. Alger said he had ordered it through the local agent for the cart's builders, who were located in Coldwater, Michigan, 120 miles southwest of Flint.

The very next day, Billy was on a train headed to Coldwater, where he met the following morning with Thomas O'Brien and William Schmedlen, owners of the Coldwater Cart Company. It was probably no surprise to Billy that the operation was smaller than a typical blacksmith shop and was strewn randomly with unfinished wood, axles, wheels, and dies.

Opening the conversation with the story of his ride and how wonderful the Schmedlen-O'Brien cart was, Billy soon asked the partners, casually, if they might be interested in selling a partial interest in the business. To his amazement, they immediately offered to sell the entire inventory and all rights to the product for $1,500. The only thing they didn't want to part with was their tools. Billy then asked if that price included the patent on the cart's suspension, its most marketable feature and the one that made it stand out from all other carts he had seen.

At first, the partners said they deserved royalties on the suspension. Soon, however, they gave in. In his unpublished papers, Billy recalled the following deal-closing conversation with the partners:

As I said before, I have very little money, nowhere near enough to make the purchase. But if you will go down to the office of your attorney with me and execute a bill of sale and assign the patent and deposit all the papers in your bank, I will go to Flint this afternoon and see if I can obtain the money, which must be in your hands within five days or no deal.[8]

SELLING BILLY DURANT, THEN SELLING THE PRODUCT

Returning to Flint, Billy decided to seek the money from a bank, but not one that was in any way beholden or affiliated with the Crapo family's business interests. He also concluded that he would need $2,000 rather than $1,500, to cover the cost of moving the parts and inventory from Coldwater to Flint.

Where and how he would begin manufacturing in Flint were another matter. With Billy, the deal always came first, the details later.

He decided to approach a man and an institution with whom he had never done business: Robert Whaley, president of Citizens

National Bank. Within minutes of sitting down in Whaley's office, Billy had his $2,000. In notes he intended for his autobiography, Billy described the scene in the third person:

A few doors north on Saginaw Street, the old reliable Citizens Bank— not as pretentious as the others, but sound as a rock—the president, a Scotchman by the name of Robert J. Whaley, son-in-law of Alexander McFarlan, one of the wealthy lumbermen in that part of the country. The young man did not know him very well, never had a business transaction with him of any kind, and was making the approach with some misgivings. A narrow pair of stairs leading to his office over the bank—not unlike many of the old-fashioned offices of early days. No elegant furniture—no fine rugs, plenty of dust and other things—a veritable curiosity shop.

The gentleman seated at the well-worn desk at the front end of the office—to the young man's surprise—recognized him. He told his story in great detail—enthusiastically of course—and when he finished he was asked the question: "Do you think it is all right?" To which the young man replied, "I would not be here, Mr. Whaley, if I did not think so."

Then the surprise: "Come with me," taking the young man down to the office of Mr. Henry Van Dusen, cashier of the bank, and telling him to make out a 90-day note for $2,000 and place the avails to the young man's credit.

But, said the new customer, "I won't be able to pay the note in 90 days," where upon Mr. Whaley, telling Henry Van Dusen to take care of it, turned on his heel and went upstairs. The credit established, the business was assured.

Possibly the reader may have mistrusted that the young man is the author of this sketch, but don't forget that Robert J. Whaley, by reason of his courage and confidence, is entitled to all the credit for having made possible the creation of a nation-wide institution which resulted later in the establishment of 12 industrial institutions in Flint, besides being the birthplace of the largest creation of its kind in the world, the General Motors Corporation.

My hat is off to, and God bless, Robert J. Whaley.[9]

Breaking the news to his friend Dallas Dort, Billy also soon had additional working capital thrown at him. Dort explained that he was bored with the hardware business and asked Durant if he could use a partner. Billy did not hesitate to say yes. Nor did he quibble when Dort offered $1,000 (half of it raised from selling his share in the hardware and the rest from his mother) for a half interest in the business. As Billy recalled it:

> I went to my office, I was in the insurance business also, and had not been there but a few minutes when my old partner, J. Dallas Dort (one of the best men that ever lived) who played the game with me for 36 years, came over to see me. He was clerking in a hardware store across the street owned by a man by the name of James Bussey.
>
> "Hello, Billy, I've missed you—where have you been?"
>
> "Over in Coldwater," I replied, "and by the way I'm in the manufacturing business."
>
> "What are you going to manufacture?" he asked.
>
> "Road carts," I said.
>
> To which came the question, "Do you mean to say that you have bought the concern that makes the cart like the one owned by Johnny Alger who works in our store?"
>
> "I do," I said, "and the concern will be moved over to Flint at once, for I have just made a deal with Mr. Whaley of the Citizens Bank who loaned me the money to buy it."
>
> "Do you own it all?" he asked.
>
> "I do," I said, "lock, stock, and barrel with the patent as well."
>
> "Will you sell me a half interest?" asked Dort.
>
> Then my story. It cost $1,500 cash, to which must be added freight, cartage, miscellaneous expenses, and a place where we can start manufacturing in a small way. I figured that $2,000 will be required and borrowed that amount from the bank upon Mr. Whaley's approval.
>
> "I would be delighted to have you for a partner and will sell you a half interest for $1,000."
>
> "It's a deal," said Dort, "if I can get the money."
>
> He left the office and returned all smiles in about half an hour and this was his story. "I had a partnership agreement with Mr. Bussey which did not expire until December 31—a salary and a percentage of the profits. The business has not been especially good this year and I did not expect my share of the profits would amount to much. I told him of your purchase and offer and asked him if he would release me from my contract which has three and one-third months to run. He congratulated me on the opportunity; thought it was a wonderful deal for me and not only gave me a release but $500 in cash besides. I think Jim

Bussey is a peach. You do not find many men like him in this neck of the woods."[10]

The partners immediately changed the name of their new business to the Flint Road Cart Company but still didn't know exactly where it would lead them. On paper, Dallas Dort was president of the company. Everyone in Flint knew, however, that Billy Durant was calling the shots. He would later quip that titles never concerned him. What did concern him was being at the center of the action, in charge—and that he was.

From his career as a traveling salesman, Billy knew that the best products always spoke for themselves. He also knew that the best sales tool beyond a physical demonstration was word-of-mouth testimony. He was absolutely convinced that once his market understood his cart's advantages, word would spread like wildfire and the cart would sell itself.

The immediate challenge was to get maximum exposure, and fast.

Billy's answer was to stage a public demonstration of the cart, similar to the way it had been demonstrated to him. The natural venue would be a county fair or similar agricultural exposition. All such events had already concluded for the year in Michigan, but the largest annual fair in the state of Wisconsin, called the Tri-State Fair (even though attendees were strictly Wisconsinites), was scheduled to open in Madison less than a week after Billy's return to Flint from Coldwater. He telegraphed the fair's president and arranged to enter his cart in a best-in-show competition with all varieties of carts and carriages.

With the fair and the vehicle-judging scheduled to open on Monday, Billy arranged to ship the best-looking of the total of two complete carts that had come with O'Brien and Schmedlen's inventory by rail car and then took a separate train himself. Arriving Sunday morning, he met with the fair's president to give a private pitch for his cart. Once again, Billy's charm proved to be as invaluable as it was irresistible: The cart failed to arrive as scheduled, but the president agreed to a plea from Billy to delay the judging.

When the cart finally arrived at the fairgrounds, Billy was ready with his order pad as the judges began making their rounds. That day, Durant's entry won the blue ribbon. On top of that, he took sales orders for a hundred units on the spot from the owner of the same shipping company (Crane & Co.) that had taken delivery of his demonstration model. He would later say that he had originally planned to call the production version "the Flint" but decided right then to change it to "the Famous Blue Ribbon Line."

From Madison en route back to Flint, Billy and his winning cart stopped in Milwaukee, where he had arranged to meet another prospective customer whose name he had obtained at the fair. This time, he took an order for one rail car of merchandise, thirty-five carts, with an option for more carloads on a regular basis.

Next stop was Chicago, where Billy met with one J. H. Fenton, a supplier of sulkies to the harness-racing circuit. Fenton asked if he could make a few modifications to make the cart better for racing. Billy agreed without hesitation. Fenton then asked if Billy would agree to change the name of this customized version to "the Fenton Favorite." Again, there was no hesitation.

By the time Billy stepped off the train in Flint, he had 600 orders in his pocket. He and partner Dort had not yet built a single cart, nor did they have a shop or factory in which to build one.

A BITTER LESSON IN PRODUCTION CONTROL

Ever the salesman, Billy personally called on Flint's leading carriage-builder, William Paterson, to secure a production arrangement. At that time, Paterson was building a variety of wagons that included only two smaller buggies a day. Billy asked Paterson if he could build 1,200 carts just like the demonstration model. Apparently taking his cue from Billy's own style, Paterson did not hesitate to say yes and asked $12.50 for each unit. Seeing no reason to tell Paterson that he was certain he could sell the finished product for nearly double that, Billy agreed.

With partner Dort still in the background, Billy once again took the initiative to evaluate Paterson's manufacturing and assembly operations. Paterson, who had actually never produced anything in a quantity near the volume he had agreed to, was open to suggestion. Focusing on the Famous Blue Ribbon Line's simplicity—few parts, all of them easily replicated and assembled—Billy, who had absolutely no manufacturing experience, quickly designed his own production line, with everything laid out and tailored to his product's components and the volume he needed each day.

With no fanfare, Billy had created the world's first vehicle assembly line. In just the first year of production, the Flint Road Cart
Company sold 4,000 units and turned a profit of $18,000.

With Paterson finally learning that Durant and Dort were selling
their wares at $22.50 apiece, however, the partners were soon in
need of a new production arrangement. Through his growing network of friends and customers, Billy learned that Paterson had approached one of Billy's key dealers in Chicago and claimed that he,
not Billy, controlled the latest (bestselling) model. Paterson further
offered to supply that carriage to the dealer at a lower price than
Billy.

Billy and his partner quickly arranged to buy an abandoned
woolen mill on the banks of the Flint River, where they started their
own production and changed their company's name to the Durant-
Dort Carriage Company. Billy Durant would never forget the bitter
lesson of what he saw as Paterson's treachery: Always control your
own production and, whenever possible, all of the links in the supply chain.

Billy described his personal reaction to Paterson's betrayal in
notes left for that never-written autobiography:

> The volume of business was a surprise and it looked as though Mr.
> Paterson's large plant would be taxed to its full capacity. No attempt
> was made to conceal the name of our customers which, of course,
> were known to Mr. Paterson.
>
> Everything appeared to be progressing in orderly fashion when we
> were confronted with an unlooked-for situation. Mr. Paterson decided
> to visit Chicago and when there called on Bristol & Gale. He told them
> that he was a carriage manufacturer in Flint, Michigan, and that he
> would like to interest them in the product. They advised him that they
> were handling a Flint product, were very much pleased with it, and at
> his request showed him a sample. When he was in position to give
> them the information, he told them that the Durant-Dort product was
> made in his factory and that they might just as well buy from the manu-
> facturer and save money by so doing. The result of his visit enabled
> Mr. Paterson to secure a good customer and our plans were immedi-
> ately changed.
>
> In order that we might not be again interfered with, we took steps
> to manufacture our own product on a different basis from any other
> carriage concern in the country. Our plan was to manufacture practi-

cally every important part of a buggy, and carrying out this idea, we did not stop until we had controlled or were interested in building a full line of bodies, wheels, axles, forgings, stampings, leather, paint, trimmings, and various other items, even whip sockets; but not until our accessory plants were in operation (16 in number) did we have a product that had no competition in value or price in the country. This gave us control of the business in that line as long as carriages were in demand.[11]

Thus did a stolen customer lead to a new business paradigm that would soon change the nature of manufacturing around the world: namely, vertical integration of the production of all components of the finished product under the manufacturer and seller's own ownership and management.

With the lesson of Paterson's betrayal sticking in his craw, what Billy did next was to redefine the carriage industry. Although he never received any credit, his carriage strategy became the model for the entire automobile industry and dozens of other industries for most of the twentieth century. That strategy was to have a broad variety of models of the same basic product; high-volume, standardized production; direct ownership and control of key suppliers (in the case of horse-drawn carriages, this encompassed axles, wheels, spokes, springs, lumber, canvas tops, paint, and varnish); and a nationwide network of franchised dealers (which Billy himself established through personal contacts, visits, and a standard franchise agreement).

Billy went on to follow this carriage model in creating General Motors; Alfred P. Sloan, Jr., whom Billy hired for his management skill, perfected it.

FROM START-UP TO INDUSTRY LEADER

As Durant-Dort's production volume increased, per-unit cost declined. And word-of-mouth testimony supplemented with advertising made the Famous Blue Ribbon Line more and more popular. By the year 1895, less than ten years after Billy's first ride in that road cart, Durant-Dort was producing 75,000 vehicles a year with gross annual revenues of $5 million. The company's wholly owned supply-and-production network included fourteen plants in the United States and Canada. In addition to the original road cart, its

sales catalog boasted a variety of models of wagons, buggies, and
carriages marketed under such nameplates as the Standard, the Vic-
toria, the Moline, and the Diamond. In addition to controlling its
own supplier network, Durant-Dort also had equity interest in competing operations such as Blout Carriage and Buggy in Atlanta and
Dominion Carriage in Toronto.

By 1900, when the automobile was just beginning to capture
America's attention and imagination, Durant-Dort was the largest
vehicle manufacturer in the United States and Billy Durant, not yet
forty years old, was a millionaire and a power broker. Employees
and business contacts not only in Flint but across the nation referred to Billy not as "the kid" or even "the boss," but "the Man."

Yet he remained soft-spoken and straightforward, always looking the other person in the eye with a slight smile, always showing
more interest in that person than in his own pitch. Years later, Billy
explained his own sales philosophy in those disorganized but passionate notes that he intended for his autobiography:

> Assume that the man you are talking to knows as much or more than
> you do. Do not talk too much. Give the customer time to think. In other
> words, let the customer sell himself.[12]

By the time Billy turned forty, with the forces that were to lead
to the showdown of 1920 still not envisioned by anyone on the
planet, he was celebrated as "the King of the Carriage Makers."

It was the height of the Gilded Age, an innocent era of optimism,
prosperity, and mobility all across America. In 1879, Thomas Edison had perfected the incandescent lightbulb. The following year,
New York City's Broadway had been transformed into "the Great
White Way," illuminated at night by electric lights. In 1893, two
brothers, Charles and Frank Duryea, had demonstrated the first
gasoline-powered vehicle built in the United States. It was a contraption almost as flimsy-looking as Billy's road cart, named after
themselves and soon to be imitated and improved by dozens of
other tinkerers, including a farmer's son from another small Michigan town, Henry Ford.

A new age was dawning, and Billy Durant was growing restless.

Meanwhile, a rail-thin, serious-minded nineteen-year-old Phi
Beta Kappa graduate of the Massachusetts Institute of Technology
named Alfred Sloan was looking for work.

CHAPTER THREE

A Quiet Student Becomes a First-Class Supplier

UNLIKE BILLY DURANT, Alfred Sloan left no private papers or doting daughters to tell the world of his life. Yet Sloan knew there would be a story, and he made sure it would be told his way.

When it came to communications, like everything else, the focus was to be Sloan's achievements at General Motors rather than himself. By the time he died in 1966, at the age of ninety, his very name was synonymous with General Motors and big business. His wife had remained in the background throughout his career and he left no heirs, but his achievements were respected across the globe, though resented by many rivals. His obituary in the *New York Times,* February 18, 1966 which garnered a full page of text (versus Billy Durant's quarter page), focused on what he had done for the company, just as Sloan would have wanted it:

When Mr. Sloan became vice president of operations of General Motors in 1920, the company accounted for less than 12 percent of motor vehicle sales in the nation; when he stepped down as chairman in 1956 its share was 52 percent. Moreover, General Motors had expanded into one of the world's largest companies. It was also among the most profitable and, operationally, one of the smoothest. These accomplishments were credited to Mr. Sloan's management policies. He centralized administration and decentralized operations, grouping together those that had a common relationship. He also realigned the company's products so that one brand of automobile did not conflict with another.

There was no mention of Billy Durant, of course. Under Alfred Sloan's leadership, Durant's name had virtually disappeared from General Motors. Today, the only remaining physical indication of the founder ever having been there is a letter D carved into the cornice at each corner off the fifteenth-floor roof of the former General Motors Building in Detroit, which was abandoned by the company and donated to the state of Michigan in the late 1990s. The building was originally to have been named the Durant Building, but Billy himself had actually opposed its construction. Whether through oversight or cost considerations, no one bothered to have the Ds removed.

Also unmentioned in any of Sloan's obituaries was his fervent opposition to the United Automobile Workers of America and any other union that dared try to organize his employees. Sloan even went as far as putting Pinkerton spies and caches of arms and tear gas in his plants. The infamous Flint sit-down strike of 1936–1937 paved the way for a far bloodier but, in the end, less consequential war at Ford Motor. Despite the 1937 strike, General Motors was the only automaker to gain market share and remain profitable throughout the Great Depression. Alfred Sloan, however, emerged from the crisis with new resentment and a hardened antiunion, antiregulatory philosophy that only intensified each remaining year of his life.

General Motors' reluctant capitulation to the unions in 1937 set the stage for such benefits as company-paid health insurance and pensions, mandatory annual wage increases, and guaranteed employment. For his part, Sloan refused to ever meet with any union leader and blamed President Franklin Delano Roosevelt for the strike's outcome and ramifications. He became one of FDR's bitterest and most determined opponents.

Yet when the United States officially entered World War II, Sloan threw himself fully behind FDR's industrial conversion program, with General Motors supplying the Allied forces with military goods worth more than $12 billion (several hundred billion in today's dollars). During the war, the General also trained or retrained more than 750,000 employees for new jobs. An unprecedented 25 percent of them were women, and they forever changed the face of American labor.

After the war, Sloan led the equally daunting feat of creating an entirely new product lineup and reconverting his hundred-plus plants and 800,000-plus employees to the production and marketing of consumer goods. Filled with new pride and confidence, both Rosie the Riveter and GI Joe soon expected and demanded more benefits and security than ever from their employers. General Motors became known as "Generous Motors," and the precedents it set in accommodating the workforce became the pattern for all American industry.

Through it all, Alfred remained the quiet, virtually unseen master planner and operator: "Silent Sloan," as many of his colleagues called him. In the end, his legacy is the deeds of the organization he put together and led. Yet beneath that image of the perfect modern CEO, there were also demons and faults. He held grudges; he suffered no fools, even if others told him they weren't fools; and he put the bottom line above all else.

STAYING ON MESSAGE

The only remnants of Alfred's career that remain in the General Motors corporate archives are copies of speeches, pamphlets, obituaries, and a twelve-page official biography that was written by the public relations staff and issued January 1, 1966, just six weeks before Sloan's death (and most likely approved in advance by Alfred himself). The Alfred P. Sloan Foundation, which he created in 1934, has an endowment in excess of $1 billion, but has no biographical material regarding the founder. The same goes for the Sloan School of Management at his alma mater, the Massachusetts

Institute of Technology, named after Alfred two years before his death.

Sloan personally created the General Motors PR department in the 1930s, when big business in general was under attack as never before, to keep reporters away from him and to make sure that they got from the company only what the company wanted them to get. (General Motors was also the first company to have a full-time in-house public relations staff.) Every message was crafted and targeted to further the company's own agenda, not Alfred's own glory—an example that many later chief executives of many corporations might wish they had followed.

Beyond the handful of early documents kept by Billy Durant and now stored at Kettering University (formerly the General Motors Institute) in Flint, Michigan, the only letters and memos bearing Sloan's signature that remain today are those selected by his team of personal researchers (hired by him rather than the company) for his book *My Years with General Motors,* published in 1963. Those documents are the core of the book's narrative.[1]

Reflecting Alfred's determination that the story left behind not only be the one he wanted told, but that it also be bulletproof on the facts it cited, the *My Years with General Motors* research team at one point included more than twenty professional researchers. Among them was renowned Harvard professor Alfred D. Chandler (the "D" standing for du Pont, who happened to be a distant cousin of the du Pont family). Chandler went on to write several management classics, including the seminal *Pierre S. du Pont and the Making of the Modern Corporation,* which was the first book to also examine the issues of corporate governance and policy that were at the core of the General Motors crisis of 1920.[2]

By the early 1930s, Alfred Sloan was widely considered to be one of the richest men in the world (Henry Ford holding the number-one spot). His portrait had also appeared on the cover of *Time* magazine, but he had no known hobbies and had never sold a single share of General Motors stock. His only known investment of either time or money in anything beyond the domain of General Motors was the purchase of a yacht at the urging of friends and his wife. Once he decided to go for it, he went big, but he soon lost interest.

As recounted in his *New York Times* obituary of February 18, 1966:

After some hesitation, the slim, dandily dressed industrialist agreed and bought a 236-footer for $1 million. He incorporated it, christened it *Rene,* hired a crew of 43 at an annual cost of $119,609, and embarked on a few cruises. But life afloat quickly bored him and the yacht was virtually laid up until he sold it in 1941 to the Maritime Commission for $175,000.

The *Rene* is also one of the few of Sloan's investments to lose money. His obituaries all emphasize that he did not smoke, hardly ever drank, and never played golf or any other sports. He was described by the *Times* as "a functional, frill-less man." John McDonald, who spent nine years working with him on *My Years with General Motors,* described him as "a very formal man out of the nineteenth century whose graven face was surrounded by the collar which had once seemed to hold up his chin but had come down over time—he was Mr. Sloan and I was John; few, and only those from far back, called him Alfred."[3]

Sloan was absolutely devoted to his wife Irene and made sure her name and image were kept private. When she died after a long illness at their Palm Beach winter home in 1956, after they had been married fifty-eight years, he resigned as chairman of General Motors but kept his feelings to himself. As McDonald recalled:

In culture and thought, Mr. Sloan was of that school for whom technology was progress, life was work, money was a measure of success, and success the goal. I noticed no religious feeling in him until just after his wife died, when he was visited by religious leaders: Cardinal Spellman came to see him twice, and Raymond [Sloan's brother] said that it was "very, very helpful." Later Billy Graham came to see him; but these visits seemed like the courtesy calls proper in crossover hierarchies.[4]

My Years with General Motors became an immediate bestseller and a manual for up-and-coming would-be corporate leaders. Alfred was no doubt pleased but refrained from comment, even when General Motors actually tried to block the book's publication. The General's legal staff claimed the book and the author's stature might be detrimental to the company's best interests in the antitrust climate of the time. When ghostwriter McDonald filed a lawsuit to free the manuscript for publication, Sloan weighed in on his side and the light turned green. When Alfred died, he was still on the bestseller list.

A MOST SERIOUS YOUNG MAN

As with Billy Durant, there was apparently nothing in Alfred Sloan's boyhood to mark or even suggest future greatness. Where young Billy was the restless dreamer, however, young Alfred was always the serious student.

The eldest of five children, he was born in New Haven, Connecticut, on May 23, 1875, the same year Billy's abandoned mother finally got her own house. In 1885, when Alfred was ten years old, his father's business forced the family to move to Brooklyn, New York. There, young Alfred quickly acquired a Brooklyn accent and a keen interest in mechanics and engineering. After high school at the Brooklyn Polytechnic Institute, he was admitted to the Massachusetts Institute of Technology in 1892 at the age of seventeen. The youngest member of his class, he graduated in just three years with a Phi Beta Kappa key and one of the highest academic records of any MIT engineering alumnus up to that time.

From that year forward, virtually all that remains for the record is Alfred's work life. In *My Years with General Motors,* a 472-page book, less than a page is devoted to his parents and his upbringing:

> My father was in the wholesale tea, coffee, and cigar business, with a firm called Bennett-Sloan and Company. In 1885 he moved the business to New York City, on West Broadway, and from the age of ten I grew up in Brooklyn. I am told I still have the accent. My father's father was a schoolteacher. My mother's father was a Methodist minister. My parents had five children, of whom I am the oldest. There is my sister, Mrs. Katherine Sloan Pratt, now a widow. There are my three brothers—Clifford, who was in the advertising business; Harold, a college professor; and Raymond, the youngest, who is a professor, writer, and expert on hospital administration. I think we have all had in common a capability for being dedicated to our respective interests.
>
> I came of age at almost exactly the time when the automobile business in the United States came into being. In 1895 the Duryeas, who had been experimenting with motor cars, started what I believe was the first gasoline-automobile manufacturing company in the United

States. In the same year I left the Massachusetts Institute of Technology with a B.S. in electrical engineering, and went to work for the Hyatt Roller Bearing Company of Newark, later of Harrison, New Jersey. The Hyatt antifriction bearing was later to become a component of the automobile, and it was through this component that I came into the automotive industry.[5]

With his top grades and fresh parchment, young Alfred was eager to find a position in his chosen field, engineering. But it was not to be. He recalled his job search the year of his graduation from MIT as "the most discouraging point in my whole life."[6]

Through his father's network of contacts, Alfred finally landed an interview with John E. Searles, head of the American Sugar Refining Company in New York. Rather than a job offer, Searles gave him a glowing letter of introduction to another company in which he was a key investor. It was a much smaller and far less prosperous firm in Newark, New Jersey, that happened to be looking for a draftsman and was offering a salary of $50 a month.

As Alfred recalled it in *Adventures of a White Collar Man* (a short book filled with personal anecdotes and observations, which may be the reason it is never cited in Alfred's later and more respected tome, *My Years with General Motors*):

Well, I am bound to admit the first sight of my opportunity was disappointing. . . . Not far from a city dump on a weed-grown, marshy plain was an old, weather-worn building, like an overgrown barn. In its indefinite yard there was a small mound of coal and a great mound of reddish-gray cinders and ashes; also a disorderly accumulation of discarded machinery of which I still seem to see one shape, the rusty cylinder of a worn-out steam boiler, all part of a junk yard next door. Once the factory had been painted brown. Only one word describes it: "dirty." Smoke from the dump carried an acrid odor. Eventually across the wall nearest the railroad track there was lettered in black this legend: HYATT ROLLER BEARING COMPANY.[7]

And things were even worse beneath the surface, with employees never knowing for sure whether the next paycheck would be there. He quietly observed and studied the company's mismanagement but also saw a broader market for its product, *if* the operation could get its act together. Sloan the MIT engineer described the Hyatt product advantage as follows:

> Roll a ball under your hand on a table and roll a pencil in the same manner. What you feel are "point" and "line" bearings. But to understand what mechanics mean by a surface "bearing," grasp a pencil in your hand and use your other hand to make it turn as a piece of shafting. Now, the lower half of the shaft is supported everywhere by contact with your hand—the upper half is not supported, merely covered. The advantages of ball and roller bearings were obvious many years ago to mechanical people. . . . Solid steel rollers, being inflexible, were not satisfactory at that stage, but a Hyatt flexible roller bearing was different. We had something. Our spirally wound tube roller had a spring-like quality, yielded to irregularities caused by poor manufacture, thus making automatic adjustments between housing and bearing.[8]

Ironically, John Hyatt (founder of the company and inventor of its flexible bearing) had never set out to design a bearing that could be used in a wide variety of machinery. He had actually been developing a sugarcane grinder for John Searles at the American Sugar Refining Company. The problem was that the grinder kept clogging as the cane was ground. Hyatt succeeded in reducing the clog by developing the flexible roller bearing, which led to Searles's backing the company.

Despite its product advantage, the enterprise continued to struggle near the turn of the century and young Alfred saw little future for himself if he stayed with it. He was courting his future wife, Irene Jackson of Roxbury, Massachusetts, and the two were eager to get married. Reluctantly, he resigned from Hyatt and went to work for another struggling company called Hygienic Refrigerator that was ahead of its time in trying (unsuccessfully) to develop and market an electric refrigerator. The electric refrigerator would actually come into its own through another company called Frigidaire, a name created by Billy Durant when he brought the operation into his General Motors empire in 1919.

Alfred Sloan married Irene on September 28, 1898, but, characteristically, left no details of the courtship or honeymoon. Although he was making more money at Hygienic Refrigerator than he had at Hyatt, he remained convinced of a bright future for Hyatt's product, *if* it could be efficiently manufactured and properly marketed.

EARLY RISK AND TURNAROUND

By the time Alfred was married, John Searles was the largest investor in Hyatt Roller Bearing and was propping it up to the point of kicking in his own money to make the payroll. When Searles finally decided to cut his losses and pull the plug early in 1899, Alfred was waiting in the wings. As he later described it:

> Mr. Searles had decided that he would put no more money into Hyatt. He declined to be its angel any longer. Unless some new backer could be found, it would be necessary to close down the works.
>
> Because of the friendship of my father and Mr. Searles, they had discussed the situation, with the result that I went back to Hyatt. My father and a man named Donner, an associate of Mr. Searles in the American Sugar Refining Company, had bought into the company. I think Mr. Donner and my father each put up $2,500. That was as far as Mr. Donner would go, but my father said he would advance more if the business showed any promise. Thereafter Pete [Steenstrup, the company bookkeeper], instead of going with the payroll to Mr. Searles, went to my father. Pete and I had become partners.[9]

Thus was Sloan given his first leadership assignment and a shot at saving the business.

Part of the deal was that Alfred and his friend Pete Steenstrup would have six months to return the business to black ink, no excuses. Their backers' gamble paid off quicker than they could have imagined. With Sloan handling production and Steenstrup handling sales, the company turned a profit of $12,000 in that first six-month trial period.

Although Alfred again left no details of how the feat was accomplished, it is not difficult to picture the meticulous MIT engineer reorganizing the plant and streamlining its bookkeeping as well as production. Sloan acknowledged only his father's support:

> Pete and I scarcely ever stopped. . . . Pete was given the title of sales manager. I was general manager. My father made that investment on my account, but I would be unfair to myself if I did not also say that he did it because he was satisfied that I could get the Hyatt Roller Bearing Company on its feet.[10]

Pete Steenstrup would remain loyal to Sloan all his life. Sloan, in turn, would give him several lucrative jobs at General Motors, beginning with the position of personal assistant to Sloan and ending with Pacific Coast sales manager for the Buick division, where one of Steenstrup's key customers would be Charles Howard, who parlayed a Buick franchise given him by Billy Durant into one of the largest fortunes in the state of California. Today, Howard is best known as the owner of the legendary racehorse Seabiscuit.

Sloan's struggle and success at Hyatt Roller Bearing during those early years always remained one of his proudest memories. When he sold the company to Billy Durant for $13.5 million in 1916, he wrote a long letter describing Hyatt's growth over the years. The letter was at Durant's request and was addressed to his lead banker for the deal, L. G. Kaufman of Chatham and Phoenix National Bank in New York, who also happened to be Durant's personal financial adviser and a member of the General Motors board of directors.

The letter is neither referenced nor mentioned in either of Sloan's books, but Billy kept it among his own papers for posterity. Alfred coolly boasted:

> I believe that the success of the company is attributable to the fact that while its organization is continually expanding, no changes have been found necessary to impair its logical and efficient development. The Works are thoroughly organized, 95 percent of the productive labor being on piece work. It is believed that the cost system is second to none; in fact, it is considered as a standard among manufacturing institutions in the East. The Works of the company are equipped with the most modern physical and chemical laboratories. Material is accepted and each step of the development of the raw material through the Works is checked with the most scientific and improved methods. It is believed that the company's laboratory equipment and organization for protecting the quality of its product is second to none. . . .
>
> The company manufactures roller bearings exclusively of the Hyatt type and this particular type of bearing is only manufactured by this company. The largest sale of the bearing is applied to motor car construction and the company numbers among its customers every motor car manufactured in America.[11]

What Alfred didn't mention in his letter was that Hyatt's growth had come from reinvestment of the company's own profits, rather than the acquisition and stock market strategy mastered by Billy Durant: a divergence of fundamental strategy that would be at the core of the General Motors crisis and showdown of 1920. In the wake of that crisis, as part of a public relations campaign to refocus public attention on the company's core business, General Motors mailed a pamphlet to all stockholders that described the activities of what were then called the company's accessory divisions, the stand-alone units building components for vehicle manufacture. Among these units was Hyatt Roller Bearing, and its competitive advantage remained what Sloan had first observed more than twenty years earlier:

> The distinctive feature of the Hyatt bearing is the helical roller, a "spiral," wound cold from chrome-vanadium steel, heat-treated to secure toughness, then ground for accuracy. The hollow rollers afford a large space for lubricant and the slots in the rollers distribute the lubricant over all bearing surfaces. There is so little wear in years of service that the bearings never need adjustment.[12]

The pamphlet also pointed out that Hyatt bearings were being used at the time in dozens of other kinds of manufacturing, including machine tools, cranes, mine cars, hoists, textile machinery, steel-mill equipment, trolleys, and locomotives. Sloan's very first success was still thriving and growing, as was the confidence in his own management ability that had led him to give it a shot back in 1899.

SEEING A NEW MARKET

When Sloan began lifting Hyatt from the ashes in 1899, the automobile industry in America was no more than the strange and wild obsession of a few tinkerers and an amusing diversion for the wealthy investors who backed them. Cars were still widely considered impractical toys and dangerous nuisances by most people. When he was first approached about doing business with one of the hundreds of small manufacturers, just a few months after his return to Hyatt, he didn't take it seriously.

Sloan received a letter out of the blue from a man named Elwood Haynes of Kokomo, Indiana, explaining that he had heard about the Hyatt bearing and wanted to know more about it. As it happened,

Haynes, a Johns Hopkins graduate, had successfully demonstrated the second functioning automobile designed and built in the United States at the Kokomo July Fourth Independence Day parade in 1894, just five months after the Duryea brothers of Illinois had demonstrated the first one in Springfield, Massachusetts. When he wrote to Sloan in 1899, Haynes claimed to have been building cars for five years but had never built more than a few a year. Later, he (like several others, including Henry Ford) would falsely claim that he had actually built a car before the Duryeas and deserved bragging rights as the father of the American auto industry; he even included the tag line "The Haynes is America's first car" in all of his advertisements.

Haynes's letter was hardly the cause of excitement at Hyatt, but Sloan nonetheless dispatched Pete Steenstrup to Haynes's Kokomo, Indiana, workshop, where he quickly secured a small order. At that point, the lightbulb clicked in Sloan's mind. As he later recalled: "That [the first Haynes order] was the beginning of our real adventures. It woke us up. If one automobile manufacturer wanted something better than ordinary greased wagon axles, why not sell to all of them?"[13]

The problem was that Haynes's order was for just a sample, and the sample had to meet Haynes's own unique specifications. After complying (and pleasing the customer), Sloan and Steenstrup were soon receiving dozens of orders from other companies claiming to be producing automobiles. Like Haynes, all were building no more than a few cars a year and all wanted a sample order to their own unique specifications.

Sloan described the new business as a nuisance for the factory, but presciently, he not only continued to comply with his new customers' requests, he started writing his own letters soliciting business from dozens of other concerns that claimed to be developing an automobile, including one led by a struggling tinkerer named Henry Ford.

Sloan's persistence in seeking a new market in the automobile soon paid off bigger than any decision he had yet made. In the summer of 1900, he finally received the order that made him rethink and refocus his entire business. It was an order for a car called Oldsmobile that would soon transform the fledgling auto industry from hand assembly to volume production and mass marketing. As Sloan recalled it forty years later:

Pete recklessly called me on the long-distance telephone. He was returning East and wanted me to meet him at the plant on Sunday; he
had a trial order from the Olds Motor Works. They wanted 120 bearings, four for each rear axle in thirty automobiles. Pete was beside
himself, and so was I.[14]

When Alfred Sloan met Pete Steenstrup at the plant that Sunday, Steenstrup reported that the chief engineer of Olds Motor
Works, Howard Coffin, had told him that Olds planned to build
more than a thousand cars the following year.

"That seemed fantastic," Sloan recalled. "If our bearing stood
up—well, that is why we talked, sketched, and planned all that
summer Sunday. If this test order gave satisfaction, we might have
to increase the size of our plant."[15]

CHAPTER FOUR

A New Machine Creates a New Order

ALFRED SLOAN'S PRODUCT and his own reputation as a businessman had put him in the right place at the right time. The helter-skelter pattern of one- or two-car assembly shops was finally about to gel into a semblance of real industry to meet America's coming love affair with the automobile.

Just a few months after Alfred and Pete Steenstrup received Oldsmobile's order, in the fall of 1900, the country's first automobile show was held at Madison Square Garden in New York City. More than 300 vehicles were on display, and more than 50,000 people paid the show's nominal admission fee to see them. By the end of the year, more than a hundred firms claimed to be either developing or selling their own unique car—two-thirds of them still powered by steam or batteries.

Neither Sloan nor Billy Durant yet saw the automobile as his destiny, but they had many traits in common with the strong-willed cast of characters who were then shaping the infant industry in America. Those same characters would influence both Billy and Alfred's view of business and, indeed, their destinies. Both men would carry the lessons learned from the early pioneers into their future endeavors. Billy, Alfred, and their General Motors changed American business, and the methods they used evolved from the long, winding, perilous, and unanticipated ways in which the automobile itself evolved in America.

AN ANCIENT IDEA SLOWLY TAKES HOLD

The automobile (a name taken from the Greek word *auto,* for self, and the Latin word *mobils,* for moving) had been a dream and vision as far back as the fourteenth century, when the Italian painter Francesco di Giorgio Martini designed a platform mounted on four wheels, with each wheel powered by a hand-turned crank and gear. Leonardo da Vinci designed a similar contraption, with battle armor added. Sail-powered carriages were being used in Holland in the 1600s, but the concept of mechanical propulsion took more than another century to evolve into a workable machine.

In 1769, the French captain of artillery Nicolas-Joseph Cugnot designed and actually built a steam-powered, three-wheeled vehicle to haul field artillery. Because it had to stop every twenty minutes to build a fresh head of steam, it was never a threat to horse-drawn caissons. In 1839 came the first electric vehicle, built by Scotsman Robert Anderson, but its battery life was as short as Cugnot's head of steam. In 1860, the internal combustion engine was invented and patented in France by Jean-Joseph-Etienne Lenoir. The German Nicholas Otto took the Lenoir concept one step further in 1876 with a four-cycle gasoline-powered engine but stopped short of trying to apply it to automotive propulsion.

One year later, a prescient American named George Selden, who happened to be a lawyer rather than an inventor, applied for a patent on a series of drawings for the design of what he called "the road engine." Although he never built an engine or a vehicle, the Selden patent eventually made the builders of all gasoline-powered vehicles built in America libel for damages if they did not first acquire a license from Selden. To make sure everyone paid up, the Association of Licensed Automobile Manufacturers (ALAM), more commonly called the Selden cartel, was created. Selden's grip held until a wildly independent tinkerer and dreamer named Henry Ford refused to pay up in 1903. The ALAM promptly filed suit and Ford fought it through the courts until 1911, when an appellate ruling declared the original Selden design to be so abstract that it had nothing in common with automobiles as they were actually evolving. Only then were American companies and individuals truly free to compete with one another in the growing automobile market.

While Selden played his lawyer game in the United States, the world's first gasoline-powered automobile was finally built and demonstrated successfully in 1885 by the German mechanical engineer Karl Benz. It was a three-wheeled vehicle, with a tiller for steering, and was patented the following January.

Also in 1885, another German engineer named Gottlieb Daimler took Otto's gasoline engine to its logical extension by adding a carburetor for injecting the fuel directly to the cylinder, under pressure. Its smaller size, lighter weight, and higher efficiency were the breakthroughs needed to make the gasoline-powered motor car practical. In 1886, Daimler adapted the frame of a stagecoach to hold his engine and created the world's first four-wheeled automobile. Today, Benz's name lives on in the brand Mercedes-Benz and Daimler's in DaimlerChrysler, the corporation that builds and sells Mercedes-Benz vehicles.

In America, the automobile was not developed until nearly ten years after the first Daimler car. It evolved independently of what was happening in Europe, and it drew little notice from the press of the day or the general public.

At the 1893 Columbian Exposition, better known as the Chicago World's Fair, the future of technology was a major theme, but there was only one internal combustion engine automobile on display. It was a Benz quadricycle (a styleless platform with a seat, engine, tiller, and four wheels) that had been brought over from Germany by William Steinmetz, the famous New York piano builder who had just acquired exclusive rights to sell Benz and Daimler products in America. The leading journal of technology and invention, *Scientific American,* covered the fair's displays of locomotives, ships, and even bicycles in depth but did not even mention the automobile.

Nor was there much interest the following year, when the first car engineered and built in America hit the road. The car was called the Duryea, after the two brothers and bicycle mechanics from Illinois who developed it. Today, it resides in the Smithsonian Institution, but the only people who took notice back then were other tinkerers trying to develop their own motor car. The Duryea was publicly demonstrated on January 18, 1894. Elwood Haynes (Alfred Sloan's first automotive customer) demonstrated his own first model just a few months later, followed by Alexander Winton, Colonel Albert Pope (whose first car was powered by steam rather than gasoline and who would, sadly, stick to steam and batteries after the rest of the industry had shifted to gasoline), Ransom Olds, Charles King, and finally, Henry Ford (who took the first ride in his own version of the quadricycle on June 4, 1896).

When the Duryea made its first run, no one knew exactly how many people in the country were either developing an automobile or had actually demonstrated one. When the *Chicago Times-Herald* decided to sponsor the country's first-ever car race a year later, the editors expected to get a handful of candidates; instead they got eighty, from all across the nation. That race would prove to be a seminal event not only in America's love affair with the automobile but in the way future manufacturers like Billy Durant would publicize their babies.

Vehicle entrants were required to have at least three wheels, run on power derived from a mechanical device rather than animal muscle, and carry at least two people, one of whom was to be an independent "umpire" assigned by the *Times-Herald*. The race was originally to be from Chicago to Milwaukee and the date was set for November 2, 1895. However, reflecting the condition of the candidates' finances as well as their vehicles, only three of the official eighty entrants showed up: the Duryea and two Benz cars, one of which was owned by the R. H. Macy Company (of department store fame) in New York. The other entrants all pleaded for a postponement. The newspaper obliged and set the new date for November 28, Thanksgiving Day.

Seventy-nine vehicles arrived in Chicago, but the city had been hit with a blizzard the day before the race. By morning, more than six inches of snow had fallen and winds were approaching sixty miles per hour. The judges decided to run the event from Chicago to Evanston, Illinois, rather than Milwaukee, a distance of just fifty-five miles. Nonetheless, all but eleven entrants dropped out rather than risk driving under such conditions.

Only two cars finished the race: one of the Benz cars (although not the Macy entry) and the Duryea. The Duryea beat the Benz's time by more than an hour and a half, giving the image of "Made in America" an instant quantum leap over the European imports of the day.

More important, the Duryea's success under such brutal conditions demonstrated vividly, once and for all, that the horseless carriage was a viable machine. No horse-drawn carriage could have pulled off such a feat under such conditions.

The umpire in the Duryea car happened to be a Toronto writer and reporter named Arthur White (who also weighed more than 200 pounds, adding an extra challenge for the car). After the victory, he wrote:

> Three and one-half gallons of gasoline and nineteen gallons of water were consumed. No power outside the vehicle was used. I estimate that enough power was used to run the motor 120 miles over smooth roads. We finished at 7:18. Our correct time was seven hours and fifty-three minutes. We covered a distance of 54.36 miles, averaging a little more than seven miles per hour.[1]

White also commented on several delays of an hour or more caused by impassable roads and mechanical failures caused by the cars striking ruts and obstacles.

When one of the rivals of the Duryeas and Haynes, Alexander Winton, later decided to garner even more publicity by driving his car the unprecedented distance of 800 miles, from Cleveland to New York, it took him seventy-eight hours and forty-three minutes. Winton blamed the poor speed on the state of roads (or absence thereof), for which he had a one-word description: "Outrageous!"[2]

The 1895 *Times-Herald* race was covered by the Associated Press and United Press International. Stories about it were run in every major city in Europe as well as the United States. When the Barnum & Bailey Circus opened in New York the following spring, the victorious Duryea car was near the head of the parade.

Also in 1896, the Duryea car was entered in the fifty-five-mile London-to-Brighton race in England. It was the only American entry; all of the forty others were either French, German, or English. The lone American was given absolutely no chance of winning but finished in first place, a full hour ahead of the second-place entry, causing even more headlines on both sides of the Atlantic. The novelty called the automobile was starting to catch on.

Detroit, Michigan, was still not a factor in either the races or the infant motor car business. Although the city was already a major manufacturing center, building rail cars and stoves as well as ships for the Great Lakes commerce, no one took notice when native son Charles King took a ride on a quadricycle he had built in his spare time. Nor did anyone notice another self-taught mechanic named Henry Ford following behind on a bicycle to study how well King's contraption performed.

ENTER RANSOM OLDS

The year 1896 was also a time of transformation for the man who would soon become the customer Alfred Sloan had dreamed of for his Hyatt Roller Bearing Company: Ransom E. Olds.

Olds was born in on June 3, 1864, (three years before Billy Durant and eleven years before Alfred Sloan) in Geneva, Ohio, sixty miles from Cleveland. His father, Pliny Olds, was a successful blacksmith with visions of owning his own machine shop. Pliny moved the family to Lansing, Michigan, where he was able to buy his machine shop, in 1880. Encouraged to take up the trade by his father, Ransom (Ranny, as he was called) quickly became an expert machinist and focused his attention on improving the gasoline engine. Soon, he and his father were building gasoline engines in a variety of sizes for factory, agricultural, and marine applications. The business quickly expanded to two shops.

In 1887, at the age of twenty-three, Ranny built his first horseless carriage, a three-wheeled, steam-powered vehicle that was never intended to be commercial. By 1894, as the family business continued to expand, he had designed a gasoline-powered car but did not have it built in time to enter the *Times-Herald* race in Chicago. He nonetheless attended the race and came away with three strong impressions: European vehicles were not unbeatable; gasoline was definitely the power source of the future; and people were fascinated by the new machines as soon as they saw them in motion. When he finally completed his first car in the spring of 1896, he told friends, "I am thoroughly convinced that had we placed our vehicle in the *Times-Herald* contest at Chicago we could have captured the first prize easily."[3]

The following year, with the family engine business thriving and growing faster than ever, Pliny Olds retired to California and left the day-to-day operations in Ranny's hands. Ranny immediately decided to shift the focus to automobile production and to secure outside financial backing to build his own car factory, the first ever built in America for the exclusive production of automobiles.

Within a year, Ranny had built his plant in Lansing. He had also engineered a second model that seated four people. However, he already realized that the Lansing plant was too small for the kind of volume he envisioned. He found new financial backing in Detroit and incorporated a new company called the Olds Motor Works on May 8, 1899, with capital of $500,000. Construction of a new plant complex began immediately. It was to include four separate buildings to house assembly, foundry, machine shop, and administrative offices on Detroit's East Jefferson Avenue (near what is now DaimlerChrysler's largest Midwest manufacturing complex). At the same time, design and engineering for the product line began, with no less than eleven pilot cars of different size and design built back in Lansing.

When the first cars rolled out of the Detroit factory, however, they did not catch on the way Ranny had hoped. Fortunately, the stationary-gasoline-engine business was still booming and offset substantial financial losses from the car business in 1899 and 1900.

Foreseeing the business model that was to forge Henry Ford's later success and fame, Ranny Olds soon became convinced that the way to create a volume market was to concentrate on a small car that was simple, dependable, and affordable. He came up with a vehicle he called the Curved Dash Oldsmobile, which was soon to become the first volume-production car in America. It was so called because the floor under the driver and passenger curved up and back, like a sleigh. The small, light, and simple design stood out from others much the way Billy Durant's first road cart had from its competition fifteen years earlier.

In his later years, Olds commented in-depth on the strategy as well as the agony and struggle of those first two years in Detroit that led to his success:

> It was our plan at that time [1899] to put out a model that would sell for $1,250. I had fitted it up with some very up-to-the-minute improve-

ments—pneumatic clutch, cushion tires, and electric push-button starter. We thought we had quite a car, but we soon found that it was too complicated for the public. That first year we ran behind about $80,000.

The prospects of the industry were not very bright. Winton was making some cars down at Cleveland, and Duryea, Haynes, and Apperson [Edgar Apperson was an early rival of the Duryeas; his name and car were soon forgotten] were all in the market. But the public persisted in the idea that it was not a practical proposition and would be a thing of the past within a year or two.

Finally, after a long sleepless night, I decided to discard all my former plans and build a little one-cylinder runabout, for I was convinced that if success came it must be through a more simple machine.

It was my idea to build a machine which would weigh about 500 pounds and would sell for around $500. The result was the Curved Dash "Oldsmobile," weighing 700 pounds and selling for $650. My whole idea in building it was to have the operation so simple that anyone could run it and the construction such that it could be repaired at any local shop.[4]

Though he rarely gets credit, Ransom Olds had laid out the product strategy and focus that would prove to be the key to success not only in automobiles but hundreds of other businesses, including computers, throughout the twentieth century and beyond.

Implementing the plan, however, was to be a bit more challenging. Before the first Curved Dash Oldsmobile was built, a fire broke out in the plant on March 9, 1901. It started with a gasoline explosion in the assembly building and leveled all the other buildings within an hour. The only things salvaged were one pilot vehicle and the mechanical drawings for building it and the other Olds models.

Olds remained undaunted. With his own plant gone, he turned to key suppliers to produce everything that would have been manufactured in-house and assembled the vehicles in Lansing while construction of a new, much larger plant began in that city. By the end of the year, the little runabout was a hit. Four-hundred were built and sold in 1901. The following year, with the new Lansing plant in operation, the number increased to 2,500, making the Curved Dash Oldsmobile the most popular car in a market that was finally blossoming.

The astounding sales jump reflected the public's desire for Olds's

innovative new model. It also reflected the impact of one more innovation that he put into his new plant: namely, the assembly line.

Henry Ford is often credited with inventing the assembly line
(just as he is often credited with inventing the American automobile), but the concept itself went back at least to the year 1798, when
Eli Whitney won a bid to supply 10,000 muskets to the infant U.S.
military. Thomas Jefferson had witnessed a demonstration of an assembly line of interchangeable parts that Whitney had devised to
prove he could produce the weapons in that quantity.

Although Billy Durant had used the assembly line in his Flint
carriage operations, marking the first time it was applied to the manufacture of vehicles, Ransom Olds was the first to apply it to the
automobile, just as he was the first to build a factory designed specifically for exclusive production of automobiles. Parts were laid
out in line at a series of work stations. Workers performed one task
(e.g., wheel and axle assembly) at one station and then moved on to
another station while another group of workers took over that first
station to perform the next task in the assembly process (e.g., en-
gine/chassis assembly). Parts were continuously brought to each
station in wheeled bins.

The Olds production system remained the model for the rest of
the industry until Henry Ford took it to its logical conclusion and
revolutionized mass production, more than a decade later, by having the assembly line itself move while the workers remained stationary.

To publicize his new car, Ranny Olds arranged for Roy Chapin
(future head of Hudson Motor Company, predecessor to American
Motors, later acquired by the Chrysler Corporation, which in turn
merged with Daimler Benz) to drive a Curved Dash Oldsmobile from
Detroit to New York, in conjunction with the second annual New
York Automobile Show at Madison Square Garden. Chapin arrived
late for the show's opening and stopped first at the Waldorf Astoria
to meet with Ranny before having the car washed and serviced for
its grand entrance on Tuesday, November 6, 1901. The *New York
Tribune* reported the occasion the following day:

> Another new machine reached the Garden yesterday for which the
> owner claims an interesting record. It arrived in the city Tuesday. . . .
> The automobile is of the gasoline sort and was driven from Detroit to

this city in seven and one-half days. The machine weighs 800 pounds
and on the trip covered 820 miles and consumed thirty gallons of gasoline. The route was through Canada, crossing to the United States over
the suspension bridge just below Niagara Falls. The owner says his
experience has shown that the lightweight automobiles are well
adapted to such tours.[5]

Word spread fast from there through other news stories and advertising. Olds was the first automaker to advertise nationally. One
of its first ads, run in the *Ladies' Home Journal,* remains a classic for
its direct appeal to both the woman driver and the (supposedly)
more technically inclined male:

The ideal vehicle for shopping and calling—equally suitable for a
pleasant afternoon drive or an extended tour. It is built to run and *does*
it.

Operated entirely from the seat by a single lever—always under
instant control. The mechanism is simple—no complicated machinery—no multiplicity of parts.

A turn of the starting crank and the Oldsmobile "goes" with nothing
to watch but the road.

Price, including mud guards, $650.00.[6]

Ransom Olds's vision and determination paid off not only for
himself but for all those suppliers who scrambled to meet his unprecedented high-volume orders: none more than Alfred Sloan's
Hyatt Roller Bearing. In 1903, sales of the Oldsmobile rose to 4,000
cars; in 1904, they reached 5,000, making it the number-one seller
by far. Soon, Olds's dual concepts—large volume production in a
plant dedicated exclusively to the automobile and mass advertising
campaigns aimed at the buyer's needs and desires—would be adopted
by all other automakers.

Despite Olds's unsung legacy, Alfred Sloan makes no mention
of his accomplishments and contributions in *My Years with General
Motors* and limits his assessment of Olds to just three sentences
in *Adventures of a White Collar Man*: "Speed! That was the most
important word of all to Ransom E. Olds. He was a pioneer in the
field of quantity production."[7]

LELAND, MASTER OF PRECISION

Of all the American automobile industry's unique and colorful characters, the one whom Alfred Sloan most admired and emulated was cold, silver-bearded Henry Martyn Leland, who also owed his start in the automotive business to Ransom E. Olds. Founder of the Cadillac Motor Company, Leland was a perfectionist who expected and demanded higher standards than any of his peers. He accepted no excuses and suffered no fools: a man after Alfred Sloan's own heart. Sloan devoted more words and detail to what he learned from Leland than he did any other person.

Born on February 16, 1843, in Barton, Vermont, twenty-five miles from the Canadian border, Henry Leland (like Sloan) was uprooted at a young age. The family moved to Worcester, Massachusetts, where young Leland (like the young Ranny Olds) quickly developed an interest in machines in general and engines in particular. He became an apprentice machinist at the age of sixteen. Denied enlistment in the Union Army because he was too young, he turned to machining the lathes used to make rifle stocks. When his elder brother Edson (with whom he had tried to enlist) was killed in action, he advanced to work on the machines that produced the rifles themselves rather than just the stocks.

The Civil War remained a vivid memory throughout his life, as it did for the rest of his generation. When he started his last car company at the age of seventy-six, he called it Lincoln, after President Abraham Lincoln. When Ford Motor Company bought that company a year later, it kept the Lincoln brand name.

After the Civil War, Leland married Ellen Hull, a Worcester native, but he could not find steady work in the community. In 1872, with two young sons, he moved the family to Providence, Rhode Island, to work for the firm of Brown & Sharpe, the leading toolmaker in the country. While there, he learned to machine tools and parts to within a thousandth of an inch of accuracy, a skill rare and respected in all kinds of blossoming industries. He also invented the first mechanical barber's clippers for a Brown & Sharpe customer (which Brown & Sharpe patented under the firm's name and soon marketed all over the world) and perfected the precision pistons and cylinders required for a new air brake system for locomotives.

In 1883, in part because of his passion for building and improving stationary gasoline engines and in part as a reward for his contributions to the company (many of which, like the barber clippers, had swelled the company's coffers but brought him only small pay raises), Leland was given sales responsibility for all Brown & Sharpe business west of Pittsburgh. He was soon calling on prospective clients in the growing city of Detroit, where dozens of small firms and inventors were building and improving the gasoline engine for different applications.

He was also soon making plans to open his own machine shop in Detroit. On September 19, 1890, with the financial backing of a local Detroit bicycle builder and a lumber baron from Alpena, Michigan (a hundred miles north of Detroit), Leland's new machine shop opened its doors for business under the name Leland, Falconer & Norton (the other two names coming from his financial backers). Leland's son Wilfred, who had been studying at Brown University and planned on becoming a medical doctor, soon dropped out of school to join his father in the new business.

Father and son quickly found themselves swamped with orders from firms that wanted the Lelands to do further grinding and machining to make their engines perform with more precision. Accordingly, son Wilfred returned to Rhode Island for further training as a precision machinist at Brown & Sharpe. After matching his father's ability to machine metal pieces to a thousandth of an inch of accuracy, he came back to Detroit and was put in charge of training (and retraining) all of the firm's other machinists. Within six months, the initial total payroll of a dozen people had grown to sixty. Among those trained by Wilfred during this early period was an employee named Horace Dodge, who went on to establish his own shop with his brother John and shortly thereafter became the head of engine production for yet another new company called Ford Motor.

As the Lelands' business continued to mushroom, so did Henry Leland's reputation as a hard taskmaster. Stories of "the old man" walking through the plant and foundry kicking and throwing faulty castings aside became legendary. Often, the parts he angrily discarded because they did not meet his own standards had actually met those of his customers, but that didn't matter to the senior Leland.

Because of that reputation, the Lelands were Ransom Olds's natural first choice to build the new, small, and unique gasoline engine for his Curved Dash Oldsmobile in 1901. They eagerly accepted the business and the durable, reliable Olds engine was soon winning customers.

Yet Henry Leland was not content with the efficiency and performance of the Olds engine, despite the success of his customer's new car. He turned his machinists and engineers loose to see if they could do better, without advising Olds Motor Works of what was going on. Soon, they had a prototype of a completely new engine that delivered 10.25 horsepower, compared to the 3 horsepower of the Olds runabout's original engine.

Yet when Leland proudly showed the new engine to the Olds Motor Works management in the summer of 1902, he was immediately rebuffed. The Olds management team, represented by the key financial backer Fred Smith rather than Ransom Olds himself, explained that the cost of redesigning the car and retooling the plant to accommodate the new engine would be more than it was worth. Leland, in turn, immediately took his prototype to another group of Detroit financiers who had joined forces just four months earlier to back a struggling tinkerer named Henry Ford and were about to pull the plug on him. The money men embraced Leland and dumped Ford.

HENRY FORD AND HIS DEMONS

The way Henry Ford lost his earliest shot at volume car production to Henry Leland remains a stark lesson for overly confident entrepreneurs and venture capitalists. It is also an early reflection of the character flaws that would later cause Ford to be mistrusted and vilified as an unbalanced bigot rather than worshiped as the Horatio Alger success that he alone believed he was.

Ford's upbringing and his values were a sharp contrast to those of both Billy Durant and Alfred Sloan. He was born on July 30, 1863, (less than two years after Durant and twelve years before Sloan) on a farm ten miles west of Detroit. The area would later be included in the town of Dearborn, although while Ford was growing up, there was nothing but isolated farmland surrounded by forest.

Like Billy and Alfred, Henry Ford did not grow up poor; however, the similarities end there. His father William's migration to America from Ireland in 1847, during the famous (catastrophic) potato famine, had been preceded by that of two of William's uncles in the 1830s. The uncles were already among the largest land owners in the Dearborn area by the time William arrived. They gave him a loan to start his own farm. By the time Henry was born, William's personal labor and determination had forged that loan into one of the largest and most prosperous farms in the region.

The eldest of six children, Henry grew up working on the family farm and hating it. Although his father was always there to help him financially, there was also always tension between the two. While the father was active in community affairs (he was even elected justice of the peace), Henry was always described as stubborn and introverted, even by his brothers and sisters. Everyone who knew him as a boy also saw resentment of his father. For example, Henry always claimed that he had wanted to be a mechanic as a boy but his father wanted him to farm and held him back, even though several of Henry's biographers refute the claim with letters and anecdotes from neighbors and relatives that show he was never held back.[8]

The various Ford biographies trace part of the resentment to the tragic early death of Henry's mother, Mary. She died of labor complications after giving birth to a still-born child in 1876, when Henry was just thirteen years old. Mary was thirty-seven years old and had been Henry's comfort and strength in his battles with his father. No doctors had been present at any of the other births, and Henry's father William called for a doctor this time only after Mary had been ill for days. Henceforth, Henry would credit the roots of all his later success to values instilled by his mother and would rarely mention his father.

Of his mother, he would say:

> She taught me that disagreeable jobs call for courage and patience and self-discipline, and she taught me also that [saying] "I don't want to" gets a fellow nowhere . . .
>
> My mother used to say, when I grumbled about it, "Life will give you many unpleasant tasks. . . . Your duty will be hard and disagreeable and painful to you at times, but you must do it. You may have pity on others, but you must not pity yourself."[9]

Of his father, he would recall only: "My father was not entirely in sympathy with my bent towards mechanics. . . . He thought I ought to be a farmer."[10]

After his mother's death, Henry grew even more withdrawn from his father and siblings, spending as much time as he could in his room tearing apart watches and clocks and then rebuilding them to understand how they worked. Two years after Mary's passing, at the age of fifteen, he ran away from home and quickly found employment as a mechanic's apprentice in Detroit. His father went searching for him and found him boarding with an aunt, where Henry told him he preferred to stay.

Four years later, Henry returned to the farm, where he was to depend on his father William for room and board until he was almost thirty years old and married. In 1886, when Henry was twenty-three (the same year Billy Durant started his first carriage business at age twenty-four), his father gave him eighty acres and a house, where Henry stayed until he finally landed a full-time job in Detroit in 1891, three years after he was married.

Not surprisingly, these years of dependence on his father draw scant attention in Henry Ford's own reminiscences and his several biographies. Luckily for both father and son, Henry spent much of his time on the road, working on and off as a traveling maintenance-and-repair man for farm customers of the Westinghouse Company throughout southeastern Michigan.

Henry's first and only full-time job was to supervise the maintenance of the generators at the Edison Illuminating Company of Detroit, an affiliate of Thomas Edison's business empire and the largest supplier of electric power to residences and businesses in Detroit. He was at last able to move back to Detroit with his wife Clara, whom he had married in 1888 after a two-year courtship. Clara, whose parents were also socially prominent in Dearborn, had lived with Henry on the farm without complaint. She also followed him to Detroit without complaint. Henry always called her "the Believer" and credited her as the only person with faith in his ideas and his dreams. (In contrast, Billy Durant credited his daughter Margery and his second wife, not Margery's mother, as the only constant believers through all his ups and downs.)

Put on the night shift, Henry soon found himself with plenty of free time at the power plant to tinker with experimental engines of his own design. At home, he was also soon tinkering with the idea of building not only an engine but a quadricycle. Henry and Clara's only child, Edsel, was born in 1893, but even that event did not distract Henry from spending most of his free time working on a quadricycle in the workshop he had built in a shed behind the house they rented.

Despite Henry's own later claims, he was apparently more obsessed with the act of tinkering itself at this time than with "inventing" an automobile that would change the world. As the Ford family biographer Robert Lacey wrote in his definitive *Ford: The Men and the Machine*:

> In mechanical terms, Henry Ford appears to have consecrated most of his twenties and thirties to the joy of tinkering. His expertise with machinery was considerable, but it was undirected: watches, farm machines, electrical generators—almost anything that whirred and got his fingers oily. Henry Ford has conventionally been depicted as forsaking his farm in 1891, in the Horatio Alger tradition, intent on devising a horseless carriage in Detroit, but this squares neither with his four years of dabbling once he got there, nor with his own testimony.[11]

Henry completed his quadricycle the evening of June 4, 1896, and could not wait to take it for a spin. Yet in his obsession with tinkering rather than planning, he had failed to think about how he would get it out of the brick workshop, whose door was far too narrow for the machine. He picked up an axe and proceeded to knock out the building's door frame and a considerable section of brick wall. At four o'clock in the morning, with Clara watching, he drove away honking his horn triumphantly.

For the next several days, Henry drove the machine all around Detroit, leading some neighbors to proclaim, "There goes Crazy Henry." That weekend, he drove it to the family farm in Dearborn, where every member of the family took a ride save one: his father.

Yet it was his father's connections that enabled Henry to pursue his first (failed) commercial venture. The mayor of Detroit, William Maybury, had made his fortune in real estate and was a close friend of William Ford and his uncles. In 1897, he gave Henry the money he needed to build a second car while still working full-time at Edison. After that car was built, Maybury put Henry in touch with William Murphy, a lumber baron (in the tradition of Billy Durant's grandfather Henry Howland Crapo) who happened to be the wealthiest man in Detroit.

Like Maybury and most of Detroit's other self-made millionaires, William Murphy was intrigued with the idea of the automobile. Upon meeting Henry Ford, who was now approaching his forties, he told him that if he could take him for a ride in the new vehicle from Detroit to the towns of Farmington and Pontiac and back (a total distance of sixty miles), he would enlist other local financiers to fund a manufacturing operation. The trip was a snap and the Detroit Automobile Company was incorporated on August 5, 1899, with Henry Ford employed as mechanical superintendent. Murphy and eleven others capitalized the company at $150,000 and gave Henry free rein to build a production car based on the one Murphy had ridden in to Pontiac.

Free to pursue what Murphy and company thought to be his passion and his dream, Henry immediately quit his job at the Edison Illuminating Company. Yet at his new enterprise, he continued to focus on tinkering rather than on delivering a marketable product. The Detroit Automobile Company was dissolved in November 1900, sixteen months after its inception, after having built a total of just twelve vehicles and losing a total of $86,000 for its backers.

Henry was back on the street looking for new backers to build another new automobile. In his ghostwritten autobiography, *My Life and Work*, Ford laid the Detroit Automobile Company's failure squarely at the feet of his financial backers, who he described as "a group of men of speculative turn of mind." His own defense was that "being without authority other than my engineering position gave me, I found that the new company was not a vehicle for realizing my ideas but a money-making concern."[12]

Ford spoke with disdain for those who put making money above realizing his "ideas," but it was his own lack of concern for making money that killed the operation. The original agreement was that Ford would build a simple car that would be marketed to the general public. Most tinkerers and inventors would have moved into high gear if given such a chance to produce their creation in volume, but Henry failed to focus on production. Instead, he toyed with a livery wagon, a race car, and several other designs, later justifying it by saying he felt none of the ideas had yet been perfected to the point of moving them into the production phase. He also spent less and less time at the shop, coming and going at his own whim (as he would later do at all his operations). As Ford's own chief mechanic, Fred Strauss, described it:

> Henry wasn't ready. He didn't have an automobile design. To get the
> shop going, Henry gave me some sketches to turn up some axle shaft-

ings. I started machining these axle shaftings to show them we were doing something. It was just to get it going but they didn't belong to anything. We never used them for the automobile. It was just a stall until Henry got a little longer into it.[13]

By now, Ford was thirty-seven years old and his son Edsel was seven. With no prospects of employment and no capital to take another shot at putting one of his automotive concepts into production, he moved the family back to the farm. During this period of unemployment and depression, a friend and fellow mechanic named Oliver Barthel suggested he read a popular book on theology and reincarnation to help regain his confidence. The book was called *A Short View of the Great Questions*. After reading it several times, Ford emerged a firm believer in reincarnation. Over the next two decades, as he overcame incredible obstacles that were often created by his own behavior, he became outspoken not only about reincarnation but his many personal biases, especially his fanatical anti-Semitism. As noted by two of his biographers, Peter Collier and David Horowitz:

He was an almanac of superstitions and prejudices. In the forefront of new technological ideas, he still worried when black cats crossed his path and about inadvertently passing under ladders. If he put a sock on inside out in the morning, he didn't change it. Whenever he saw a red-haired person he immediately looked for a white horse and vice versa, believing for some reason that the two went together. On Friday the thirteenth it was difficult to get him out of the house.[14]

Such superstitions and prejudices were no doubt bolstered by the way "Crazy Henry" was to reenter the automobile business in the early 1900s, only to fail again and then be given yet another chance.

LELAND IS IN, CADILLAC IS BORN

Less than a year after the failure of the Detroit Automobile Company, Henry Ford was again saved by William Murphy, the man who had put that doomed enterprise together. Still the wealthiest and one of the most powerful men in Detroit, Murphy was also still determined to dabble in the car business, which continued to get more and more publicity across the nation, thanks to the popularity of racing.

When Ford told Murphy he could build a single race car that would take on all comers (rather than a car that might make money), Murphy agreed to give him the financing he needed to produce just that one vehicle. With full enthusiasm, Ford built his car and entered it in a race against the world's speed record holder, Alexander Winton. The race was held on October 10, 1901, at a brand-new track in the town of Grosse Pointe, Michigan, which at that time was nothing more than a collection of a few lakeshore summer mansions surrounded by forest. The race drew no fewer than 8,000 spectators and, like all others of its kind, was covered by the national press. Driving his own car, the unknown Henry Ford was the underdog from the start.

The stars seemed to be again aligned for Ford, however. Winton's car developed mechanical problems early on. With his engine spewing blue smoke, Winton managed to finish the race but Ford, who had never raced before, took the lead after a few laps and kept it.

The name Henry Ford burst into the headlines across the country. Thanks to the publicity, he again found the financial backing he needed to form a new automobile company less than two months after that first Grosse Pointe race. This time, the company bore his own name to capitalize off his fame. However, Ford's new operation was at the mercy of yet another group of local Detroit millionaires who were eager to make money rather than headlines. Led again by William Murphy, the five investors each put in $10,000 and issued 6,000 shares of stock priced at ten dollars each, with Ford granted one-sixth of the shares in return for his granting the company his designs, his expertise, and his name.

Again, the investors' intent was to produce a marketable, practical car. Yet Ford again set out to build another racer that would bring him more glory. As biographer Robert Lacey put it: "He knew how to win commitment, but he did not know how to give it."[15]

The patience of Ford's backers quickly wore thin. They were desperate for options to recoup their investment. Word of their dissatisfaction spread quickly throughout Detroit's small circle of automakers and suppliers. The news especially caught the attention of Henry Leland, whose new engine had just been rejected by the management group at the Olds Motor Works. After learning that the group of investors was about to pull the plug on Henry Ford, Leland asked if he could demonstrate his engine to them. Aware of his reputation for quality and production, they agreed enthusiastically.

When Leland made his presentation, the investors were immediately sold: At the end of the meeting, Ford was out and Leland was in at the company that bore Henry Ford's name. Ford was given $900 cash and the rights to continue developing a race car that he had been working on in defiance of what he had agreed to do for his backers (namely, build a practical car that would sell in volume, like the Curved Dash Oldsmobile).

On August 27, 1902, the board of directors of the Henry Ford Company formally agreed to dissolve the company and restructure and recapitalize it to build a new car with Leland's engine. They let Leland himself pick the name. He chose Cadillac Automobile Company (which became Cadillac Motor Car Company in 1904) in honor of the French explorer who had founded Detroit in 1702, Antoine de la Mothe Cadillac. The Cadillac name was much in vogue that year of Detroit's bicentennial. Leland also adopted the Cadillac family coat of arms as the emblem of the new company (which remains the core of the Cadillac brand logo today).

The first Cadillac was built within months of Ford's ouster and was introduced to the world as the Model A at the 1903 New York Automobile Show. Building on the foundation of Henry Leland's personal reputation for quality, precision, and durability, the car was soon respected for all those traits. It was also the first car designed by a team of engineers rather than a single man. Two thousand were built in 1904, putting it right behind the Oldsmobile in car sales in America.

Among the technical advances in Leland's first Cadillac was a large, more durable crankshaft, which also happened to require larger and more durable bearings to support it. The bearings were subcontracted through the supplier that provided the car's axles: a firm called Weston-Mott, based in Utica, New York (which would eventually be moved to Flint, acquired by Billy Durant, and run by Alfred Sloan as part of the General Motors accessory group).

Weston-Mott turned to Hyatt Roller Bearing, which had by now also established itself as the quality leader in its business, for the Cadillac's unique bearings. Hyatt won the business after Leland found fault with several other bearing-makers that Weston-Mott had used. When the old man (now sixty years old) also found fault in the Hyatt bearings, however, he took his wrath directly to Hyatt rather than Weston-Mott. Leland called Alfred Sloan himself into his private office in Detroit for one of the most severe tongue-lashings Alfred would ever experience.

As Sloan described it in *Adventures of a White Collar Man*:

> The white beard of Henry M. Leland seemed to wag at me, he spoke with such long-faced emphasis.
>
> "Mr. Sloan, Cadillacs are made to run, not just sell."
>
> On his desk were some of our roller bearings, like culprits before a judge.
>
> "Your Mr. [Pete] Steenstrup told me these bearings should be accurate, one like another, to one-thousandth of an inch, but look here!" I heard the click of his ridged fingernail as he tapped it against a guilty bearing. "There is nothing like uniformity here."
>
> Precision-trained Henry Leland seemed to be out of patience with all bearing manufacturers. But he had some excuse to be short-tempered with us, as I discovered when he challenged me abruptly, "Mr. Sloan, do you know why your firm received this order?"
>
> As I started to answer, he got up, strode over to a window, beckoning me to follow. He pointed into the factory yard, where a lot of axles were piled up like cordwood.
>
> "The bearings in those axles out there did not stand up under the Cadillac load," Leland explained. "The balls and braces broke and crumbled. We canceled the order, but the manufacturer has continued to ship them. Unless you can give me what I want, I'm going to put five-hundred Weston-Mott axles out there beside those rejects. . . .
>
> A genuine conception of what mass production should mean really grew in me with that conversation. I was an engineer and a manufacturer, and I considered myself conscientious. But after I had said good-by to Mr. Leland, I began to see things differently. I was determined to be as fanatical as he in obtaining precision in our work. And entirely different standard had been established for Hyatt Bearings.[16]

It might be argued that Sloan's recollection, forty years after the meeting with Leland occurred, was embellished by both the passing of time and his admiration for Leland. Nonetheless, the fact that this one meeting merits three pages of text in *Adventures of a White Collar Man,* far more space than any other incident or decision re-

counted in the entire book, is itself testimony to the impact that Leland and his insistence on precision and quality had on Sloan's life and career.

In his one other recollection of Leland, in *My Years with General Motors,* Sloan is more sparing of praise, yet he gives the founder of Cadillac his due far more than he does Ransom Olds:

> Early Cadillac engineering had an important influence on the industry and upon my operations in Hyatt. This was largely due to Henry Leland, who, I believe, was one of those mainly responsible for bringing the technique of interchangeable parts into automobile manufacturing. . . .
>
> Mr. Leland was one of my early acquaintances in the industry. He was a generation older than I and I looked upon him as an elder not only in age but in engineering wisdom. He was a fine, creative, intelligent person. Quality was his god."[17]

ALFRED MEETS HENRY . . . AND HENRY RISES AGAIN

While Leland's devotion to precision and quality represented all that Alfred Sloan admired in business, Henry Ford was at the opposite end of the scale: impulsive, defiant, and incapable of taking advice or orders from anyone. By the time the Henry Ford Company's financial angels dropped him and adopted Leland, Ford had managed to alienate every investor and partner he had ever worked with: a feat unmatched by anyone else in the freewheeling early automobile industry.

Yet in his later years, Sloan went out of his way to give Ford credit for lasting contributions to the industry that had actually been originated by others. These included the concepts of mass production and precision parts, which began with Olds and Leland and were then applied by Ford on a massive scale to his moving assembly line (which itself was not a new concept—Billy Durant had actually pioneered a moving carriage assembly line at the Durant-Dort plant in Flint, only no one took notice at the time).

Sloan and Ford first met at the 1902 New York Automobile Show, where Hyatt was one of dozens of supplier exhibitors. Sloan and Pete Steenstrup were attending the show to network with potential new customers. The Hyatt exhibit area was in a gallery over-looking the show's central arena, where the various automobiles being presented were put through their paces much the way Billy Durant's first road cart had been at the Wisconsin Tri-State Fair. Steenstrup already knew Ford and brought him over to meet Sloan. As Alfred described those events:

> I heard Pete hail someone in the throng passing the counter. A tall, slender man stopped and, after shaking hands with Pete, lifted his derby hat to wipe his forehead. After tramping around the show, he was tired.
>
> "Come in," insisted Pete. "Where could you find a better place to rest? Sit down at the railing and see the show from a box seat." Then he introduced me. The visitor's name was Henry Ford . . .
>
> Much was to come out of our association with Mr. Ford; fabulous orders for roller bearings. But I did not suspect that I was talking with a man who was to take a foremost place among the individual leaders of all times. No one has made a greater contribution to industrial progress. I have already stated that the primary conception of mass production is a system of interchangeable parts. But it is more than that. It is the technique of the factory system, involving the continuous flow of these interchangeable parts through the various steps of manufacture, finalized in a continuous system of assembly. Right there lies Mr. Ford's outstanding contribution to industrial progress.[18]

Characteristically, Sloan did not mention how his own genius for product innovation and marketing eventually left Henry Ford in the dust.

When Alfred and Henry Ford met at the New York Automobile Show in 1902, Ford had just found yet another financial angel: this time, a renowned and well-off professional bicycle racer named Tom Cooper who, like the rest of the country, was intrigued with automobile racing. That summer, with Cooper's money, Ford proceeded to build two virtually identical racers, which he called the Arrow and the 999.

Named after a locomotive that had broken the New York-to-Chicago speed record, the 999 was one of the largest and most powerful vehicles built up to that time, measuring ten feet in length and producing seventy horsepower of thrust from a massive four-cylinder engine. It was basically a bare chassis with only the engine and a primitive seat for the driver, with no hood and nothing atop the rear wheels.

Learning of Henry Ford's new project, Alexander Winton challenged Ford to a second race, at the same track in Grosse Pointe. This time, Ford's entry was the 999 and the driver was Barney Oldfield, a friend of Cooper's who had a winning record as a bicycle racer but had never raced an automobile.

The race was held on October 25, 1902. Again to the delight of the press, the novice Oldfield not only beat Winton but set a new world speed record, completing the five-mile race in five minutes, twenty-eight seconds. Barney Oldfield was carried off the track on the fans' shoulders and became an instant celebrity. True to form, Henry Ford had a falling out with Cooper and ended up selling him the 999 (keeping the Arrow for himself) and never doing business with him again.

Yet the gods again smiled on Henry Ford. Even before breaking with Cooper, he had begun looking for more funding, again telling prospective backers that his plan was to build "a car for the common man."

He found his angel this time in Detroit's biggest coal merchant, Alexander Malcomson, who also had dozens of other ventures and, like all other members of Detroit's Old Boy network, wanted to get into the car game. In August 1902, they formed a partnership called Ford & Malcomson, Ltd.

Because Malcomson was spread thin with his other ventures and knew of Ford's own penchant to go off in many directions at the same time, he assigned the head clerk at his coal yard to watch over day-to-day operations and manage the accounting. The clerk's name was James Couzens, who soon proved to be one of the few executives able to tolerate working directly with Henry Ford for more than a few months. Couzens was far closer in character and temperament to Alfred Sloan than Henry Ford—stern, almost humorless, focused on the bottom line—but the two managed to tolerate each other and offset each other's strengths and weaknesses.

With the 999's well-publicized victory, Ford & Malcomson changed its name to the Ford Motor Company before building a car. Remarkably, Henry Ford kept his word this time and focused on producing that car for the common man. Launched in 1903 and called the Model A (not to be confused with Leland's Model A Cadillac or Ford's own more famous Model A, introduced later in 1927), the car featured a radically improved engine, with the cylinders placed vertically rather than horizontally to reduce vibration and increase power. Ever since, all internal combustion cylinders have been placed in virtually that same position.

With the original Model A's success, Henry Ford's future finally appeared bright. But more demons and more breakups with partners and backers lay ahead, as did fame, success, and controversy that neither Ford nor anyone in his family or hometown had ever imagined possible.

Meanwhile, the wildly successful entrepreneur and salesman named William C. Durant was growing restless and bored with the horse-drawn carriage business and with his own life in Flint, Michigan.

Not caring for automobiles, it is doubtful that Billy Durant knew or cared much about Henry Ford's unique ability to win financial backing for new ventures each time he created one that failed. Billy did not yet know failure. Nor had he fallen out with any backers or partners. That, too, still lay in Billy's future.

CHAPTER FIVE

Restless in Flint, Antsy in New York

ALTHOUGH HE BECAME a player in the auto industry much later than either Alfred Sloan or Henry Ford, Billy Durant had actually taken his first automobile ride long before either of them, even before Ransom (Ranny) Olds and Henry Leland had begun their serious development work with the internal combustion engine. The year was 1889, when Billy's own horse-drawn carriage business was booming, and the machine was a steam-powered vehicle owned by a cousin in Flint. Annoyed by its noise, clumsiness, and slow pace, Billy saw it as no threat to the carriage and buggy.

Durant did not come to picture the automobile as a practical machine, let alone a viable business, until he was in his forties and already wealthy. Not until he finally drove a car that stood out from all the others (just as the Schmedlen-O'Brien cart had stood out in 1886) did the motor car capture his imagination. Once it did, it became his new passion.

Daughter Margery recalled Billy reacting with shock and horror when she informed him of her own first automobile ride in 1902, when she was fifteen years old. That same year, Henry Leland was starting the Cadillac Motor Company after Henry Ford's sad ouster from the company that had originally borne his name. The car was a Panhard, one of the industry's very first brands (soon to fade into oblivion along with hundreds of others), and it belonged to the father of a girlfriend from school. The plan was to take a jaunt into the country, leaving from the schoolyard and returning there. For the occasion, Margery even bought goggles and a veil to tie under her chin to hold her hat on.

Yellow with red leather upholstery, and driven by a mechanic hired by her friend's father, the Panhard shook, rattled, and sputtered so loudly that the two girls in the back seat hugged each other for dear life. Chugging along a dirt road, terrifying a team of horses pulling a wagon, it abruptly stalled and died. A crowd of gawkers quickly gathered and was soon taunting the driver with the common cry of "Get a horse!" When he finally got it started and managed to return the girls safely to the schoolyard, Margery's face and clothes were caked with dust and her ears were ringing.

Yet she could not wait to get home and tell her father about the great adventure.

"Pops, I've ridden in a horseless carriage!" she cried to him. Billy made Margery repeat the statement and then told her in an uncharacteristically firm and cold voice: "Margery, how could you—*how could you* be so foolish as to risk your life in one of those things!"[1]

Just three years later, Billy was sitting at the family dining room table talking automobile strategy with his original partner, Dallas Dort, and Charles Nash, his top lieutenant in a start-up car company that he had taken over and put in turnaround mode. That company's name was Buick Motor. Billy told his two friends that the day would soon come when a single car company would sell 10,000 and even 100,000 vehicles in a single year.

No American, not even "Crazy Henry" Ford, had yet voiced such a vision. Nash turned to Dort and declared: "Dallas, Billy's crazy."[2]

Nash had been hired at a wage of a dollar a day by Billy to work as a blacksmith at the original factory of the Flint Road Cart Company. Seven years after that dinner, he was elected president of General Motors. Four years after that, he was fired by Billy.

But all of that, like Henry Ford's equally grandiose visions and business feats, was still unimaginable when Billy chastised his daughter for riding in the Panhard.

THE GOOD LIFE IN FLINT

By the time Margery took her secret ride in 1902, her father's carriage and buggy business had grown beyond his or anyone else's wildest dreams. Billy's vision and success had brought the good life to hundreds of families in Flint, Michigan, who otherwise would never have seen any horizon beyond the farm. Company-paid holiday parties were held at the plants, and the company even gave wedding gifts to employees. Bonuses were also often given to employees with the most seniority. Though wages for most employees averaged between four dollars and ten dollars a week, and they worked nine hours a day, six days a week, both the pay and the hours were in line with those in other industries.

More important for Billy's own relations with his workforce, the work itself was far less stressful than in other manufacturing industries such as steel and locomotives. The parts for the carriages and buggies, even those that were of metal rather than wood, were small and light enough for one or two people to assemble without strain or aid of heavy machinery. The way the parts fit could be fixed or improved by a little manhandling or pounding of metal and wood: a far cry from what would soon be required to assemble the automobile with its hundreds of precise mechanical parts.

Durant would often stroll through all the plants unannounced and stop to chat with his workers. During one such visit, he learned from Charles Nash, who at the time was supervising the buggy-trim operation in Flint, that several people were holding up production because the tacks they were using to nail the trim to the buggy were inferior. The workers would hold the tacks in their mouths (like most carpenters), but the heads were unfinished and had sharp edges, cutting their lips and forcing them to spit them out and then bend over to pick them up again. Observing the problem firsthand, in front of the workers, he told Nash on the spot to order better tacks. The issue was resolved, trim-line production increased, and Nash was soon promoted to supervise all production in Flint.

SPARED THE STRIFE . . . FOR THE TIME BEING

Life in Durant's plants was also far removed from the unrest that was already bubbling up in other industries, where the work was monotonous and backbreaking, the pace was dictated by strict production quotas, and wages were low and uncertain.

Even when labor strife reached a peak with the so-called Panic of 1893, the country's first industrial recession, Durant-Dort managed to keep all its plants operating: a tribute to both the desirability of Durant's products and his loyalty to his employees. There is no record of unrest among the workers or of any worker quitting because of dissatisfaction with pay or work conditions. Nor is there any record of any attempt to unionize the workforce, despite the growing labor movement.

Such stability and contentment were already on the way to becoming rare in the rest of the country. The year 1886, when Durant and friend Dallas Dort started the Flint Road Cart Company, saw the Haymarket Riot in Chicago, in which eight policemen died trying to break up a protest demonstration in demand of an eight-hour workday at the McCormick Harvester factory. That same year, the American Federation of Labor (AFL) was created. In 1890 came the Sherman Antitrust Act (though it would not be willfully enforced for another decade, at the hand of Teddy Roosevelt) and the birth of the militant United Mine Workers of America.

This was followed in 1892 by the Homestead Strike at Carnegie Steel's Pittsburgh mill complex, with 300 Pinkerton guards and the Pennsylvania National Guard brought in to break up a three-month strike over wages. The Homestead Strike resulted in ten deaths and the banning of all unions from the steel industry. Two years later, it was the railway workers' turn, with Eugene Debs leading the Pullman Strike in Chicago and crippling passenger railroad service across the country. The issue this time was reinstatement of wage and workforce cuts of 25 percent that had been imposed in the Panic of 1893. The Pullman Palace Car Company refused to increase either employment or wages and the U.S. Army was called in to break the strike on the grounds that U.S. mail was being unlawfully disrupted.

Remarkably, workers in Flint would not see or feel such emotions and violence in the workplace for another forty years, when the country was in an economic depression that made 1893 look like a hiccup. By then, Alfred Sloan rather than Billy Durant was the man identified as "the Boss." With Sloan determined to keep General Motors profitable, a relationship of mistrust and animosity came to replace the paternalism and loyalty of the previous century.

As the Gilded Age of the 1890s drew to a close, however, life in the Durant-Dort Carriage Company and Flint, Michigan, was good, and the future looked even better. By 1901, Durant-Dort had eight factories in Flint alone and was the city's largest employer. In seven of the ten years between 1892 and 1902, the company added at least one new subsidiary or division to its empire.

Billy Durant had personally designed several new models of lightweight vehicles that had become hits, including one called the Diamond that was simpler and lower-priced than anything else on the market; the Diamond was actually brought to market in less than six months from the day Billy first envisioned it. He had also been proving the future business model of vertical integration (even though the term itself had not been devised at that time), buying major producers of the product's key components: subassembly (the equivalent of the chassis for an automobile), wheels, axles, and even varnish.

A DIFFERENT ROUTINE FOR BILLY'S EXECUTIVE TEAM

While such growth meant unprecedented prosperity for Durant-Dort's workers and their families and community, life was not as simple for the lieutenants of the hard-charging Durant. He expected his executives to push themselves as hard and fast as he pushed himself, which was further and faster than most normal people (especially those with families) could endure over an extended period of time. Each member of his core management team had a clear and crucial position: Dallas Dort, administration; Fred Aldrich, finance; A. B. C. Hardy, coordination of plants and logistics; and Charles Nash, production. Each man also knew that Billy would take any liberty, at any time, to offer new ideas and suggestions as well as questions (a style that would later be called micromanagement and would drive Walter Chrysler out of General Motors on the eve of the crisis of 1920).

To a man, they all admired Billy and shared his dreams of further growth. They considered themselves more than a team, almost an extended family. They all lived within a few blocks of each other and they walked to work together and even dined together. The main office of Durant-Dort itself was laid out more like a living room than a typical office of the day, with no walls separating one man's area from another and with sofas and potted plants in lieu of desks and filing cabinets.

While such collegiality led to open communication, it also led to a workload and schedule determined by Billy Durant's own lifestyle rather than the time clock. He was always focused on how to improve the last big idea or how to implement the next one. He cared nothing about his team's physical appearance or personal habits. What mattered was the person's performance, whether an executive or a plant worker. He would ease up if he saw the person really trying, but he also expected no excuses. And, as daughter Margery recalled with the flattery to be expected of a doting daughter, he always demanded even more from himself:

> My father always drove himself as he drove his men. Harder, if anything. How he stood it, we never knew. He was slight, though wiry; and he practiced none of the hygienic fads then in vogue. He smoked cigars almost incessantly—I almost never saw him without one.
>
> He slept only two or three hours a night. Like Edison, he felt that too much sleep was unnecessary for some men. I suppose his intense pleasure and complete engrossment in his work buoyed him up. It was his daily tonic. Where other men might be expending precious energy in night work, he was actually stimulating and refreshing his nerves by exploiting some new idea among those who sat with him.
>
> And yet he was very considerate of other men who did not have his nerves of steel or his powers of recuperation. If he saw a man buckling, he did not resent the fact. . . . When he found a man's level in the scale of endurance, he kept him there, goading him only sufficiently to get the best out of the worker without injury.
>
> Time to him was one of life's most precious elements. While he gave ungrudgingly of his time to those he felt deserved it, while he

spent uncounted hours on any detail he thought important, the waste
of a minute was in his eyes an affront to the Divine Creator.[3]

Margery vividly recalled one incident when her father was dis-
satisfied with the quality of the wood being used for one of his new
buggy models. Rather than have his lieutenants resolve the problem,
Billy jumped in himself. He ordered samples from suppliers all
across the country, but none matched his own vision. Finally, he
boarded a train and traveled to San Francisco, alone. From there, he
traveled by horse and buggy all the way to Oregon, scouring the
region for exactly the right kind of wood that would meet his own
standards of durability and attractiveness. He found what he
wanted in Oregon. By the time he had secured his order and returned to San Francisco for the train trip home, however, he had
barely enough money left on his person for a ticket back to Flint.
Eating one meal a day for a week, he finally reached the Flint railroad depot with twenty-five cents in his pocket; but he had found
the quality of wood that he was looking for.[4]

Despite Margery's understandable bias and sentimentality, not
even Billy's worst critics would ever charge that he lacked energy
and drive. The problem was focusing that energy and drive. His
own haphazard schedule always took priority, even if it meant disruption of other executives' duties and schedules. As historian Bernard Weisberger wrote in his 1979 Durant biography, "Durant
seemed to enjoy limitless work, although as the planner, the trav-
eler, and the contact man he was spared the tedium and repetition
and not maddened by trivial and personal problems that consumed
the energy of static executives."[5]

Billy's frenetic style would eventually lead one of his closest
associates and employees to quit just to escape the pressure. That
same man would go on to start the first automotive company located
in Flint, Michigan, and pave the way for Billy's own fateful entry
into the automotive business.

A HARDY MAN TAKES THE PLUNGE WITHOUT BILLY

Alexander Brownell Cullen Hardy (A. B. C., as his friends and business associates always called him) was twenty years old and work-

ing at a competitor's small carriage plant in Davison, Michigan, when Billy Durant met him in 1889 and offered him a job (a year before Durant hired the future General Motors president, Charles Nash). Hardy immediately earned Billy's trust with his grasp of inventory management and production flow and his willingness to put in long hours. When Billy came up with the idea for that low-priced buggy called the Diamond, Hardy was the man he appointed to make it happen.

The Diamond was to be a reincarnation of the original Flint Road Cart: a new cart for the masses, simple, low-priced, and sold in high volume for cash only. Billy got the idea during the Christmas holidays in 1895 and immediately called his original partner Dallas Dort on the telephone to explain the concept and enlist his support. Dort was in the middle of dinner and voiced initial skepticism to the idea, questioning whether it could generate the volume required to make a profit at a low price. After two hours on the phone, Dort finally gave the project his blessing.

It is not known if Durant was having dinner with his own family at that moment, but Dort and Hardy both later recalled Billy telephoning Hardy just a few days later, also at the dinner hour, with an offer he couldn't refuse. Hardy was in the midst of a holiday turkey dinner with his family, but by the time "the Boss" hung up, he had agreed to take on the new assignment of organizing and supervising production of a new subsidiary to be called Diamond Buggy.

Within six months, Hardy had brought the Diamond from concept to market. It was an immediate success, adding to Durant-Dort's coffers and market share. While Dort managed the growing empire's day-to-day operations and Durant focused on new acquisitions and markets, Hardy soon became Durant's unofficial surrogate during his absences from Flint, which were becoming more and more frequent.

By 1898, Dallas Dort was feeling the emotional toll of the long hours and endless unexpected calls and requests from Billy, whose own office was now a suitcase. With his wife ill, Dort requested and received a two-year sabbatical to the dry climate of Arizona. With Nash uninterested in matters outside the realm of production and efficiency, that left A. B. C. Hardy as the only one Billy felt free to call on at any hour and for any issue.

Hardy, like the others, felt nothing but admiration and loyalty for Durant. However, like Dort, he was unable to escape the endless telephone calls and messages from Durant. By the time Dort returned from sabbatical in 1900, it was Hardy's turn to request a leave of absence to revive his energy and enthusiasm. With Dort now back in the fold, Billy immediately granted Hardy's request.

Rather than Arizona, Hardy chose Europe, where he proceeded to fall victim to the same virus as so many successful men of the era: the automotive bug. He attended all the continent's auto shows and toured several plants, studying production techniques as well as engineering. Returning to Flint, he met with Billy and is said to have advised him to "get out of the carriage business before the automobile ruins you."[6]

Billy still didn't have the bug and dismissed Hardy's warning. Yet he apparently voiced no objection when Hardy decided to strike off on his own to establish his own automobile manufacturing enterprise.

Unable to find investors in Flint, where the horse-drawn carriage was still king and sales were still strong despite the publicity of the automobile, Hardy put up $5,000 of his own money to establish the Flint Automobile Company in 1901. Within a year, he built his first Flint Roadster and exhibited it at the Chicago Auto Show. The small, practical car got good press, but it was priced higher than the popular Oldsmobile, which still dominated the low end of the market. Hardy's Roadster failed to stand out from the pack. To make matters worse, Hardy was sued by the Association of Licensed Automobile Manufacturers (ALAM) for not paying royalties under the Selden patent. In 1903, after having built just fifty-two cars, the Flint Automobile Company was history and the carriage-makers of Flint, Michigan, were again without competition from any upstart automobile plants.

Despite his failed adventure, Hardy was to remain a close associate of Billy Durant and played a key role in making the Chevrolet Motor Company an early success. Billy actually welcomed Hardy back to his close circle of advisers after Hardy's automotive venture failed: a gesture of compassion as well as an acknowledgment of talent that neither Alfred Sloan nor Henry Ford would ever show toward any executive who dared to quit and strike off on his own. Hardy would end up a vice president of General Motors under Alfred Sloan and would retire in 1925 for health reasons. He would also remain loyal to all the local civic and business leaders he had known in Flint since the 1890s, despite their refusal to back the Flint Automobile Company.

One of the people Hardy had approached for backing was Billy's top rival: James Whiting of the Flint Wagon Works. Whiting was nearly twenty years Billy's senior (born in Connecticut in 1842 and relocated to Flint at age twenty-one). Unlike Billy, however, he followed Hardy's automotive efforts closely. While not ready to declare the horse-drawn carriage dead, Whiting was ready to hedge his bets and test the automotive waters when he learned that yet another tinkerer from Detroit was in dire financial straits.

Meanwhile, Billy Durant had dropped out of the picture, for the moment.

BILLY TAKES A SABBATICAL

When A. B. C. Hardy returned from Europe in 1901 and warned that the automobile would soon replace the horse-drawn carriage, Billy Durant was forty years old and successful by all measures. Father of a precocious daughter and a quieter son, he was the most admired and respected man in Flint, Michigan. His company was the largest and most profitable in its industry. His business advice and endorsement were sought after by all. He never spent money foolishly, yet he was never known to be afraid to take a chance on something he believed in.

By 1901, however, with Durant-Dort's sales and earnings continuing to grow under the management team of Durant, Dort, Nash, and Aldrich, he had become bored with the lack of new challenges. That year, Billy left Flint for New York City and remained there for two years, without his wife and children and far from his carriage business.

The only explanation for the move from either Billy or his business associates was that he had decided he needed to learn more about the stock market. He opened an office under the name Durant-Dort Securities Company at 52 Broadway, where he began trading in stocks and building a personal network with investment bankers and other financiers. He continued making his phone calls and even made occasional surprise visits to Flint, but the New York office became his official address. Wife Clara occasionally wrote to him there, but he never answered her letters. His only known personal correspondence was with his mother, who also still resided in Flint.[7]

What was the real story behind Durant's move to New York? Did he feel so good about the state of business at Durant-Dort Carriage Company that he felt he deserved a sabbatical, like Dort and Hardy? If so, why the constant phone calls and visits back home?

Was he frustrated with the confines of Flint's small-town culture? Did he see the stock market itself as the logical next personal challenge, a chance to prove that he could succeed where his father had failed so dismally?

Was he bored with Clara, or vice versa?

Was Clara, unlike the more meek spouses of Henry Ford and Alfred Sloan, unwilling to follow any decision and endure any sacrifice in the name of her husband's career? Did she have her own interests and dreams apart from her husband's? Or did she want Durant to spend more of his time with her and his children than with his business associates and his constant new ideas? Had Billy failed to balance those priorities of family and business and forced Clara to show him the door? Was their separation a prequel to the tensions and strains that would become almost a stereotype of high-profile CEO marriages by the end of the twentieth century?

All armchair psychoanalysis aside, the answers will never be clear. Most of that two-year period from 1901–1903 remains a void in Billy's recorded life.

It is clear, however, that he was an active stock trader, working with a number of established brokerage houses. He also made his name known and respected among several key banking houses, including that of J. P. Morgan. He even tried to float at least one big deal. Having observed how easily the House of Morgan had persuaded several inefficient and threatened steel mills and smelters to combine and form a billion-dollar company called U.S. Steel, Durant proposed to James Whiting that they combine their carriage operations and then enlist others to form a similar wagon trust. Although the idea never got off the ground, Billy returned to the concept a few years later, after succeeding where all others had failed in building automobiles in Flint, Michigan.

By the end of 1904, Billy was back in Flint and laying the foundation for a new business empire that would dwarf his carriage empire. It was called the Buick Motor Company, named after another tinkerer who was to lose control of his creation while others made fortunes from it.

DAVID BUICK TAKES HIS SHOT

Like Ransom Olds, Henry Leland, and Henry Ford, David Dunbar Buick had a genius for mechanical innovation. His business sense and personal temperament, however, were worse than any of the others. He watched from the sidelines as the car that bore his name became the industry sales leader under Billy Durant, and he died in poverty and obscurity.

Buick was born September 17, 1854, in the town of Arbroath, Scotland, but immigrated to the United States with his parents at the age of two. The family settled in Detroit, at that time a lumber and transportation hub, but his father died when David was just five years old. His mother found work in a candy factory to support herself and her son. At age eleven, David was "put out" (the term used back then) to work on a farm in return for room and board and a small stipend for his mother, who soon remarried. He returned to Detroit on his own at the age of fifteen and went to work full-time for the Alexander Manufacturing Company, a producer of plumbing fixtures that specialized in toilet bowls and water closets.

No details remain of Buick's adolescent years or his early twenties. He worked his way up to foreman at Alexander Manufacturing before it folded in 1882. That same year, he and a former schoolmate named William Sherwood managed to buy the defunct operation for a song and renamed it the Buick and Sherwood Company, with Buick holding the title of president and Sherwood vice president.

Sherwood focused on sales and finances while Buick devoted himself to production, where his inventive side quickly blossomed and flourished. His many inventions in the next few years included not only a better flushing mechanism for the toilet but a new lawn sprinkler and, most important, a new process for bonding enamel to porcelain. This patented process marked the obsolescence of metal plumbing fixtures and made possible the bathtub that we know today. It also paved the way for the infinite variety of shapes and colors of bathroom and kitchen fixtures available today. Indeed, Buick's same basic bonding process is still in use.

With the plumbing fixture business taking off, it was now David

Buick's turn to be smitten with the automotive bug, to the detriment of all existing business and personal relationships. Although he remained president of Buick and Sherwood, he was soon devoting all of his energies to stationary and marine gasoline-powered engines. In 1899, his former schoolmate and partner Sherwood told him it was time to either refocus on the plumbing business or leave. Buick angrily sold his interest to Sherwood for $100,000 and used the money to start his own engine company, which he called the Buick Auto-Vim and Power Company.

Buick concentrated initially on adapting stationary and marine engines for automotive applications, but he made only a few sales to actual automakers. In 1902, he reorganized the operation as the Buick Manufacturing Company to develop his own automobile as well as its propulsion system.

That same year, he built his first car with a new partner and fellow tinkerer named Walter Marr. It featured the first engine to apply "valve-in-head design," known today as overhead-valve design. With the valves and pistons extending from the top of the engine block through holes bored directly through the engine head, it proved not only easier to service but also delivered more power than the so-called flathead engines of the day, which were heavier and more difficult to access for service. Overhead-valve technology would soon become the industry standard, but Buick managed to nearly bankrupt his company in the process of developing it. Marr and Buick had a falling out over which of them deserved credit, and Marr tried without success to start his own company (only to eventually end up back at the Buick Motor Company under Billy Durant).

At this time, Oldsmobile was still the only profitable volume automaker. Henry Leland was making money supplying the Olds Motor Works with engines, but financiers in general and banks in particular were still leery of anyone who claimed to have a great new idea for a great new car. Only the adventurous Detroit millionaires like William Murphy and William Maybury, Henry Ford's angels, were willing to put up money, and they rarely did so in the quantity required to start a true manufacturing operation. It would take natural salesmanship as well as financial genius to break out of the pack and secure substantial funding, and luckless David Buick proved to have neither.

ENTER THE BRISCOE BOYS AND WHITING OF FLINT

Buick found his first frail financial lifeline in the brothers Walter and Benjamin Briscoe, who at the time were the major suppliers of sheet metal to Olds and a few other smaller automakers. The Briscoes would later also play a major role in one of the many turns in Billy Durant's career. When they met Buick, however, they were just testing the waters for a possible venture in engine production and vehicle assembly. David Buick, for his part, was theirs for the taking.

The Briscoes ended up restructuring the operation as the Buick Motor Company in 1903. It was capitalized at $100,000, but $97,700 of the stock was held by the Briscoes and just $300 by Buick himself. In addition, the Briscoes issued Buick a personal loan of $3,500. In reorganizing the company, they gave him six months to pay back the loan. If he did so, 100 percent of the company stock would revert to him; if he failed to pay up, however, the Briscoes would take total control of the company's assets, including its small factory in Detroit (which may have actually been what the Briscoes were after from Buick, initially).

The Buick operation was small potatoes for the Briscoes, who also had their eye on another car company named Maxwell (started by Jonathan Maxwell and later to be taken over by Walter P. Chrysler, who renamed it after himself). The Briscoe brothers also soon realized there was no chance of the volatile and financially inept David Buick coming through and paying off his loan. In the summer of 1903, less than six months after reorganizing Buick's company and just days before Buick's marker was to come due, they met with James Whiting and the board of directors of his Flint Wagon Works to see if he might be interested in buying them out.

Having heard about the new valve-in-head engine while also watching A. B. C. Hardy's start-up problems, Whiting listened closely to the Briscoes' pitch. He was one of the few carriage-builders who took Hardy's warning of the coming obsolescence of the horse-drawn vehicle seriously. He was also among a handful of local business leaders who thought Flint was equal, if not superior, to Detroit or Lansing (where Oldsmobile's production was then located) as a venue for automotive production.

Although Flint still had fewer than 15,000 residents, it also had a capable workforce and a solid manufacturing infrastructure, thanks to the various carriage operations. It also had excellent water and rail transport connections. The Flint River gave direct access to Michigan's best pine forests and had spawned some of the biggest lumber mills in the country, and their product was vital to automobiles as well as buggies.

Despite his lack of mechanical knowledge or experience, Whiting was ready to enter the automotive game. After a visit to the Buick plant in Detroit and a test demonstration of the car over some of the worst roads in the region, he was hooked. He and his directors ended up buying out the Briscoes for $10,000 in cash (borrowed from Flint banks in order to keep the venture completely separate from the Flint Wagon Works, which was still growing and profitable at the time). David Buick stayed on as an employee in Detroit to continue developing a marketable car, but Whiting moved engine production to a workshop adjacent to the Flint Wagon Works' main plant in Flint. Whiting also rehired Walter Marr to work in the engine operation.

The entire town of Flint quickly took notice. Hardy's flop was history and hopes were high that Whiting would put Flint on a par with Detroit as a center of automotive production. The purchase of Buick Motor Company was reported in the *Flint Journal* on September 11, 1903, with the story noting that a new plant was to be built to produce "stationary and marine engines, automobile engines, transmissions, carburetors, spark plugs, etc." The very next day, the *Flint Journal* ran an editorial making the case for a new automobile industry located in town:

> Flint is the most natural center for the manufacture of autos in the whole country. It is the vehicle city of the United States and in order to maintain this name, by which it is known from ocean to ocean, there must be developed factories here for the manufacture of automobiles.

Despite the hopes expressed in the *Flint Journal*, the Buick Motor Company fared no better under Whiting than under the Briscoes. It was again reorganized and recapitalized at $75,000 in January 1904, with most of the money coming this time from Whiting himself and local Flint banks. In July, the first prototype Buick with the famous valve-in-head engine was finally built. Walter Marr took it on a test drive to Detroit and back. Although it performed flawlessly, there was still no production line and no distribution network. In August, the car officially went on sale as the Model B, but only thirty-seven were built that year. Whiting had by now committed not only his own reputation but that of the city of Flint to the failing Buick Motor Company.

If Buick failed, Flint's self-proclaimed title as "The Vehicle City" would be endangered and several of its leading citizens would take a financial bath. Both Whiting and his community saw only one potential savior: the town's own Horatio Alger, Billy Durant, who had lately been spending most of his time alone in New York City rather than with his family in Flint.

CHAPTER SIX

The Dropout's Next Big Thing

WOULD BILLY DURANT have remained in New York, alone, if the Whiting interests had not sought him out to help save Buick Motor?

Once again, there are no clear answers. And, as with his first ride across Flint, Michigan, in Johnny Alger's new horse cart in 1886, the details of Billy's return to Flint vary from one source to another.

One thing that all agree on is that the final catalyst for getting Billy to return to Flint was a visit from Fred Aldrich, who was still secretary of the Durant-Dort Carriage Company and had been in touch with James Whiting of the Flint Wagon Works. Whiting had just bought Buick and moved engine production to Flint. Whiting told Aldrich about Buick's financial problems and the need for someone to turn the business around. Aldrich gave him Billy Durant's name, but Whiting was apparently reluctant to approach him.

He asked Aldrich to broach the subject to Billy, and Aldrich agreed. Sometime during the summer of 1904, Aldrich met Durant in New York to plead Buick's (and Flint's) case.

On September 4, 1904, at Aldrich's request, Billy was back in Flint to take what may have been only his third automobile ride. This time, however, he was immediately taken with the car, just as he had been immediately taken with the road cart in 1886.

The car he rode in this time was not a factory prototype but one of the first Buick Model B's sold to the public. Its owner was Dr. Herbert H. Hills, one of Flint's most prominent physicians and civic boosters, who paid $950 for the car. Hills also happened to be an acquaintance of both Whiting and Durant. By some accounts, Whiting personally asked the doctor to take Billy Durant for the fateful ride.

Billy knew absolutely nothing about how motor cars worked, let alone what it took to build them, but he still trusted his own instincts about what made products sell. Hills, in turn, was (like the rest of Flint) eager to do anything he could to get Billy involved with saving Buick. Hills ended up agreeing to let Billy take virtual possession of his car for two months so he could test it and investigate the business case for pumping new money and life into the Buick manufacturing operation.

During this time Durant, a nontinkerer and nonmechanic, took the Model B through its paces in a way that neither Henry Ford, Henry Leland, nor Ransom Olds had ever done with their products. He personally tested the car not only for its performance and durability under differing driving conditions but for its comfort, visual appeal, and ease of operation and maintenance. He quickly concluded that it was the perfect car for the nontechnical operator. The Buick-developed overhead-valve engine was capable of conquering mud and hills (which larger cars and engines could not tackle) and was far simpler to maintain and repair than other engines. As the official General Motors historian Arthur Pound observed in 1934:

> With no technical experience of his own to guide him, Mr. Durant applied the only test he could make, but he did so with a thoroughness which to this day is recalled in Michigan. He drove that two-cylinder Buick back and forth over a wide range of territory devoid of good roads, save for a few gravel turnpikes built by toll companies. He put it

through swamps, mud and sand, and pitch-holes for almost two months, bringing it in for repairs and consultations and then taking it out again for another strenuous cross-country run. He had every sort of mischance chronic in the motoring of the period, often, of course, being stalled in out-of-the-way hamlets for lack of repair parts or fuel and oil. During these enforced waits, perhaps in a country blacksmith shop which someday would be a garage, this impetuous and eager mind wrestled with the future of transportation.[1]

Billy was convinced that the Buick car had what it took to be a winner. Like Whiting and the banks, he also knew that the biggest challenge was to secure new capital and do it fast.

But he was also determined that if he were to throw himself fully into the Buick turnaround, he needed and deserved full authority. He agreed to undertake the challenge only if he were granted full operational control of all aspects of the business. And he got it with no questions asked. On November 1, 1904, Durant officially assumed management responsibility of Buick Motor Company. He abandoned the Durant-Dort Securities office in New York and moved full-time to Flint: fully committed, fully focused, and fully energized.

He also moved back in with Clara, who was still living at the first house Billy had bought back in his early twenties. Apparently, whatever problems that plagued the marriage were either put aside or made temporarily irrelevant by Billy's total immersion in the Buick challenge. He was once again a whirling dervish of new ideas, deals, and plans. And, once again, he expected and assumed the same commitment and energy from everyone touched by the project. As daughter Margery recalled, the Durant home became a virtual twenty-four-hour office, with people coming and going and on the phone without any prior notice or schedule.

Night after night men came to our house in Flint. All kinds of men: bankers, lawyers, executives, foremen, mechanics. Some came because Durant sent for them. Some came because it was the only way they could get enough of Durant's time to have ten minutes consecutive conversation with him. Some had axes to grind. Some longed to help him grind his bright new gasoline-buggy axe—hoping that they would be permitted to use it later for a little chopping on their own account.

There were men at dinner. There were men at the front door. The parlor was often full of men, and behind closed doors there were other men. Earnest men, emitting an unending stream of facts, figures, suggestions, protests. They sat with their heads forward, elbows on knees. They talked and they listened; but my father mostly listened. When he did talk it was like a violin beginning to play. Those present had to listen. I know: they all said the same thing then that they do now:
"Durant is the greatest salesman I ever knew."[2]

MAKING IT A GO

One of Billy's first decisions was to keep David Dunbar Buick on as an employee, despite Buick's growing bitterness and constant riffs with the engineering team. He also decided not to change the company's name. As daughter Margery described the decision:

"Buick—Buick—" he'd mutter. "Wonder if they'd call it Boo-ick."
"Why not call the car a Durant?" Almost everybody suggested that.
He'd shake his head. I know he was thinking of two things: the appeal of the name, and the man who had invented the engine. Perhaps on such occasions there jumped into his mind the picture of the little red shed where he and I went and listened to Mr. Buick explain the mechanism; just a little outhouse with shelves full of tools and metal parts, greasy and cramped and dark. Just the kind of place you'd think might be the cradle of a great invention. And he'd feel the justice of perpetuating the name.[3]

Billy knew he had the moral support of the entire local community and was no doubt grateful for it. He took on the dual challenges of raising new money and generating public interest in the Buick car with the same energy and absolute confidence he'd displayed for his first road cart nearly twenty years earlier, moving on several different fronts at once.

On the finance front, the experience and firsthand knowledge that he brought home from New York City were apparently just the pedigree he needed to bolster his own natural sales skills. Within less than a month, he increased the Buick Motor Company's capital from $75,000 to $500,000.

How did he manage to generate such backing for an operation that was bleeding red ink and had no brand awareness and no sales track record?

In part, he used his own established base: No fewer than a third of Buick's total shares were bought by the Durant-Dort Carriage Company. The rest of the shares were bought, quite simply, on faith and speculation. The stock market itself was virtually unregulated at the time, and it was not uncommon for shares to be issued in new companies whose tangible assets would seem to justify only a tiny fraction of the money actually raised—not unlike the way capital was generated for so many near-assetless dot-com start-up companies in the 1990s. In essence, Billy was selling shares of his own confidence in the company's growth potential, rather than shares of anything tangible, and investors were buying it. (Unlike the dot-com investors, however, Durant's investors would soon see their money grow rather than evaporate.)

Part of his sales pitch to the new investors was that the Buick car was, as he described it, a self-seller. To demonstrate it, he exhibited a Model B at the 1905 New York Automobile Show. He even manned the exhibit himself. While all exhibitors and attendees took note of the new valve-in-head engine's unique technical advantages, Billy also no doubt regaled them with tales of his own exploits in testing the car under the worst weather and road conditions imaginable. After the show closed, he returned to Flint with a total of 1,108 orders. No other exhibitor at any auto show had ever taken so many orders for a new product: a feat all the more remarkable because the Buick itself was a new and unknown brand.

That was the good news. The bad news was that Billy once again had no idea how to fill the orders, just as he'd had no idea where or how he would build his road cart in volume after stunning his fellow carriage exhibitors with the orders he brought home from the Wisconsin Tri-State Fair in 1886. As of the day he wrote up the last of his 1,108 new orders, fewer than forty Buick cars had actually been built.

The immediate, short-term solution was found in a Durant-Dort plant in Jackson, Michigan, 80 miles southwest of Flint, which happened to be vacant at the time. For the first year, the engines were still built at Whiting's plant in Flint and shipped to Jackson for final vehicle assembly.

At the same time production began in Jackson, however, Billy began plans for a new facility in Flint that he envisioned as the largest automotive production complex yet built anyplace in the world. He bought a 220-acre parcel of farmland just north of Flint's city limits with that dream in mind.

To put the plan in motion, he first let the Flint banks know what was on his mind, to whet their appetite. He then gave the same message to the civic and financial leaders of Jackson, who also saw great potential for Buick production in their town and begged him not to build in Flint. Soon, he had the Flint crowd convinced that if they didn't pump more money into the enterprise, Jackson might end up winning all future Buick production. He thus set the precedent for what would later become known in the auto industry as "whipsawing," offering threats and incentives to states and local communities as an inducement for them to come up with their own incentives for companies to locate or expand production in their area.

In the spring of 1905, three Flint banks agreed to purchase a new issue of shares for a total price of $100,000 in exchange for Billy's firm commitment to proceed with the new plant in Flint and phase out production in Jackson. Construction of the new plant commenced almost immediately, and Billy soon leveraged the groundbreaking to issue even more stock. In September of that year, the state of Michigan approved the issuance of an additional $900,000 in common stock and $600,000 in preferred stock. It was quickly a sellout. In papers Durant kept for his never-completed autobiography, he boasted: "In the small town of Flint, where I started Buick, in forty-eight hours I raised $500,000, and I am certain that few of the subscribers had ever ridden in an automobile."[4] Even William A. Paterson, the former nemesis in carriage-building whom Billy always believed had betrayed him, bought the new Buick stock.

At the same time he was looking for investors, Billy was looking for new salespeople. Initially, he used the Durant-Dort Carriage network of sales agencies to sell Buicks as well as buggies, but he knew he needed a nationwide, stand-alone sales and distribution network for the kind of growth he had in mind. Again, his own personality and reputation as a salesman were the only pedigree needed to attract some of the most astute promoters in the country. His 1,108 orders at the New York Automobile Show did not go unnoticed. He soon had people who wanted to sell the Buick *calling on him.*

One of these was Charles S. Howard (future owner of the legendary racehorse Seabiscuit), who had fought with Teddy Roosevelt's Rough Riders and, according to his own account, ended up in San Francisco with twenty-one cents in his pocket at the end of the Spanish-American War. When Billy took over Buick, Howard was making his way selling bicycles in San Francisco but saw his own future, and the country's, in the automobile.

Upon hearing about what Billy was up to (and with the kind of chutzpah that he undoubtedly knew Durant would admire), Howard took a train to Michigan and called on Billy unannounced, like so many other would-be partners and vendors. Although he had no experience selling automobiles, he left the meeting with rights to become the sole distributor of Buicks in eight western states, including California. By 1910, Buick's annual production had risen to more than 30,000 units, and one out of every ten Buicks sold in the country was through a Charles Howard distributorship, soon making him one of the wealthiest men on the West Coast.

By the end of 1905, Billy had a national network of thirteen Buick distributors (including Howard), in addition to the Durant-Dort sales network. He chose each man not only for his sales skills but his potential to train other salesmen and, more important, recruit businessmen with the capital and zeal required to open new dealerships within the distributor's territory. It was a model that would create dozens of multimillionaires and would become the pattern in the auto industry until the mid-1920s, when the manufacturers began buying out the distributors and selling their franchises directly to local dealers of their choosing.

ANOTHER INDUSTRY PRECEDENT, AND AN EARLY JAB FROM ALFRED

Also in 1905, Durant ran into a supply bottleneck that ended up changing the face of Flint and the nature of automotive manufacturing.

The Weston-Mott Company of Utica, New York, was now supplying axles to Buick as well Cadillac. It was also still relying on Alfred Sloan's Hyatt Roller Bearing Company for all the roller bearings used in its axles, and Sloan had developed a close friendship with its principal owner, C. S. Mott (who was also Sloan's age). With Buick production expanding and Weston-Mott pressed to meet demand from all its customers, Buick was soon experiencing delays in shipping that forced delays in vehicle production.

With typical boldness, Billy Durant asked Mott if he would be interested in building a new plant in Flint, adjacent to the Buick plant. Mott wasn't interested, but Billy didn't give up. He coaxed Mott into visiting Flint several times, and with each visit he offered various new sweeteners to the deal (as he had done in playing the towns of Jackson and Flint against each other). Finally, Billy and his own largest investors offered Mott a deal he could not refuse: $100,000 in new capital, an outright grant of the land needed for the new plant, a guarantee that Mott would henceforth receive 100 percent of all Buick's axle business, and no constraints on selling to other automakers as well as Buick. Mott was hooked.

This colocation of the axle supplier's operation with the vehicle manufacturer's assembly plant was the real beginning of vertical integration in the auto industry (i.e., the vehicle manufacturer either owning or controlling the production of all the vehicle's essential components). It was also the beginning of a supply flow and inventory control system that the Japanese industry would later expand and take credit for: *kanban,* or just-in-time parts inventory and delivery.

Alfred Sloan later recalled the decision and its importance:

> It was not too long before Charley Mott had given me assurance that he was still the boss of his business, in spite of his move to Flint. Nevertheless, to finance the building of his new Flint plant, he had been compelled to sell an interest in Weston-Mott to the Buick people. . . . Mott and his partner, W. G. Doolittle, calculated that their assets were worth $400,000. Durant and Dort provided them with $100,000 cash, so that they would have sufficient capital to move and build a new plant. . . .
>
> Why had Durant and Dort been so anxious to get Weston-Mott's axle plant established next door to the new Buick factory in Flint? Every piece of the motor car is essential in the sense that the automobile is not complete unless every part is available. Delay in delivery of any part stops the work. A dependable supply of parts might well make the difference between success and failure.[5]

By this time, the term *genius* was often being applied to Billy Durant's name when it appeared in the press. Alfred Sloan could not resist taking an indirect shot at Durant in expressing his admiration for Mott:

> Weston-Mott continued some operations in its Utica plant after the new one was established in Flint, and we [Hyatt] had to keep in touch with both, of course. I liked to work with Mott. His training had made him methodical. When he was confronted by a problem, he tackled it as I did my own, with engineering care to get the facts. Neither one of us ever took any pride in hunches. We left all the glory of that kind of thinking to such men as liked to be labeled "genius."[6]

That same tone of resentment would come through in virtually everything else that Sloan left for the record of his feelings toward Durant. Even in those earliest days, before they were dealing directly with each other and before anyone foresaw the crisis of 1920, they were oil and water in all respects.

BILLY FINDS A NEW FLAME

With the new Flint plant under construction, Billy soon found himself dividing much of his time between Jackson and Flint when he wasn't traveling to more distant points to drum up sales interest in the Buick. Although he had moved back in with Clara, they clearly spent little time together.

As his daughter Margery recalled, his mind was always on Buick. He barely noticed what he was eating at mealtime, always consumed with yet another problem or idea related to the business:

> We had a comfortable house in Flint. Comfortable chairs; a pretty little garden; the kind of place a man could come to after a hard day in the office and sink down with a sigh into his favorite rocker and enjoy this domestic refuge from the care of his business.
>
> Not my father. He waved the same "magic wand" at home that he did away from it; the wand that was but a symbol for unending toil and application, planning and scheming, hoping. . . .
>
> I can still see my father at the table. He weighed only 118 pounds, while I weighed 120. He ate very little; still does. He would help himself mechanically; would dispose of part of it almost breathlessly—put

aside his plate; then take out a pencil and begin to draw on the back of an envelope.[7]

Yet while Billy Durant loved the new activity and risk, he also soon found new love of another kind in the midst of it all. In the summer of 1906, during one of his visits to Jackson, Margery introduced her father to Catherine Lederer, who was nineteen years old and working in the Jackson post office. Margery was also nineteen at the time, and just a few months earlier she had married Dr. Edwin Campbell, a Flint physician closer in age to his father-in-law than to his bride.

Once again, the details of the introduction and the ensuing relationships vary with the source. The facts leave enough gaps and suggestion to whet the appetite of any would-be screenwriter.

After Margery returned from her honeymoon, Billy left Clara again and moved in with Margery and her new husband, who eventually quit his medical practice to work full-time as an executive assistant to his father-in-law. With typical boldness and confidence, forty-five-year-old Billy called on nineteen-year-old Catherine's mother during one of his visits to Jackson to ask permission to see her socially. Not surprisingly, given that he was married and that his own daughter was Catherine's friend, the answer was no. Within a few weeks, Billy hired Catherine as a secretary. Clara Durant, on the advice of her son-in-law, Dr. Campbell, then put herself in a rest home in Pinehurst, North Carolina.

There is no record of any further contact between Billy and his first wife Clara. Clara filed for divorce on grounds of "wanton and extreme cruelty." On May 27, 1908, two years after Billy was first introduced to Catherine, the divorce decree was granted by the circuit judge for Genesee County, Michigan, where Flint is located. The record was ordered suppressed and there were no reports in the area newspapers.

The very next day, May 28, William C. Durant and Catherine Lederer were married in New York City. Portions of those "suppressed" records that Durant preserved among his other papers for that never-finished life story show that Clara received $150,000 in cash and securities. She moved to California with son Clifford, who was then nineteen years old, and apparently never saw Flint or Durant again.

Neither Catherine nor Clara is mentioned by name in daughter

Margery's book. Margery herself soon began encountering her own demons shortly after her father's marriage. By all accounts, Catherine was everything that Clara was not, and everything that Billy needed. As described by Durant biographer Bernard Weisberger:

> That the marriage was exciting for Catherine was beyond doubting. Durant was at the peak of his powers and energies, still attractive, still youthful-looking, eager to love in his fashion. Catherine was, in her turn, a perfect match for his needs. She was beautiful, innocent, uncritical, and shy, the perfect princess to install in the castles he was building in his mind. . . . Her great strength was loyalty, and in a far future time it would be tested and found good.[8]

BUICK TRIUMPHANT

Whatever the reason—whether this new interest in his life spurred even more creativity or whether he might have driven himself even harder if he had not met Catherine—Durant continued to interject himself into all aspects of the business and to voice his own opinion, even in areas where he had no direct expertise (as he would leading up to the crisis of 1920 at General Motors).

Although the valve-in-head engine was already establishing a new industry standard, Durant the nonmechanic did not hesitate to take a gamble on what he thought might be a better version (unlike the Olds Motor Works management team when it turned down Henry Leland's engine improvements and opened the door for the creation of Cadillac Motor Company in 1902). Walter Marr of Buick had recruited a fellow engine aficionado from Cadillac whose name was Arthur Mason. Mason was working on a new engine that he claimed could double the revolutions per minute (RPM) of the Buick-Marr engine. Word of the project quickly reached Billy.

He hired an outside "expert" to examine the new engine in his and Mason's presence. Billy was cautioned against taking the risk. He recalled the consultant telling him, "I would suggest to whomever buys one of these cars to purchase a bushel basket with it in order to be able to collect the pieces."[9] After that visit, Mason pleaded his case directly with Billy. According to Durant, Mason bent over, put his arms around the engine, pressed his face against its head, and told him, "Start it up, if it goes, I may as well go with it."[10] Durant immediately took Mason's side over the expert's and ordered development and production to proceed. The Mason engine performed so well that it became the new selling point for Buick. Again, according to Billy himself:

> Power, the achievement of Mason's long experience and hard work became synonymous of Buick. We played on that one item: Power! Power to outclimb, power to outspeed anything on wheels in our class. With Buick we sold the assurance that the power to perform was there.[11]

As he had with his carriage business, Billy also decided to offer a variety of different product models to the growing auto market. The tinkerers of the day, and even the successful Ransom Olds and Henry Leland, were all more narrowly focused on making each new model car better than the one before it, which meant that they usually either stopped actively marketing previous models or stopped building and selling them altogether to focus exclusively on what was "newest and best."

Not Billy, however. He was as committed to continuous improvement as any of his peers, but he had also learned from his carriage business that there was synergy in selling more than one model at the same time under the same brand: another concept that he pioneered in the auto industry that would eventually become doctrine for all of the twentieth century.

In 1906, Buick introduced two new car models: the Model F, a larger and more expensive car than the preceding Model C, and the Model G, a runabout in the price range of the Model C. The following year, Billy introduced four more new models (the Model D and Model H at the high end of the market, and the Model K and Model S at the low end), but he kept building the Model F and Model G for three more years. No other brand was offering its customers so much choice. Nor was any selling as fast.

Aware of what the publicity generated by racing had done for Henry Ford and his driver Barney Oldfield, Durant also put together a full-time team of Buick race drivers. At the same time, his regional distributors hired professional drivers and entered their Buicks in high-profile local races. The early Buick race teams won more than 500 race trophies, more than any other brand.

Finally, with all these initiatives under way, he further cemented his growing reputation as a genius and "the wizard of Flint" by taking a gamble on the U.S. economy. In the spring of 1907, the stock market and business in general began a sharp decline. A handful of relatively large companies actually went bankrupt and several major stock traders were forced to withdraw money from banks to cover their losses. As word of the failures spread, more depositors began withdrawing money from their banks. With no official central bank or regulatory controls, smaller banks feared a run on their deposits.

In the end, the "panic" was averted when the financier and banker J. P. Morgan (who soon became one of Billy Durant's personal enemies) assembled an informal network of larger banks to pump more money into the smaller banks that were in danger. Working from Morgan's own library, the group labored around the clock for three weeks to find new lines of credit (many of them overseas) and buy stock in threatened companies. In less than a month, the panic was over. Yet during that brief period, all kinds of manufacturing enterprises shut down production and could not move inventory or maintain cash flow.

Of all the automakers, Billy Durant was the only one who decided from the outset that the "panic" was just that, a short-term blip that would be followed by a sharp rebound. Accordingly, Buick production was not decreased but pushed to full capacity. With his usual charm, Billy was able to put off his creditors and keep his plants running twenty-four hours a day, as was his new associate C. S. Mott, while his new distributors and dealers watched anxiously. At one point, new Buicks were being stored anyplace available, even barns. By the end of the year, however, the economy was on the upswing and Buick was the only car maker with enough inventory to meet renewed demand. Buick pulled ahead while the rest of the industry struggled to catch up.

By the spring of 1908, less than four years after Durant's arrival on the scene, Buick had overtaken both Oldsmobile and Cadillac in sales. The new Flint complex was the largest in the world, just as he had envisioned, and it employed a workforce of more than 2,000 people. The plants were running twenty-four hours a day, with three labor shifts, pumping out more cars in just one day than Buick had in the entire year of 1904.

At the start of 1908, Buick was the number-one carmaker in America in sales, although the phoenix-like Henry Ford was emerging as a greater competitive threat than either Olds or Leland. For his part, Billy Durant was about to restructure the industry with an even grander vision.

More than fifty years later, Alfred Sloan summed up the growing competition this way:

> No two men better understood the opportunity presented by the automobile in its early days than Mr. Durant and Mr. Ford. The automobile was then widely regarded, especially among bankers, as a sport; it was priced out of the mass market, it was mechanically unreliable, and good roads were scarce. Yet in 1908, when the industry produced only 65,000 "machines" in the United States, Mr. Durant looked forward to a one-million-car year to come—for which he was regarded as a promoter of wildcat ideas—and Mr. Ford had already found in the Model T the means to be the first to make that prediction come true.[12]

NO LEGACY FOR DAVID

And what of David Dunbar Buick, the man whose own initial vision had sparked Durant's new success?

He ended up watching everything from the sidelines, as Durant himself would two decades later in the wake of the crisis of 1920.

Unlike Durant, however, Buick never found another dream to chase. By 1905, he owned just one share of Buick stock and was destitute. When Billy's attorney, John Carton, informed him that Buick owed him $92.58 in legal fees, Billy immediately sent a check to Carton with a cover letter stating, "Mr. Buick wishes me to say that until a few moments ago, this [$92.58] was more money than he had in the world. He disliked very much to make this admission and possibly this is the reason why you have not heard from him before."[13]

Before the end of the year, David Buick moved back to Detroit, unemployed. Two years later, Billy Durant bought his remaining share in the now-thriving company that bore his name for $100,000.

David Buick proceeded to squander all of that money in a series of bad investments, first in California oil exploration and then in Florida real estate. He ended up back in Detroit, where he had started, in a series of menial jobs. He died on March 5, 1929, of colon cancer, in the charity ward of Detroit's Harper Hospital. That year, Buick the man turned seventy-four and Buick the car company sold more than 196,000 cars.

In 1937, General Motors' Buick Motor division changed its logo to the original Buick family crest, which remains the symbol for the Buick brand to this day. On September 15, 1974, 120 years after David Buick's birth, the *Sunday Post* of Arbroath, Scotland, where he was born, ran a special tribute to its most famous and forgotten native son. The short article asked the rhetorical question, "Do you recognize the name?" and noted:

> David started the company that grew into the General Motors Corpora-tion of America, the mightiest car-making empire in the world. Over 17,000,000 cars bearing his name and crest have rolled off production lines, yet he was involved in making only 120 of them. . . .
>
> The house where David Buick was born no longer stands. It was demolished years ago to make way for new council houses. But as the birthplace of a man who greatly influenced transport, its setting is ap-propriately close to the burgh's new four-lane throughway, Burnside Drive. Arbroath could do worse than rename it Buick Way, as a tribute to Scotland's most remarkable forgotten son.

David Dunbar Buick remains a forgotten son, and the burgh's throughway remains Burnside Drive.

A SHAKEOUT ON THE HORIZON

By the late fall of 1907, when Buick Motor was on a roll, the automo-bile had become the one product all consumers dreamed of, even if most people still couldn't afford it. Billy Durant and Henry Ford both had a vision of millions of Americans owning their own auto-mobiles, but each would follow a very different strategy to make it happen.

The growing automobile industry was still characterized by chaos and speculation. The phenomenal popularity of the Curved Dash Oldsmobile had sparked the birth of more competitors, but also put more pressure on each one to increase its sales volume. In 1904, the United States overtook France as the world's number-one automobile-producing country, with 19,000 vehicles built and sold. By 1907, annual U.S. production exceeded 60,000 vehicles. The

U.S. industry had sprouted more than 240 new companies with the stated purpose of building automobiles. However, the top-ten producers—led by Buick, Ford, Reo (created by Ransom Olds after a falling out with his Oldsmobile management team), and Cadillac—accounted for 75 percent of total production. Buick and Ford alone built 18,689 of the total 53,387 cars sold by the industry's entire field of forty-five "major" competitors in 1908. Below Buick and Ford, more than half of the rest of the pack sold fewer than a thousand vehicles each.[14]

Although conventional wisdom assumed that the big fish would eat the little ones (as it is still almost always assumed, often wrongly, when industries face structural imbalances), no one foresaw who the biggest long-term survivors and winners would be. In the end, one of the biggest winners of all was actually a supplier rather than a manufacturer: Hyatt Roller Bearing, then still owned and managed by Alfred P. Sloan, Jr., who was watching the action closely but playing his own cards close to the vest during the winter and spring of 1907–1908.

CHAPTER SEVEN

Birth of a General

UNLIKE BILLY DURANT AND HENRY FORD, Alfred Sloan preferred to be in the background rather than under the spotlight, even as his reputation as a shrewd executive continued to grow. He felt that the automobile business was attracting "as sugar draws flies, a host of persons who had strong appetites for excitement."[1]

Sloan saw himself as a different breed, dealing with those persons with "strong appetites for excitement" only when there was a need for what he saw as his own unique technical expertise. Yet he actually admitted to enjoying a meeting of the minds when the topic was an engineering problem.

"Mix with them?" he mused. "I felt I had more important work to do at the Hyatt plant. But the mixing was important then precisely because there was so little stability in the haphazardly growing industry. When a sales problem concerned engineering, then I could help. It was interesting when some technical problem involved a meeting with another manufacturer. It was fun to find myself at some convention in the company of men whose training and experience made us kindred spirits. . . . But what fascinated us were engineering problems, whereas Pete [Steenstrup] functioned as our head salesman without regard to technological evolution."[2]

Wisely, Sloan let partner Pete Steenstrup serve as his company's primary customer interface. While Sloan was turned off rather than thrilled by the sales process, Steenstrup believed in establishing relationships with anybody and everybody who had even the slimmest chance of ever building and selling a successful automobile. Like hundreds of other automotive suppliers' representatives (today as well as back then), he virtually lived out of a suitcase in the eternal quest to keep current customers happy and make sure potential new ones knew what his company had to offer.

Steenstrup was also blessed (like Billy Durant) with the born salesman's rare ability to empathize with any customer, regardless of personal tastes, habits, or convictions. Sloan recalled both his own reticence and his partner's charm:

> The kinds of things Pete Steenstrup had been doing for Hyatt [Roller Bearing Company] in the early 1900s did not appeal to me. Once in a while in the early years Pete would urge me to go to Detroit, just to mix, as he expressed it. There were always so many problems at our plant [in Harrison, New Jersey] that I would argue my job was to build the bearings. But Pete was persistent.
>
> "Hell, Alfred! I'm not a mechanical expert. I'm just a strong Norwegian with a frolicsome disposition. I need you on some of my trips. Those fellows want engineering authority for what I tell them. You are the only one to answer their questions. Loads. Performance. Durability. Design. Above all, deliveries. So, you come along."
>
> If I still resisted, he'd argue: "Don't make work out of these trips. Enjoy yourself."
>
> Pete enjoyed himself, and without seeming to need much sleep. I've never known a man with more vitality to share with people. He could have just as much fun with Henry Ford, who did not drink, as with the Dodge brothers [Ford's key suppliers], who did. To Pete, three o'clock in the morning was not one bit different from three o'clock in the afternoon.[3]

As Steenstrup constantly rode the rails between New Jersey and Michigan, his most regular point of call was soon the Pontchartrain

Hotel in Detroit, where Billy Durant also stayed whenever he was in town. In the heart of the city's growing downtown area, the Pontchartrain (which was later torn down and replaced by a high-rise hotel with the same name a mile away) was where the action was for tinkerers in search of backers, backers in search of tinkerers, and inventors and suppliers looking to make a sale. It was the place where the rumors were planted and spread, and where the whiskey flowed as freely as the tall tales. Sloan described it as "the heart" of the young industry, where Steenstrup could track down anyone connected with the automobile game, especially suppliers and dealers still located in the East, as was Hyatt itself. As Sloan put it:

> The Pontchartrain was where motor car gossip was heard first. New models customarily had debuts there. As word spread that So-and-So's new Whizzer was parked at the curbstone, the crowd would flock outside to appraise the new rival of existing cars. Even on ordinary days, when the crowd thinned out of the dining room, the tables would be covered with sketches: crankshafts, chassis, details of motors, wheels, and all sorts of mechanisms. Partnerships were made and ended there. New projects were launched.[4]

In this freewheeling, informal, and unstructured environment, it was actually to Hyatt's advantage for the more introverted Alfred Sloan to stay back in New Jersey whenever he could. His absence from the back-slapping and rumor-mongering arena only enhanced his reputation as one of the few men who seriously studied and understood all the dynamics of not only the machine called the automobile, but the complex network of differing functions and skills required to put it on the road at a profit.

A HYATT CUSTOMER PREPARES TO SHIFT INTO HIGH GEAR

Pete Steenstrup's quirkiest and most important customer was not Billy Durant or any other member of the Pontchartrain crowd. It was Henry Ford, who (like Sloan) disdained the kind of braggadocio and wheeling and dealing that went on at places like the Pontchartrain Hotel.

Steenstrup's unlikely relationship with Ford actually went back to 1902, during Ford's darkest days. It had started not with a personal sales call from Steenstrup but rather a written query from Ford, shortly after he had been shown the door and replaced at the Henry Ford Company by Henry Leland and the Cadillac brand. As Sloan recalled it:

> Their acquaintanceship began long before the name of Ford became famed. I think the first contact resulted from Pete's follow-up on a letter of inquiry from someone associated with Mr. Ford; Mr. Ford was building a racing car and wanted to know something about our bearings, what a set would cost him. In those days such letters commonly came to us mottled with the stains of oil and graphite. The desks on which they were written were workshop benches.
>
> Anyway Pete had found Mr. Ford and C. Harold Wills, who was drafting for him—if my memory is right—designing a car in a room on the fourth floor, above a machine shop. They could be found there only in the evenings. Each had another job by day. The place had no heat. They would draw until their fingers got too cold to hold a pencil. Mr. Wills tells how they would put on boxing gloves and flail each other until they felt warm. That was how they finished the drawings of Mr. Ford's famous racing car, the 999, the one with which Barney Oldfield made a lot of records. Its straight rear axle had no differential, but it turned on Hyatt roller bearings.[5]

Whatever "Crazy" Henry's latest project might be, it was always near the top of the list of gossip and rumors being spread or denied at the Pontchartrain's bar. After joining forces with local coal magnate Alexander Malcomson in 1903, Ford managed to stay focused on practical automobiles; and, to the surprise of many of the Pontchartrain regulars as well as his former financial backers, each model he built was successful. The Model A of 1903 was followed by the Models B, C, F, K, N, R, and S. By the end of 1907, the Ford Motor Company was actually closing in on Buick's sales and Ford was tinkering with the design of a car that would fulfill his earlier though somewhat vague vision of a car "for the common man"—a car to be called the Model T.

Control of Ford Motor Company itself, however, still rested with Ford's partner Malcomson and two other former mechanics: the hard-drinking, hard-living Dodge brothers, who were regulars at the Pontchartrain and many other saloons. While the administration of the Ford Motor Company was in the hands of James Couzens, who remained an employee rather than a partner, the Dodge brothers had become partners through the back door when they cut a unique deal to supply all mechanical components to the newborn Ford Motor Company back in 1903.

John Dodge was four years his brother Horace's senior. The two were virtually inseparable all their lives, but John was clearly the dominant mind and personality. On one occasion, a drunken John held his pistol aimed at a saloonkeeper while equally drunken Horace proceeded to throw shot glasses at the bar's mirror. On another, at a formal banquet, John rose and proceeded to walk across the tops of all the tables, smashing all the lightbulbs and chandeliers of one of Detroit's most elegant ballrooms apparently because he felt like it.[6] As Ford biographer Douglas Brinkley put it, "Henry Ford was only a year older than John Dodge, but exemplified another of the era's archetypes entirely with his righteousness, independence, and doggedly homespun values. . . . Throughout their lives John and Horace continued to frequent working-class bars most weekend nights, specifically to get very, very drunk."[7]

Trained as machinists, the Dodge brothers had opened their own shop in Detroit in the late 1890s and supplied transmissions to Ransom Olds for his early Oldsmobiles. Because few other suppliers were willing to take the risk and make such a large commitment on the still-unproven Ford name, they were selected by Malcomson, Couzens, and Henry Ford to supply nearly all of the mechanical components (including engines and axles as well as transmissions) for the Model A. Knowing that the Ford Motor Company needed them more than they needed it, the Dodge boys agreed to deliver a total of 650 engines, transmissions, and axles but demanded that they be paid cash-on-delivery rather than on the standard sixty-day terms agreed to by all other suppliers. The total value of the contract was $162,500. It stipulated that if the manufacturer/customer defaulted on payment of any delivery, the Dodges would take full ownership of all the company's machinery and unsold product.

With Henry Ford himself in charge of engineering for the Model A, the Ford Motor Company ran into a cost overrun and budget crisis before the first Model A had been built. Facing financial ruin if the Dodge brothers were not paid, Malcomson and Couzens were forced to beat the bushes to find investors (while disdainful Henry Ford remained above the process). As it turned out, the Dodge brothers were as eager as any other red-blooded male Detroiter to get an ownership stake in the car game. To Henry Ford's chagrin, they agreed to accept shares of stock in Ford Motor Company valued at $5,000 in lieu of part of the cash due them after their first delivery. Ford now had yet another set of "partners" more concerned with making money than with his own love affair with the automobile.

The deal with the Dodge brothers also made Henry Ford an indirect partner with Alfred Sloan. Sloan and his own partner Pete Steenstrup realized that they would now have to do whatever it took to maintain a relationship with Ford as well as the Dodges. Sloan described the relationship this way:

> These two [John and Horace Dodge], who were to become great automobile makers, acquired wealth as parts makers and partners of Henry Ford. They made his first engines, after their initiation into the field as makers of transmissions for the early Oldsmobiles. They made Ford axles, too. These, like Weston-Mott axles, turned on Hyatt roller bearings.
>
>   Well, that made us almost the same as partners of these two, and in the same way we realized ourselves to be in an informal partnership with Mr. Ford. Every time he sold a Ford car he sold a set of Dodge axles and a set of Hyatt bearings as well. . . . Smooth relations with the Dodge brothers depended on smooth relations with the Ford Motor Company. Fortunately for us, Pete Steenstrup and Henry Ford were on good terms.[8]

HENRY FORD'S DIFFERENT PRODUCT STRATEGY

With the Model A's success, and with the Dodge brothers and all other creditors no longer worried about Ford Motor making payment, Alexander Malcomson soon had his own falling out with Henry Ford. Again, the divisive issue was product strategy.

Malcomson believed the company should build on the Model A's success by producing a variety of large cars, which were more profitable than the small Model A. Henry Ford had no objection to putting larger and more powerful engines in some models, but he was determined to concentrate on the low end of the market, where he believed that high volume would drive costs down and at the same time feed even more demand for the product. It was a fundamental difference in philosophy, one that would reemerge several times among all automakers during the rest of the twentieth century as market demand and consumer preferences fluctuated in line with economic cycles.

James Couzens, who had been brought in from Malcomson's coal business to hold Henry Ford in check, ended up siding with Ford rather than Malcomson. Malcomson in turn went to the board of directors to try to have Couzens removed, but he got no votes of support. One of Henry Ford's and James Couzens's strongest supporters on the board happened to be John Dodge, who with his brother controlled the second-largest block of stock.

To force Malcomson out, Henry Ford himself proposed the creation of a new company to be called Ford Manufacturing Company. The new entity would have full responsibility for all parts used in Ford Motor products and actually sell the parts to Ford Motor. The idea was for Ford Manufacturing to set arbitrary prices and force Ford Motor to cough up all its profits to the new entity, thus diluting the value of Malcomson's Ford Motor stock.

The idea worked. A defeated Malcomson finally sold all his 225 shares directly to Henry Ford on July 12, 1906, for $175,000. Shortly thereafter, Henry Ford was finally elected president of the company that bore his name and John Dodge was elected vice president. Ford then proceeded to buy out as many other stockholders as he could, with the exception of Couzens and the Dodge brothers, who were still supplying all of the crucial mechanical parts for Ford's various models.

Ford was now finally free to focus all his attention on what he referred to as the "universal car": a car that would be lighter, more durable, simpler to maintain and repair, and less expensive than any other on the road. In the fall of 1906, he sealed off a room at his thriving new Piquette Avenue plant in Detroit (the second plant he had built for his growing concern). The room was to be used exclusively by him and the small team of engineers he picked to work on his new obsession. They continued working in secret throughout 1907. When they finally introduced a car called the Model T in the fall of 1908, it immediately changed the way people looked at the automobile and the industry that built it.

BILLY TAKES ANOTHER CALL

While Alfred Sloan remained focused on quietly expanding the customer base for his roller bearing business and Henry Ford proceeded to develop his Model T, forty-seven-year-old Billy Durant was also looking to expand his empire—this time, with his new young bride Catherine at his side. Unlike first wife Clara, Catherine was thrilled to accompany Billy in his travels and adventures, both of which were about to accelerate to a pace that even his daughter Margery wouldn't think possible.

The biggest adventure of all began with what Billy described as an unexpected phone call from Chicago.

The caller was Ben Briscoe, who had established close relations with the all-powerful House of Morgan in New York City after dumping his interest in the failing Buick enterprise on James Whiting in 1904. J. P. Morgan and Company agreed to back Briscoe with a bond issue of $250,000 to acquire Jonathan Maxwell's automobile enterprise, which at the time was only slightly healthier than David Dunbar Buick's business. The Morgan bankers were finally taking notice of the automobile industry's potential and saw the underwriting of Briscoe as a low-risk way to enter the market. They also wanted to make sure that the concentration of manufacturing operations in the Midwest was offset by at least one major operation in the East. At the insistence of Morgan, the renamed Maxwell-Briscoe Company proceeded to build a new plant in Tarrytown, New York, on the banks of the Hudson River. Within a year, the plant was up and running.

The first Maxwell-Briscoe cars were immediately successful, but by the spring of 1908, Briscoe (like so many others) was convinced that the inevitable shakeout among manufacturers would come sooner rather than later. Accordingly, he had an idea to run by Billy Durant. As Billy described it:

> I was dining with my daughter, Mrs. E. R. Campbell, when I was called to the phone. Chicago on the line, Briscoe calling.
>
> Briscoe: "Hello, Billy, I have a most important matter to discuss with you and want you to take the first train to Chicago."
>
> Durant: "'What's the big idea, Ben?"
>
> Briscoe: "Don't ask me to explain, it's the biggest thing in the country, there's millions in it, can you come?"[9]

Durant told Briscoe he couldn't come to Chicago, he was too busy; but he would have breakfast with him in the morning if Briscoe could catch the evening train to Flint. Briscoe agreed, and Billy met him at the Flint train depot at seven o'clock the next morning. They had a quick breakfast at the nearby Dresden Hotel and then proceeded to Billy's office at the Buick plant to discuss Briscoe's big idea.

The big idea was a consolidation of carmakers on the lines of U.S. Steel, whose creation in 1901 had been orchestrated by J. P. Morgan himself. Morgan now wanted Briscoe to feel Durant out on the idea of a similar automotive merger. As Billy recalled it:

> One of the partners of J. P. Morgan & Co. had made a small investment in the Maxwell-Briscoe Co. when it was first organized. Pleased with the progress the company was making and recognizing the possibilities, he asked me if a sufficient number of motor car concerns could be brought together to control the industry. How would the leading companies regard a consolidation? Would Briscoe canvass the situation and report [to Morgan]? At that time trusts and combinations were the order of the day—promotions of all kinds encouraged by big banking interests. Briscoe had no well-considered plan but wanted to get my ideas.[10]

Despite his years as a professional stock trader in New York before taking on the Buick challenge, there is no record of Billy Durant having ever dealt directly with the House of Morgan before Briscoe made his pitch. If he had, he may well have told Briscoe good-bye on the spot. Durant's business record (like that of all the other strong-willed auto industry leaders of the day) indicates a temperament that would never willingly cough up the kind of money and operational control that was the J. P. Morgan and Company policy in underwriting mergers. That policy was spelled out by Morgan partner George Perkins, who eventually became the lead intermediary in trying to put together the first automotive merger:

> Morgan and Company would investigate, consulting and questioning the various producers in the field as to their interests and opinions. Then the firm would prepare a plan and submit it to the chief corporations in the industry. If approved, the House of Morgan would estimate the working capital necessary to organize the new concern, and form

a syndicate to raise the money. If $10,000,000 were needed, the syndi-
cate would issue $15,000,000 in stock, the extra millions representing
the syndicate's "bonus" . . . Morgan would also insist upon choosing
all the officers and directors of the new company. This point Morgan &
Co. have found indispensable in making their combination.[11]

Perkins's description of more than a century ago remains a remarkably accurate depiction of the way most investment banks still
put deals together today. It also explains why they were feared, respected, and needed all at the same time, then as now.

At his meeting with Durant in Flint, Briscoe suggested bringing
together no less than twenty companies for discussions. He then
asked Billy what he thought. Billy told him he did not think it was
workable, with so many different parties and too many conflicting
interests to be reconciled.

Billy asked, "Why not modify your ideas, Ben, and see if you
can get together a few concerns committed to volume production in
the medium-priced class, all having a common objective, all head-
ing for a highly competitive field?"[12] He went on to suggest Ford,
Maxwell-Briscoe, Buick, and Reo, then the four dominant companies of the industry. (Reo had been formed by Ransom E. Olds after
his falling out with his financial backer Fred Smith and his Oldsmobile management team and was now actually outselling Oldsmobile.)

Durant further suggested that Briscoe meet personally with
Henry Ford before any of the others, explaining that Ford was "in
the limelight, liked publicity, and unless he could lead the proces-
sion, would not play."[13] He told Briscoe, "Get Ford if possible, then
take the matter up with R. E. Olds. When and if everything is arranged to your satisfaction, advise me the time and place and I will
attend your meeting."[14]

Regardless of how much each player actually knew of the Morgan bankers' modus operandi, a new game was afoot. The fact that
all the players quickly agreed to what Billy suggested that morning
is testimony to how nervous and uncertain each man was about
who would survive in the young but ruthlessly competitive and
wide open automobile industry.

BILLY BRINGS THE BIG FOUR TOGETHER . . .

With J. P. Morgan and Company still in the background, Briscoe
informed Durant two weeks after their Flint breakfast that Henry

Ford and Ransom Olds would like to meet with the two of them in Detroit. The designated place was the Penobscot Building (then Detroit's tallest building, still standing and occupied today) rather than the more popular Pontchartrain Hotel, where Durant and all other self-respecting nonresident auto barons always stayed.

When Billy arrived, he saw the others waiting in a crowded public area with a cadre of "associates and advisers." He immediately feared that they would draw attention and headlines. As he observed:

> I sensed that unless we ran to cover, plenty of undesirable publicity was in the offing. As I had commodious quarters in the Pontchartrain Hotel and as the luncheon hour was approaching, I suggested that we separate (in order not to attract attention) and meet in my room as soon as convenient, giving the number of the room and how to locate it without going to the office. This was accomplished and I had the unexpected pleasure of entertaining the entire party until mid-afternoon.[15]

Durant let Briscoe open the meeting. Not one to beat around the bush, Briscoe explained that the objective was to come up with a plan for merging the four companies that might appeal to J. P. Morgan and Company.

Then came what Billy called "a painful pause."

Durant himself broached the subject of the value of the companies, throwing out a figure of $10 million for Ford Motor, $6 million for Reo, and $5 million for Maxwell-Briscoe, but *not* offering any figure for Buick.

When Briscoe finally asked what Buick was worth, Billy replied only that "the report of the appraisers and auditors and the conditions and terms of the agreement" would answer that question.

With tension already in the air, the discussion then moved quickly to the nitty-gritty of all merger negotiations: How would the new entity be managed? Who would be the boss? How would the different companies be represented in management?

Briscoe and Durant led the discussion, and their differing views remain a remarkably accurate summary of the debate over centralized control versus operational independence that is still conducted within large companies and among potential partners every day.

As Billy Durant recalled the discussion:

> Briscoe took the position that the purchasing and engineering depart-
> ments should be consolidated, that the advertising and sales depart-
> ments should be combined, and that a central committee should pass
> on all operating policies.
>
> I took the position that this would only lead to confusion; that there
> should be no change or interference in the manner of operating, that
> the different companies should continue exactly as they were. In other
> words, I had in mind a *holding company*. Briscoe came back jokingly
> with "Ho! Ho! Durant is for states' rights; I am for a union."[16]

Eerily, it was the same difference in opinion and philosophy
that would eventually lead to the General Motors crisis of 1920 and
the final parting of Billy Durant and Alfred Sloan.

Billy also noted that Henry Ford was the only person who remained silent during the meeting. Despite the sharp differences between Durant and Briscoe, the discussion kept going, with Billy
recalling, "Business conditions and the future of the industry were
forecast, the hazards and uncertainties were gone into thoroughly,
the desirability of a controlling organization agreed upon, the meeting breaking up with the best of feeling with a statement from Mr.
Briscoe that he would see his people and report, and that, in all
probability, we would be invited to meet in New York in the near
future."[17]

From that point, the House of Morgan took charge of the game,
and none of the players would end up happy with its rules.

HENRY FORD KILLS MORGAN'S BIG DEAL

The exact dates of the various meetings following that initial session
in Detroit are contradicted by the various players: James Couzens,
Henry Ford's point man, and Ransom Olds both left sketchy diaries
that put the most intense meetings in January 1908, while Billy Durant puts them in May (around the time of his divorce and remar-
riage). Most historians give credence to the January time frame but
also concur with Durant's recollection of the substance of the con-
versations.[18]

Regardless of the exact dates, the House of Morgan contacted all
four principals shortly after Briscoe's report. The next meeting was
arranged in New York and held at the law offices of Ward, Hayden

and Satterlee at 120 Broadway rather than the fabled House of Morgan at the corner of Broad and Wall Street (opposite the New York Stock Exchange). Herbert Satterlee was a partner in the firm and happened to be J. P. Morgan's son-in-law. Satterlee led the discussion and immediately asked the kinds of questions that today make all executives wince in the presence of competitors and in the absence of their own attorneys: How much capital did each bring to the table? What would each gain by the merger? Would a consolidation attract or discourage competition? What were their objections, if any, to the merger?

Significantly, only Henry Ford raised any objection. As Durant recalled, "He [Ford] thought the tendency of consolidation and control was to increase prices, which he believed would be a serious mistake. He was in favor of keeping prices down to the lowest possible point, giving the multitude the benefit of cheap transportation."[19]

Ford's comment reflected his determination to build that "universal car" for the masses, but it also reflected his lingering mistrust of financiers and other businessmen. The mistrust went back to his early failures. Those experiences actually led him to resent many of the basic tenets of capitalism itself, especially the way financiers and investors were driven by the profit motive rather than what he saw as the more noble desire to create a product that would benefit the human race. Ford expressed his bitterness and suspicion when recalling his ouster by the financial backers of the Henry Ford Company in 1902:

> What I most realized about business that year is this: (1) That finance is given a place ahead of work and therefore tends to kill the work . . . (2) That thinking first of money instead of work brings on fear of failure and this fear blocks every avenue of business . . . (3) That the way is clear for anyone who thinks first of service, of doing the work in the best possible way. The money influence . . . seemed to be at the bottom of most troubles . . . I was not free. I could not give full play to my ideas. Everything had to be planned to make money; the last consideration was the work.[20]

Despite his comment in Satterlee's office, Henry Ford expressed no other objection to the merger at that meeting. It was agreed by all parties, however, that the session was to be considered "purely informal," that there would be no publicity, and that none of the parties had made any kind of commitment.

Billy Durant left the meeting confident that a deal would be made. That same evening, he took the train back to Flint, where he instructed his attorney John Carton to draft a proposed agreement on behalf of Buick stockholders, authorizing him to act on their behalf in exchanging their Buick shares for shares of the new company. The agreement was quickly drawn up and approved. During the spring and summer, several more meetings were held in New York as the House of Morgan proceeded with the appraisal and audit of each of the four enterprises.

With new bride Catherine traveling with him and supporting his vision, Durant was again thinking and dreaming big. Sometime during this period of heated negotiations in a hot summer, Billy declared, "The time will come when 500,000 automobiles will be manufactured and sold in this country every year." To which Morgan banker George Perkins (who had so eloquently described the Morgan philosophy of business) replied: "If he has any sense he'll keep those notions to himself if he ever tries to borrow money."[21]

During one trip to New York, Billy was asked by Perkins to meet with one of the attorneys in Satterlee's office. At this meeting, he was informed that J. P. Morgan himself wanted him to meet instead with the firm's lead attorney, Frederick L. Stetson. Billy was personally escorted to Morgan headquarters at Broad and Wall Street, the "corner" as it is still called, and taken to Stetson's office in a "private elevator." As Billy recalled:

> Mr. Stetson was very cordial, said he had heard some very nice things about Buick, and understood that I was in complete control with authority to execute the agreement. I told him he was correctly informed; that the stock was deposited in the First National Bank of Flint with the understanding that if the merger was completed, the exchange of the securities would be made if the terms were satisfactory to me. Mr. Stetson asked if the depositors had knowledge of the new securities or any of the details regarding the new company, the size of the capitalization, etc., etc., etc. I told him the stockholders had confidence in me and that the matter was entirely in my hands.[22]

Stetson then challenged Durant's authority to act on behalf of the Buick stockholders and told him it would be necessary to draw up a new agreement. Billy replied that he had full authority but would consult again with his own attorney. At that moment, his confidence in both the House of Morgan and the likelihood of a deal began to crumble.

With the seeds of doubt already planted in Billy's mind, another meeting of the four principals and the Morgan representatives and attorneys was called at Satterlee's office on Broadway. The bankers reported that they had completed their audits and appraisals. They also reported that they had already instructed their attorneys to draw up contracts to be approved by the stockholders and directors of the four companies.

The conversation then turned to the actual underwriting of the issuance of stock in the new company, and Henry Ford quickly killed the deal by announcing that he wanted cash rather than stock. This turn of events might have been expected from the outset if the other parties had followed a bit closer Ford's prior dealings with bankers and investors As Durant recalled:

> We were told that generous subscriptions on the part of the manufac-turers would have a favorable effect upon the public acceptance of the issue and Mr. Ford was asked how much of the preferred stock he would subscribe for. He replied that when he was first approached by Mr. Briscoe, he told Mr. Briscoe that he would sell his company for cash, but would not be interested in or take stock in any merger or consolidation. This was a great surprise and the bankers who were expecting a large subscription from Mr. Ford were quite disappointed.[23]

The number Ford threw out that day was $3 million in cash plus a share of the new company's stock. Ransom Olds immediately declared that if Ford wanted to get cash, he did, too. Olds's number was also $3 million.

A stunned and embarrassed Satterlee asked Durant to step into an adjoining private room. Durant told him that Ford's statement was news to him, and he suggested they bring Briscoe into the room. Incredibly, Briscoe told them that what Ford had said was true. Again, Billy recalled:

> Briscoe said that Mr. Ford had correctly stated the case, but that he had shown such an interest as the matter progressed that Briscoe,

whether rightly or wrongly, inferred that Mr. Ford had changed his mind and that he would go along with the others.[24]

With that, the deal that would have combined the Big Four automobile makers into a single enterprise was dead. One can only speculate how America's auto industry, its economy, and even its culture would have been different today if the merger had proceeded. Would Henry Ford have still had the freedom to proceed with the Model T? Would Ford and Durant have been able to coexist in the same organization? Would the House of Morgan have put its own management team and business strategy in place? Would Alfred Sloan have remained a small independent supplier?

Regardless of the could-haves and should-haves, Billy Durant was not ready to give up on a merger. He had put his own credibility on the line by securing the Buick stockholder agreement authorizing him to execute a deal. After the meeting, he confronted Satterlee:

> I told him I had come to New York several months earlier, and had been led to believe that the consolidation sponsored by the Morgan firm was being seriously considered and had so informed my people; that the Buick stock had been deposited and if released could never again be collected in the same form, nor would I have the courage . . . to make such an attempt. I must have a consolidation.[25]

Satterlee's response was, "Mr. Durant, you only have the Buick, how can you have a consolidation?" And Billy replied that he would have "no difficulty in securing another company."[26]

BILLY CUTS HIS OWN DEAL

Over the next few weeks, Durant and Briscoe continued meeting with the Morgan bankers. Their grandiose vision had been reduced to a merger of just their two companies. But even that was not to be, despite Billy's determination.

As the talks with Briscoe and Morgan went on, Durant refused to comment to the news media, but Briscoe could not keep his mouth shut. Inevitably, rumors of a merger of Buick and Maxwell-Briscoe began floating at the Pontchartrain Hotel in Detroit and on Wall Street in New York.

On June 29, 1908, Briscoe spoke with a newspaper reporter. In the interview, he not only confirmed that a merger was in the works, he also declared that the new enterprise would be a consolidation of all operations rather than the holding company Durant had envisioned all along.[27] A month later, on July 31, an expanded version of the story broke in the *New York Times*. The *Times* article described the deal as "the first big combination in the automobile world" and even reported that it would be capitalized at $25 million. It did not mention the House of Morgan but did mention Herbert Satterlee as an "interested party." It further reported that the new company would be called International Motors and would be "ready for operations" by September 1.[28]

The reaction of the secretive House of Morgan was predictable: The talks were off.

Having come so close to victory only to be tripped again at the finish line, Durant expressed his frustration in a letter to his friend and attorney John Carton:

> If you think it is an easy matter to get money from New York capitalists to finance a Motor Company proposition in Michigan, you have another guess coming. Notwithstanding the fact that quoted rates are very low, money is hard to get owing to a somewhat unaccountable feeling of uneasiness and a general distrust of the automotive proposition.[29]

Billy was still not willing to give up on his latest dream, however. In fact, he had begun work on plan B right after the House of Morgan and its attorney had questioned his authority to act on behalf of Buick's stockholders.

Without informing either Briscoe or the Morgan bank, Durant had met privately with Fred Smith back in Lansing, Michigan. Smith was now in charge of Oldsmobile, and Oldsmobile's business was in the tank. Like Briscoe and Whiting four years earlier, Smith was looking for an angel; and there was still no more powerful angel in Michigan than William Crapo Durant.

After the deal with Briscoe and the Morgan bank was killed, Durant took a train from New York to Lansing, Michigan. He arrived near midnight. In his typical style, he immediately called Smith at home. At three in the morning, Billy was given a plant tour of the Olds Motor Works. While walking through the machinery and assembly line, he laid out his proposition: a holding company that would acquire both Buick and Oldsmobile. With Oldsmobile losing money and carrying huge debt, Smith agreed to a one-to-one exchange of three-fourths of the outstanding 200,000 shares of Oldsmobile stock in exchange for shares in the new holding company.

NO HEADLINES FOR BILLY'S NEWBORN

With Oldsmobile in his pocket, Billy then met one more time with Satterlee. This time, there were no questions about his ability to act on behalf of the Buick stockholders. Satterlee and the Morgan Bank now had no objections to the deal; it was, after all, small potatoes compared to what had originally been envisioned. While Oldsmobile was bleeding red ink, Buick was the most profitable and highest-volume producer in the industry: The new venture appeared to be a safe bet.

When the discussion finally came down to what name to give the new company, Billy suggested "International Motor Company," which had been suggested originally by Morgan partner Perkins.

Perkins, on behalf of the House of Morgan, said no—that name would be held by Morgan because it might fit with some other future merger of manufacturers, whether they be automotive or nonautomotive.

On September 10, Satterlee sent Durant a letter recommending the name "General Motors Company." It was a name that his firm had come up with and had researched to make sure it was not being used by any other manufacturers or supplier.[30] After checking again to make sure that Smith and Oldsmobile were still in, Durant instructed Satterlee to proceed with drafting and filing the papers of incorporation for General Motors. The deed was done on September 16, 1908.

At Billy's request, the papers were filed in New Jersey rather than Michigan because New Jersey law had no restrictions on the amount of stock a company might issue regardless of its actual assets. He thus had virtual free rein to use his new baby to generate capital through the issuance of new stock: a game he had learned to play much better than his father during his two-year sojourn in New York. To avoid drawing attention to himself or the new entity, Durant's own name did not appear on the articles of incorporation on September 16.

This time, the deal went unnoticed in the business world, just as he wanted it. The biggest business news story in the *New York Times* on September 16, 1908, was the announcement by the White Star Line shipping company that it was to begin construction of the world's largest ocean liner, to be called *Titanic.*

Twelve days later, on September 28, acting on behalf of Buick's stockholders, Billy Durant proposed to sell the Buick Motor Company to General Motors in a one-for-one exchange of shares of stock. The deal was immediately approved by the three men he had picked as the first "directors" of General Motors, none of whose names were known on Wall Street or among the press. Three months after that, General Motors acquired control of Oldsmobile in a similar exchange of three-quarters of all Oldsmobile stock rather than cash.

The birth of General Motors was not reported in the press until the end of December 1908, when Billy's baby was already rumored to be on the verge of several more acquisitions. *Horseless Age,* the auto industry's only nationwide publication, ran the following item:

> The formation of the General Motors Company as a New Jersey corporation and offers of an exchange of stock made to stockholders of the Olds Motor Works of Lansing, Michigan, have started anew rumors of the consolidation of automobile manufacturing interests. Considerable secrecy is maintained in regard to the new company, which is said to be capitalized at $12,500,000, divided into $7,000,000 Preferred stock and $5,500,000 Common stock, each share having a par value of $1. At present the new company is said to embrace the Buick Motor Company, of Flint, Michigan, and the Olds Motor Works of Lansing, Michigan. . . . The General Motors Company has an office in the Terminal Building, Forty-first Street and Park Avenue, New York City, but the manager was said to be "extremely busy" and could not be seen. The plan is said to be to continue the different works as at present under their proper names, assigning to each the manufacture of certain types of vehicles. The General Motors Company will act as a holding company and appoint the directors of the subsidiary companies.[31]

At the time the holding company called General Motors Company was incorporated, the Buick Motor Company's outstanding stock was valued $3,750,250. Four years earlier, when the Briscoe brothers took control from David Buick, it had been valued at $75,000.

Billy's remarkable record now gave both Wall Street and his competition ample reason to watch his next moves closely. He had just begun to realize his vision. As he wrote with no little pride in his notes for the never-completed autobiography:

> I had made the first step, the responsibility was mine and it was up to me to make good. Enormous capital was required. How was it to be obtained? My experience and success with the Buick gave me the idea. I figured if I could acquire a few more companies like the Buick, I would have control of the greatest industry in this country.[32]

Billy was about to embark on the fastest, largest series of acquisitions in the history of business, laying the foundation for what Alfred Sloan would transform into the largest and most successful industrial enterprise the world had ever seen. Like everything else in his life, however, Billy Durant's next ride would be wild, unmapped, and filled with hairpin turns and bumps.

CHAPTER | **EIGHT**

Shooting for the Stars

HAVING FINALLY PULLED OFF the auto industry's first meaningful consolidation against all odds and in spite of the opposition of both Wall Street and the New York bankers' club, Billy Durant had proved himself the miracle worker once again. While the world took little notice of General Motors' birth, the communities of Flint and Lansing, Michigan, saw it as one more wave of the genius's magic wand; and they were just as confident as Billy in more wonders to come.

Many executives in Billy's enviable catbird seat would have been eager to step back from the New York scene and focus on the tasks of building momentum for the new company's two divisions, Buick and Oldsmobile. Not Billy. While he took bold, unprecedented, and drastic measures to turn Oldsmobile around, he remained focused on broader, more abstract horizons. For him, the thrill was always in the next deal, not in the nuts-and-bolts of daily operations. In his mind, empires were built by conquest, not through internal growth. And the road to conquest was through other people's money and other people's confidence in his genius, rather than the quiet, conservative road of knowing the fundamentals of manufacturing and marketing, as was followed by the likes of Henry M. Leland and Alfred P. Sloan, Jr. In notes left behind with his other papers, Durant explained:

> I felt confident because of the hazardous nature of the automotive business that if money in sufficient quantity could be obtained, a reasonable number of good companies could be induced to sell out or become members of a central organization that would provide engineering and patent protection and minimize the hazards which were constantly developing.
>
> Reviewing the situation, I found that there were 423 companies in this country organized to manufacture automobiles, over 100 of which had passed the experimental stage and were preparing to enter the market.[1]

Each successive deal to add new outposts to his General Motors empire only made Durant more frantic to pull off the next one, and each failed deal only added to the fervor. In a period of just eighteen months, from General Motors' creation in September 1908 through the summer of 1910, he attained full or majority control of at least one new manufacturing or component supplier every thirty days. Bankers and brokerage houses alike scoffed at both his methods and his sanity, but he had no time to worry about them. He operated like a man on a holy mission, with absolute confidence and unrelenting drive, as if the addiction of financial speculation that had ruined his father had come back to his own soul in the form of a guiding angel rather than a demon.

As company historian Arthur Pound noted, "General Motors swallowed so many companies in its first two years that acute indigestion followed as a matter of course."[2] For Billy himself, it would prove a bit more than indigestion.

PUTTING THE HOUSE OF OLDS IN ORDER BY CUTTING THE BABY IN QUARTERS

Within days of closing the Oldsmobile deal at the end of 1908, Billy was back at the Olds Motor Works in Lansing to demonstrate his idea for turnaround to a demoralized management team. Once again, he dazzled all with his speed, decisiveness, and confidence. Within months, Oldsmobile was on the rebound.

How had Oldsmobile stumbled?

Following the success of the Curved Dash model, Oldsmobile had dazzled the competition with the industry's first midsize six-cylinder engine car. It had the highest brand recognition in the country, reinforced by the popularity of the song "In My Merry Oldsmobile." People all over the country were humming the tune and the company didn't have to pay a dime in advertising. It was even the first U.S. brand to be exported, with permanent export dealers and sales representatives established in France, Germany, England, and Russia in 1904.

Yet by the fall of 1908, Oldsmobile's plight was almost as bleak as Buick's had been before Durant returned to Flint in 1904. Sales had fallen from 5,000 cars in 1904 to just a thousand in 1908. Worse, only fifty-five of those 1908 sales were accounted for by the newer midsize six-cylinder engine. While the company founder Ransom (Ranny) Olds was flying high (for the moment) with his new company Reo (the name taken from his own initials—R. E. O.), Oldsmobile was stumbling most spectacularly without him.

Put simply, Oldsmobile was being run by men more concerned with near-term profit than high-quality cars (as Henry Ford's original backers had been). They had expected the midsize six-cylinder car to produce the same kind of volume as the smaller, less expensive Curved Dash vehicle. They had also expected it to yield a much higher profit margin, but neither expectation held true. The growing field of competitors, led by Buick and followed by Ford, was offering new models with the same performance as the midsize Oldsmobile (and in many cases better quality) at a lower price: The Oldsmobile team had no new product in the pipeline and no financial resources to remedy the situation.

Billy Durant was well aware of the situation when he made his deal to bring Oldsmobile into General Motors, but he also knew the brand had tremendous recognition. One of the jokes when he concluded the deal was that he had paid a million dollars for nothing more than a nationwide collection of roadside billboards (Oldsmobile being the automotive pioneer in roadside advertising).

His response to the challenge was again from his own head. Rather than convene a meeting of minds with the Oldsmobile team, and rather than solicit ideas from his own successful Buick engineering team, Billy paid another unannounced visit to Lansing. There, he gathered the Oldsmobile engineers and managers around him and proceeded to perform the automotive equivalent of King Solomon's act of cutting the baby in half. In his typical over-the-top salesman's style, he had arranged to have the body of a Buick 10 (also called the White Streak) delivered to the plant. At that time (and into the 1920s), all automotive bodies were made of wood rather than steel. Durant ordered the body put on sawhorses and then asked for a crosscut saw.

Billy described the show and the ensuing business plan this way:

> . . . I sent to the Oldsmobile factory by truck one of these bodies in the white, following with my engineer and production manager.
>
> Arriving at the plant, I had the body placed on two ordinary horses and asked the plant manager if in their equipment they had a crosscut saw. When it was produced, I asked to have the body cut lengthwise from front to rear and crosswise in the center from side to side, giving me an opportunity to widen and lengthen the body, changing the size and appearance completely.
>
> For the chassis, we redesigned the Model 10, increasing the length and width, making these changes with a minimum of expense.
>
> I do not know of an automobile ever created in the short space of time and at as low cost as the publicly accepted small Oldsmobile.
>
> When finished, it was a handsome creation, painted and trimmed to meet the Oldsmobile standard and priced to the trade at $1,200. This gave the Oldsmobile dealers a very handsome small car without interfering in any way with the Buick Model 10.
>
> [It was] a happy solution of the problem—placing the newly acquired Oldsmobile Motor Division of the General Motors Company immediately on a profitable basis.[3]

The new Oldsmobile was christened the "Model 20" and went into production within months. During its first year, 1909, more than 6,500 units were sold and Oldsmobile returned to profitability—its first profitable year since 1906.

By creating a distinctive Oldsmobile car from Buick design and components, Billy had cut Oldsmobile's lead time and development costs to a fraction of what they would have been if Oldsmobile had tried to develop the car on its own. It was another industry first: the use of shared components among different brands. By the 1980s, the use of shared components and incremental design and engineering changes among different models sharing the same basic architecture had become the pattern across the industry.

The synergies of Durant's vision of the new holding company were already paying off, as even Alfred Sloan later acknowledged. Sloan's account of the Lansing demonstration is actually more colorful than Durant's:

> None of us knew what was in store for the Oldsmobile, but Durant wasted no time in getting its plant started.
>
> Mr. Durant sometimes tells friends how he drove from Flint to the Oldsmobile plant in Lansing, riding in a Buick Model 10, a fine little car. No new Oldsmobile had been designed, so Durant got hold of the company's engineer, and showed him the car in which he had driven from Flint. Then he ordered its wooden body taken off and placed on a couple of sawhorses.
>
> "Get a crosscut saw," ordered Durant.
>
> This was brought and Durant directed workmen to saw it in half lengthwise. Next the halves were sawed through at the middle. When the four pieces were placed together on the ground, Durant moved them until each piece stood inches apart from its fellow members.
>
> "We'll make a car a little wider than this Buick," he said. "We'll have it a little longer; more leg room. Put your regular hood and radiator on it. It will look like an Olds and it will run. Paint it; upholster it—and there's your Oldsmobile for the coming year."
>
> Buick's Model 10 was selling for $1,000. The "new" Oldsmobile was put on the market at $1,250—and they couldn't build them fast enough for the trade.[4]

Billy was already focused on the next galaxy of deals before his new Oldsmobile prototype even went into production.

First came a start-up company called Oakland, less than a year old and still struggling to make a place for itself when Billy bought it for a song in January 1909. Oakland was headquartered in Pontiac, Michigan, twenty miles north of Detroit. Its first car, the Model K, was a dud in the marketplace despite a spurt of national publicity after winning the 1907 national hill-climbing championship. Only 278 Model Ks were sold in all of 1908.

Strapped for cash, Oakland's founder Edward M. Murphy (not to be confused with William Murphy, Henry Ford's early backer) was eager to sell to Billy. In the pattern of tragedy that followed so many early automotive entrepreneurs, he died within days of the deal's completion. Neither Murphy nor Durant had any idea that the Oakland brand would eventually be transformed into a new General Motors division called Pontiac under the later leadership of Alfred Sloan.

CADILLAC MAKES ITSELF THE WORLD STANDARD . . . DESPITE SLUMPING SALES

Billy correctly saw even more brand power in Cadillac than Oldsmobile or Oakland and proceeded to move just as boldly to add it to his General Motors stable. Like Oldsmobile, Cadillac had seen its sales decline: from 4,300 cars in 1906 to 2,700 in 1907. Durant smelled another bargain. The owners of the Cadillac company, father and son Henry and Wilfred Leland, had other ideas for their jewel.

Before the doomed negotiations with Henry Ford and the Morgan gang during the summer of 1908, the Lelands took the unprecedented gamble (for an American company) of entering Cadillac in the Royal Automobile Club of London's Dewar competition, the most rigorous and prestigious testing and judging of manufacturing precision and excellence in the world. Each year, the club awarded the Dewar Trophy in recognition of the most significant improvement in automotive technology. Bringing home the Dewar would be just what the Lelands needed to jump-start Cadillac publicity and sales.

Cadillac's claim was that it had achieved the industry's highest standards of precision and interchangeability of parts. To put it to the test, the Royal Automobile Club picked three Cadillacs randomly from its London sales agent's inventory. The cars were then shipped to the club's own test track, the Brooklands, just outside London. There, the cars were completely torn apart and their parts scrambled by a team of mechanics. Then, a different team of mechanics was assigned to reassemble the vehicles using only hammers, wrenches, and screwdrivers. With each vehicle now containing a variety of parts taken from the others, they were then each driven 500 miles on the Brooklands test track. Each performed flawlessly, and Cadillac was immediately awarded the Dewar Trophy.

Cadillac had demonstrated to the world once and for all that quality and mass production *could* go hand in hand. The trophy immediately boosted Cadillac's prestige in Europe and in America. In 1924, the original Cadillac U.K. sales agent, F. S. Bennett, looked back on its lasting impact in a letter published in the *Automobile* trade journal:

> It had the effect of giving the Cadillac car in particular, and the American-made car in general, a place in the sun in this country. On this side of the water it answered completely the adverse criticisms against the American-made car and opened wide the gate for many American manufacturers to come into this market.[5]

Competitors and customers alike now fully understood and appreciated Henry Leland's devotion to precision and quality: a devotion going all the way back to his days in the machine shop of Leland, Falconer & Norton and the morning of his fateful scolding of Alfred Sloan for not adhering to the same principles. Cadillac's official motto was now *Craftsmanship a Creed, Accuracy a Law*, and no one doubted its veracity.

WOOING THE LELANDS

If Billy Durant thought that Cadillac's 1907 sales slump would lessen the brand's value in the eyes of its creators and owners, he soon got a rude awakening. He first approached Henry and Wilfred Leland about bringing Cadillac into General Motors early in 1909, shortly after the Oakland purchase. They replied that they would be glad to for $3.5 million in cash (with no stock transaction) and would need the money within ten days.

General Motors had nowhere near that much cash on hand, and Billy knew that neither his own board of directors nor any of the large banks would be willing to authorize a bond issue or loan of that size. The offer expired and the Lelands refocused on improving their own balance sheet and bottom line. When Billy returned a few months later, the Lelands raised their asking price to $4.125 million (in cash, again). By this time, Cadillac was back in the black and its owners sat even more firmly in the driver's seat.

He made one more offer, in June 1909, in a private meeting with the Lelands at the Pontchartrain Hotel in Detroit. This time the Lelands not only again raised the price (to $4.75 million) but demanded a $500,000 deposit, with the full balance to be paid in thirty days. The $500,000 would to be forfeited if these terms were not met. With both Oldsmobile and Buick now solidly profitable, Billy agreed. Rather than issue more General Motors stock or seek more loans, he again used Buick as collateral. Bank notes were issued against Buick rather than General Motors and the deal was done.

Why were the Lelands willing to sell? In a nutshell, they had nothing to lose. The actual net worth of all Cadillac's assets at the time was less than $3 million. Billy considered the difference between this figure and the $4.75 million asking price to be "goodwill." Moreover, he promised the Lelands absolute operational independence under the General Motors umbrella, with no change in the company's name or identity: a promise he also made to virtually all the equally strong-willed, hands-on owners who brought their operations into the General Motors family. This pattern of continued autonomy under the very hands of the men who had sold their companies to General Motors would come back to haunt the empire with a vengeance during the crisis of 1920 and its aftermath.

Durant was actually pleased when the Lelands issued their own news release reassuring customers, employees, and suppliers that they, not Durant, would continue running Cadillac. Written by Wilfred Leland, the statement read:

> We have written assurance of the purchaser that the Cadillac Company will continue to carry on its business as though it were an entirely independent organization. It is not tied to any company, or to any policies. On the contrary, Cadillac standards, Cadillac policies, Cadillac methods, and the entire Cadillac organization will be carried on without alteration, and exactly as though the transaction recently consummated had never taken place. Mr. H. M. Leland will continue to have full charge of the management of the company.[6]

Once again, there was method (and genius) behind Billy's apparent madness. Within one month of the sale to General Motors, Cadillac reported its earnings for the fiscal year 1909. The number came in at $1,969,382. Billy had already recouped nearly half of the cash he had put up for Cadillac, and Cadillac's continued profitability was doubted by no one. He had scored the auto industry's biggest deal yet. Buick and Cadillac alone now accounted for half the industry's sales.

Cadillac's results were reported on August 31, 1909. Just one month later, General Motors reported its own results for its first full year of existence. Billy's baby reported sales of $29 million and net income of $9 million, once again defying all the bankers and other moguls and skeptics who had dismissed it a year earlier. To further encourage investors and give himself even more room to play the acquisition game, Durant went to his board of directors for an additional $60 million in authorized capitalization and a 150 percent increase in the shares of common stock.

Both requests were immediately granted, and Billy resumed shopping, keeping his promise not to meddle with Cadillac's products or operations. In fact, he deliberately refused to even visit the Cadillac plant in Detroit. As he explained:

> It was several months before I had occasion to inspect my purchase although I received many invitations from the Lelands to do so, giving as my reason "pressure of important business."
>
> The real reason was that I was negotiating for the purchase of many other concerns, some of whom were fearful that a connection with General Motors might mean a change of policy and management. To meet this situation, it was only necessary to refer them to the Cadillac Management, who could truthfully say that Durant had never been in the Cadillac Plant. In passing, I might add that the Cadillac earnings in 14 months returned the entire purchase price, $4,750,000.[7]

ONE MORE RUN AT HENRY FORD

With the ink on General Motors' first profit-and-loss statement barely dry, Billy proceeded with his boldest bid of all: outright purchase of the Ford Motor Company. Hardly a year had passed since Henry Ford's sabotage of the original consortium that Durant had attempted to create through the facilitation of the Morgan bankers. The bitter memory of that betrayal no doubt made the dream of owning Ford Motor especially sweet.

After the launch of the Model T in 1908, Henry Ford had discontinued production of all other models. He was putting all his bets (and his company's future) on that low-priced "car for the common man" that he had dreamed of for so long, which was the exact opposite of Billy Durant's strategy of having a broad variety of brands as well as models. The Ford Motor Company reported $9 million in sales and a most respectable $2.5 million in earnings for the year 1908, but most analysts of the day (particularly banks and other auto executives) remained dubious of Ford Motor's long-term prospects without any larger, higher-profit entries.

Billy approached the more levelheaded and business-minded James Couzens, who was now in charge of operations and administration at Ford Motor, rather than deal directly with the unpredictable Ford. Couzens was thirty-seven years old and the father of three children whom he seldom saw because of the demands of the business. He had somehow endured five years as the right-hand man to "Crazy Henry" but was now suffering migraine headaches. Durant later claimed that he was not surprised when Couzens told him that he personally supported the idea of selling and would approach Ford on Durant's behalf.[8]

While most historians discount Henry's sincerity (Ford biographer Douglas Brinkley in particular goes to great length to downplay the likelihood that Henry would have ever sold his own baby), he nonetheless agreed to meet Durant in New York City. According to Billy, part of Henry Ford's motivation was his ongoing legal battle against the patent cartel of George Selden. Billy recalled Couzens telling him:

> Mr. Ford is very much concerned about the Selden patent suit and its outcome. The prospects of winning or losing the case are about equal. To lose means the payment of a very large sum of money. He is not a member of the license agreement, and on general principles, he has opposed the right of any man to control this patent situation. General Motors, with its several companies holding licenses, would probably be able to make a very satisfactory adjustment with Selden if they owned the Ford Motor Company.[9]

Ford and Couzens checked into the Belmont Hotel, near General Motors' New York office. When Billy arrived in the lobby for the meeting on October 5, Couzens greeted him alone. Ford was up in his room, in too much pain from an attack of lumbago to come down, and authorized Couzens to speak for him. Billy offered a total of $8 million. Of this, $2 million would go to Couzens in the form of stock. Couzens was confident that Ford would allow him to increase his own holding in the company to 25 percent as a reward for his loyalty. Couzens was also willing to accept stock rather than cash for his share. For the remaining $6 million, Billy offered to pay $2 million in cash up-front and the remainder over a period of three years at 5 percent interest.

Couzens carried the message back to Ford, whom he found lying on the floor of his room trying to ease the pain in the back. Ford's response was, "All right, but gold on the table!" When Couzens asked what he meant, he answered, "I mean cash. And tell him I'll throw in my lumbago."[10]

Billy left the hotel feeling confident that he was about to pull off his biggest coup yet. All he had to do was secure the $2 million cash, and General Motors' track record should make it a cinch.

Alas, the New York banking club still did not trust Durant or the automobile business. He decided to approach National City Bank, which happened to have close ties to J. P. Morgan and Company, and met privately with the bank's president, Frank Vanderlip. Vanderlip claimed to be most interested. He ordered a thorough study of General Motors' ledgers and invited Billy to lunch at the Belmont Hotel a few days later. In Billy's own recollection:

> During the luncheon at the Belmont Hotel, diagonally opposite my office, he [Vanderlip] encouraged me to believe that the loan following the usual procedure would be favorably considered with the remark that the meeting of his Board of Directors would be held on the following Tuesday, a loan committee passing on such items the following Wednesday, and that I would have an answer directly following that meeting. Asking me where I would be that day, I told him at the Buick office in Flint, and that he could reach me there by phone.
>
> The answer, by long distance telephone, was not favorable, with the explanation that the business was new, that the bank had just recently been severely criticized for a sizable transaction with the Amalgamated Copper Company, and the committee felt that it would be unwise to have it understood that they were sponsoring an automobile venture. It must be remembered that the banks, as a rule, were not at that time in favor of the automobile industry. As a matter of fact, they

were extremely antagonistic. I made no further attempt to secure the $2,000,000 and notified Mr. Ford that the purchase could not be financed at the present time.[11]

Giving up the quest for Ford Motor Company, Billy turned his attention back to smaller manufacturers and suppliers more likely to be available for the exchange of stock rather than cash. Couzens stayed on the Ford Motor payroll for six more years, despite his personal burnout and Henry Ford's increasingly erratic personal behavior and ideas. He also held onto all his Ford Motor stock until 1919, when Ford bought all outstanding shares and took his company private. In 1922, Couzens was appointed by the governor of Michigan to fill a vacancy in the U.S. Senate. The vacancy had been left by Truman Newberry, who had defeated Henry Ford himself in a close election and was then forced to resign amid charges of campaign fraud.

Politics still lay ahead for Henry Ford in 1909, when his Model T overtook Buick as the sales leader in the United States, a position it held until the mid-1920s, when General Motors took the lead under Alfred Sloan. As Ford's sales continued to soar in 1910, he began plans for yet another new plant to be devoted exclusively to "the Tin Lizzie," as many of the loving owners of the Model T called it. In 1911, he also finally won his legal battle with the Selden cartel, a victory that was again portrayed as a triumph of "the little man" over the Powers That Be. On his own, Ford was at the top of his game.

In a final footnote to what could have and may have been, Durant relayed the following chance meeting between him and Couzens sometime in the early 1920s, long after the deal had been forgotten:

I was riding from New York to Detroit, having taken the late afternoon train. It was an extremely warm day, and in the door of my compartment, where I was working with papers strewn around in great confusion, my usual custom, when I looked up, I saw Senator Couzens standing in the doorway. I immediately made room for him. The subject discussed was not politics, but automobiles. Without wasting much time, he referred to the Ford deal and the one-quarter interest which he was to purchase for a consideration of $2,000,000. He asked the following question: "What do you think the company is worth today?" I told him I had not the slightest idea. He said, "Three-hundred-and-fifty million dollars, the value based upon ten times the earnings which last year amounted to $35,000,000."

By the way, Mr. Vanderlip never forgave himself for not obtaining the $2,000,000 for me, and it was a standing joke for years whenever we happened to meet.[12]

Once again, there is no bitterness in Billy's tone. Nor did any of his colleagues or associates ever recall him stooping to personal criticism of any of the dozens of rivals and one-time allies who were to derail his dreams.

THE GREAT RACE . . . AND MORE GREAT OPPORTUNITIES

Neither Billy's confidence nor his energy was abated whenever a deal failed to pan out. For him, failure was only a temporary distraction.

As soon as the Ford deal died, he made a bid for another infant company that, like Oakland, had attracted nationwide publicity with its very first model. The E. R. Thomas Company, named after its owner, was located in Buffalo, New York. Its car was called the Thomas Flyer. Although no more than a handful had been sold in the United States, the car had gained international fame as the winner of the so-called "Great Race" of 1908. Billy saw the potential of another well-publicized brand name where others saw only debt.

The Great Race captured the imagination and attention of the international press and the motoring public even more than the first Chicago race and Henry Ford's early victories. It was billed as the first around-the-world automobile race and was sponsored by both *Le Matin* of Paris and the *New York Times*. In the end, the Thomas Flyer went up against just five other entries, all of them European and heavily favored to beat the upstart American. The six vehicles left New York City on February 12, 1908, and proceeded to San Francisco via Wyoming and Utah. The Flyer arrived in San Francisco a full ten days ahead of its three European rivals, sparking headlines across the world.

After crossing the Pacific by ship and stopping in Tokyo, the second and final leg of the race was across Asia and Europe, beginning at Vladivostok and following the route of the Trans-Siberian Railway across Russia. Daily reports of the Flyer's progress appeared in both the American and European press. The victorious Flyer entered Paris on July 30, 170 days after leaving New York. The unlikely Flyer had beaten all records for endurance and many for speed. Its legend was immortalized by Hollywood in the 1965 film *The Great Race,* starring Jack Lemmon, Tony Curtis, and Natalie Wood.

In addition to being swamped in debt, the Flyer venture lacked a nationwide dealer network. Billy Durant's new General Motors would seem to have offered a natural haven and opportunity for it to grow. Steeped in his own fleeting glory, however, E. R. Thomas refused to sell. Billy again moved on to other cherries ripe for the picking, and the E. R. Thomas Company ended up bankrupt and forgotten.

Billy continued to focus on two fronts at the same time: first, automotive manufacturers, and second, component suppliers. It was actually an extension of the same vertical-integration strategy he had followed successfully in putting together the Durant-Dort Carriage empire. The major differences were the scale and speed of execution. As Billy described it:

> My twenty years' experience in the carriage business taught me a lesson. We started out as assemblers with no advantage over our competitors. We paid about the same prices for everything we purchased. We realized that we were making no progress and would not unless and until we manufactured practically every important part that we used.
>
> We made a study of the methods employed by the concerns supplying us, the saving that could be affected by operating the plants at capacity without interruption, and with practically no selling or advertising expense. Having satisfied ourselves that we had solved our problem, we proceeded to purchase plants and the control of plants, which made it possible for us to build up from the standpoint of volume the largest carriage company in the United States.[13]

After bringing Weston-Mott and its crucial axle production into the General Motors fold, Durant either bought or acquired controlling interest in more than a dozen lesser-known but critical suppliers of such parts as wheel rims, forgings, engines, transmissions, gears, bodies, and countless other small parts. In each case, the seller agreed to an exchange of stock rather than cash. For his part, Billy let each continue to run its own business, as he had the Lelands and Cadillac. Each new acquisition's top priority was to guarantee the steady flow of parts to the General Motors production network, but it was also free to do business with non–General Motors customers: a win-win for all parties, as long the business and the industry kept growing.

One of his most brilliant component deals resulted from another chance meeting, this time in Boston. Billy happened to be at the Buick northeastern regional sales office when a man with a strong French accent appeared unannounced. Impressed with the caller's chutzpah, Billy agreed to talk to him. His name was Albert Champion, and he had developed a new porcelain spark plug. He had also demonstrated it at the bar of the Pontchartrain Hotel in Detroit and managed to get enough backers to start producing in small volume in Boston.

Billy got his own demonstration there in the office and was impressed. At the time, Buick was paying thirty-five cents apiece for spark plugs that were clearly inferior to Champion's. Billy asked if Champion could beat that price. Champion answered yes with no hesitation. Billy then asked for a tour of the man's shop, which occupied a portion of the third floor of a warehouse. His eyes again on the stars, he asked Champion to visit Flint and the Buick operation. If he liked what he saw, he would back him to start an "experimental" plant. At that point, Champion admitted that he did not own the business. As Billy recalled:

> He said that a man by the name of Stranaham was sole owner; had invested $2,000 in the project; had named it Champion Ignition Company (not incorporated); that he [Champion] was working on a salary and was to be given an interest in the business if it was a success.[14]

Billy told Champion to tell Stranaham he was ready to buy him out. Stranaham agreed to sell the patents and tools, but wanted to keep the company name for himself. Billy saw this as no problem, but Champion was most distressed, telling him, "I am very much interested in the name. That is my name."[15]

Billy's response: "We will have little use for a name unless and until you make good, but it would seem to me that a company bearing your initials—A. C.—would answer every purpose."[16]

Thus was born the AC Spark Plug division of General Motors. Billy set Champion to work in an unoccupied corner of the Buick plant. The division was soon supplying Buick with spark plugs at a cost of twenty-five cents apiece. It was also soon supplying other General Motors car lines and selling to non-GM customers. With the company's new financial structure within General Motors, Champion was granted one-sixth of its stock, valued initially at $25,000. Within a decade, Albert Champion's stock in AC Spark Plug was generating yearly dividends in excess of $500,000.

A WHIRLING DERVISH UNCONSTRAINED

At the same time he was building his vertically integrated infrastructure, Durant also expanded into trucks, with the purchase of the Reliance Truck Company of Lansing, Michigan, and the Rapid Motor Company of Pontiac. Shortly after the purchase, a Rapid truck became the first truck to climb Pikes Peak. These two units were combined to form the GMC Truck division in 1911.

He also laid the foundation for the empire's expansion beyond the borders of the United States. In 1907 he entered into an agreement with the McLaughlin Motor Company of Oshawa, Ontario, owned by the colorful "Colonel" Sam McLaughlin. Like Billy, Colonel Sam had made his fortune in horse-drawn carriages and was eager to move into automobiles. He was most impressed with the Buick and secured the licensing rights to build and sell Buicks in Canada. With the creation of General Motors, Billy bought 40 percent interest in McLaughlin's company, bringing it directly into the fold and leading the way for the creation of General Motors of Canada as a separate operating subsidiary in 1918.

In 1909, Billy scored General Motors' first outright non-U.S. acquisition with the purchase of Bedford Motors, Ltd., in the United Kingdom. Bedford was one of the U.K.'s earliest truck builders. Under General Motors, it expanded its geographical and product markets, becoming the leader of heavy-duty commercial vehicles in Europe and Asia in the immediate post–World War II years.

Through it all, he continued to focus on his baby's future sales growth rather than its growing cash flow needs. With each new acquisition, General Motors relied more and more on the core Buick and Cadillac vehicle operations to generate revenue to cover day-to-day operating expenses. No one knew all the details except Billy himself, and he saw no reason to delegate either creativity or administration. As *Motor World* magazine noted in 1910:

> It was quickly made plain that General Motors was a "one-man institu-
> tion." Durant was its general and he was his own colonel, his own
> major, and his own lieutenant. He dominated it from top to bottom and
> brooked no interference. He is a prodigious worker and the wonder is
> how he attended to so many details, great and small, and lived through
> it all. He kept one eye on his factories and another on the stock ticker,
> and all the while he dreamed of world conquests.[17]

The one truly disastrous link in Durant's chain of acquisitions was an ill-fated company called Heany Lamp, purchased in January 1910 through stock exchange and bonds valued at $7 million (almost as much as Durant would have paid for Ford Motor). At the time, there were still no reliable electric lights for automobiles: Gas lamps were the only alternative, and they were notoriously undependable in wind or rain. Most drivers simply chose not to drive at night or in bad weather. John A. Heany claimed to have developed a workable electric light for the automobile by "improving" the basic incandescent lightbulb sold by the General Electric Company. He filed a patent but still had no production when Billy took the gamble of buying his company. As it turned out, Heany Lamp had made no more progress than General Electric: Heany's attorney was actually jailed for tampering with dates of several patent applications to make it look like Heany's work had preceded General Electric's.

In the end, Heany's patent for automotive lighting was also thrown out by the courts and General Motors was forced to write off the entire investment: a decision that was not only embarrassing to Billy Durant but also provided strong ammunition to Wall Street traders and bankers who were already questioning his methods and his reach. Some even charged that he had known Heany Lamp to be worthless and proceeded with the deal only as another excuse for issuing more General Motors stock.[18]

Billy, of course, was still undaunted. He also continued his old habits of calling on any executive at any hour or in any place whenever a new idea burst into his mind. One of the more famous, colorful, and revealing anecdotes of his whirling dervishlike energy came from Lee Dunlap, general manager of Oakland. In his diary, Dunlap offered the following description of a visit from Durant and the problems left in his wake:

> When Mr. Durant visited one of his plants it was like the visitation of a cyclone. He would lead his staff in, take off his coat, begin issuing orders, dictating letters, and calling the ends of the continent on the telephone, talking in his rapid easy way to New York, Chicago, San Francisco. . . .
>
> On this visit of which I am thinking, early in 1910, I expected he would stay several days as we were to discuss the whole matter of plant expansion. But after a few hours, Mr. Durant said, "Well, we're off to Flint." In despair I led him on a quick inspection of the plant. Instantly he agreed that we would have to build and asked me to bring the expansion plan with me to Flint the next day. There wasn't any plan, and none could be drawn on such short notice, but his will being law and our need great, something had to be done.
>
> So I called in a couple of our draftsmen to help me and that night we made a toy factory layout—existing buildings in one color, desired buildings in another. We drew a map of the whole property, showing streets and railway sidings, and then glued the existing buildings to it in their exact locations. Feeling like a small boy with a new toy, I took this layout to Flint and rather fearfully placed it before the chief. I needn't have been alarmed at our amateur layout. He was pleased pink. We had a grand time fitting our new buildings into the picture as it was spread on his desk. In the whole history of America, up to that time, buildings had never arisen as swiftly as those did. . . . But, of course, we could not be equally swift in paying for them. That was something else. But for the time being none of us worried too much over that; we figured "the Little Fellow" would find the money somewhere. Which he did, in the end, even though we knew there was trouble before the bills were receipted.[19]

By the fall of 1910, General Motors had more than 14,000 employees and accounted for 21 percent of all automobiles produced in the United States. Within a period of less than two years, its total assets had grown to a value of $54 million. Billy Durant had paid only $33 million for the entire maze, and less than $7 million of that sum had been in cash. He had indeed earned his unofficial titles of genius and wizard.

CHAPTER NINE

Down but Hardly Out

THE GENIUS WAS NOT IMMUNE to either criticism or crisis. It took just one unexpected hiccup in the vehicle market to expose his baby's cash flow problem and send Billy Durant scrambling to the despised banking community for help.

By the spring of 1910, the feared market saturation that had sparked J. P. Morgan's first effort to put together an automotive combine seemed to have finally arrived. With Henry Ford's Model T continuing to soar, makers of luxury cars were trying to add lower-priced models. The market for large cars suddenly dried up (a drought that would prove to be very short-lived) and General Motors was suddenly in a financial crisis.

Billy's baby was now offering twenty-one different models, produced by ten different manufacturers who were now part of the General Motors family. Because each one of these manufacturers still ran independently (as Billy had promised the original owners and management), the duplication of administrative and production costs and parts inventories came home to roost when sales stalled.

Buick and Cadillac, the crucial cash cows of General Motors' network, were hit especially hard. By midsummer, Buick alone owed $2.7 million in short-term loans and $5 million in bills due to suppliers. On top of that, General Motors' employee payroll came to nearly $200,000 every two weeks.

Inevitably, Billy was forced to begin a desperate quest for loans. Rather than go hat-in-hand to New York, he first scoured the Midwest, seeking help from dealers and his own dwindling Durant-Dort Carriage operation as well as local banks. He toured the region by train with Wilfred Leland and Arnold Goss, Oldsmobile's sales manager.

No one was eager to help. The scorn that Morgan banker George Perkins had shown for Billy Durant's grand vision of the auto industry's growth in 1908 was suddenly shared by the entire banking community. Consensus was that the market was indeed saturated and that automobile executives as a group, who continued to glut the market with new vehicles, were poor businessmen at best and unstable dreamers at worst.

Billy's own image took a 180-degree turn overnight. The "genius" was seen as a foolish speculator. Some bankers claimed that if the loan were only for Cadillac, there would be no problem, but there was no way they would stake the General Motors combine. Others claimed (rightly) that it was impossible to calculate the extent of General Motors' true debt because of the lack of central bookkeeping and the plethora of different accounting systems among the different business units.

After one unsuccessful trip to Kansas City, St. Louis, and Chicago, Durant and Goss were joined for the journey back to Flint by A. B. C. Hardy, who had been calling on banks in Indiana. As Hardy later recalled:

> The train stopped at Elkhart, Indiana, in a pouring rainstorm. Far down the dark and dismal street shone one electric sign—BANK. Durant shook Goss, who was dozing dejectedly in a corner.
>
> "Wake up, Goss,'" said the leader. "There's one bank we missed."[1]

Despite Billy's continuing ability to crack a joke at his own expense, drastic measures now replaced the bold wheeling and dealing of just a few months earlier. A total of 4,250 employees were laid off, cutting the workforce to 10,000. Yet the debt continued to mount. As company historian Arthur Pound observed:

> The longer the situation waited, the worse it grew, partly because decreasing confidence brought demands, partly because investigations revealed growing liabilities, a situation easily explainable in view of the independent operations of the various units and the lack of uniform accounting. One item in the minutes makes it quite clear, for instance, that the directors, on September 19th, did not know how much money Oakland owed.[2]

Finally, Billy was forced to acknowledge that, at least in the eyes of his creditors and the banking world, he personally was both the problem and the solution. Painful pleas to the large banks in New York and Boston made it clear that if a bailout was to be arranged, the angels (or vultures, depending on one's perspective) would demand a restructuring, and there would be no place for Billy Durant in the new management team.

To save his baby from receivership or total breakup, he finally threw himself at the mercy of one of the biggest investment banks in his native Boston: Lee, Higginson and Company, which had also happened to have close dealings with Alfred Sloan's father in the tea-and-coffee business and was to eventually offer Sloan a job when his own future at General Motors looked doubtful during the crisis of 1920.

BILLY SAYS GOODBYE . . . FOR NOW

The terms of the bailout were harsh if not downright selfish by any measure, then or now. A syndicate of no fewer than twenty-two banks led by Lee, Higginson and Company would issue General Motors a total of $15 million in notes to be repaid in five years at 6 percent interest. The notes would be secured by mortgages on all General Motors property and assets. In turn, General Motors would be given $12.75 million in cash. On top of those brutal terms, the bank syndicate would receive a "bonus" of $6 million in General Motors stock. Finally, management of the company would be in the hands of a five-man directorate for the period of five years: Billy Durant would be allowed to be a member of the directorate, but his vote would be just one of the five on all matters. In effect, he would give up his baby to save it.

The terms were worked out at a marathon meeting at the headquarters of Chase National Bank, with Lee, Higginson's point man, James B. Storrow, taking the lead in the discussion. Durant and his management team were grilled until six o'clock, when the meeting adjourned and the bankers asked Wilfred Leland to resume the discussions in one of their suites at the Belmont Hotel.

This time, Billy was not present to defend himself. Initially, some of the bankers argued for dumping all the pieces of General Motors except Cadillac, the crown jewel. Leland favored keeping the holding company intact, arguing that if there were a breakup, there would be no chance of investors recouping their losses. The meeting went on until 2:30 A.M., with Leland steadfastly defending Durant and at one point refusing an offer to take personal charge of General Motors' day-to-day operations. The group reconvened at 10:30 A.M. the next morning, October 10, with Durant summoned again to be informed of the final terms of the agreement.

Billy was again on the street and on his own, just two years after having created General Motors. Yet in his own mind, he was neither down nor out. In his own words:

> With no idea of being disloyal, it seemed to me that it would be better to let the new group handle the business to suit themselves and if ever I expected to regain control of General Motors, which I certainly intended to do, I should have a company of my own, run in my own way. In other words another one-man institution, but taking a leaf out of Henry Ford's book—No Bankers.[3]

Ironically, Billy's basic strategy had been one that would later carry General Motors to unparalleled success under Alfred Sloan: namely, a vertically integrated manufacturing network and a family of different brands and products that would create more volume and market leverage than the more narrowly focused competition could match. As he described it to the early automotive historian Lawrence Seltzer (whose one book is long out of print):

> Durant bought a lot of different companies, most of which were not much good; but he paid for them largely in stock. He didn't want the actual assets of these companies; most of them were head over heels

in debt, anyway. He wanted to have a lot of "makes," so that he would always be sure to have some popular cars. I heard him explain this one day in this way:

"They say I shouldn't have bought CarterCar," he said. "Well, how was anyone to know that Carter wasn't to be the thing? It had the friction drive and no other car had it. How could I tell what these engineers would say next? And then there's the Elmore, with its two-cycle engine. That's the kind they were using on motor boats; maybe two-cycles was going to be the thing for automobiles. I was for getting every kind of car in sight, playing it safe all along the line."[4]

A CASE OF CONSPIRACY OR PRUDENCE?

Ironically, the crisis that had sparked the creditors' and bankers' panic and mistrust of Durant evaporated as quickly as it had emerged. Within weeks of the creation of the bankers' trust, Buick and Cadillac sales were on the rebound and cash was coming in, with Buick alone receiving 14,000 new orders for cars by year's end.

Billy Durant saw the quick recovery as a vindication of his decisions and his vision, arguing (as did daughter Margery in her book, nearly twenty years later) that the problems at the new company had proved to be not nearly as severe as the creditors and bankers had alleged. The bankers, of course, saw the recovery as a vindication of their own wisdom and decisiveness in restructuring Billy's baby.

Were the bankers in fact seizing on a momentary blip to seize control of his empire purely for their own financial gain, as Margery implies? Margery's book offers the only documented defense of her father and the only direct criticism on record of the creditors' and bankers' unprecedented dismantling of a young enterprise whose balance sheet today would warrant nothing like the drastic measures taken in 1910:

By 1910 General Motors carried, in addition to its many doubtful manufacturing plants, a preferred stock of over $10,000,000 and a common stock of $15,819,830, large figures twenty years ago for an industry not then fully accepted in the business world.

Furthermore, outside the sale of this "speculative" stock, the Buick Company was bearing the brunt of financing both operation and expansion of General Motors. Due to my father's original sound organization and splendid distribution throughout the country, Buick sales reached the extraordinary total of approximately $50,000,000 in 1910.

However, he now found himself in the position of a man who has encouraged his friends to join him in building a community barn; and when the roof isn't yet on they lose their heads and attack him because the barn won't keep out the rain!

In my father's case the barn was General Motors, the roof was adequate financing, and the rain a horde of anxious creditors. . . .

It is well known that the bankers did their end of the job with praiseworthy thoroughness. Under the voting-trust agreement they held a majority of the stock in General Motors.

It is significant that all of the General Motors notes were bought up before they were offered to the public.

Notice then this curious fact: on one hand the banking fraternity led by one of the finest and oldest firms in the country was so apprehensive of the future of General Motors that they combed its assets for security to cover the money they advanced. On the other hand were investors who were so anxious to buy General Motors' stock that they competed with one another to get as much of it as they could.[5]

The charges made in Margery's book were never answered, and Billy chose to put the entire incident behind him as he plotted even grander conquests.

Reflecting on the events more than thirty years later, Alfred Sloan (who would end up the biggest winner from all of Billy Durant's crises at General Motors) dismissed the entire episode in just a few sentences. Uncharacteristically, however, Sloan actually gave Billy at least an indirect compliment for all he had done in those first two years:

Everybody said Durant was amazingly resourceful. Some said he was reckless to the point of danger. Perhaps both viewpoints were to an extent right, but neither really reflects the great contribution Durant made. Partly due to a too-rapid expansion, partly to an undeveloped organization and an inexperienced management, and partly due to the problems incident to an entirely new industry, General Motors became financially involved a year or two after it was started. A banking syndicate was organized; $15,000,000 of the company's notes were sold and a new start made.[6]

It was to be a new start for both General Motors and Billy Durant. The next ten years would see the automobile redefine American industry and life, defying the logic of all the negative bankers of 1910, including the House of Morgan. Two companies in particular soared above the rest and stayed there. They were Ford Motor and General Motors.

HENRY PULLS AWAY. . . AND BRINGS AMERICA WITH HIM

Between 1908, the year Durant created General Motors, and 1910, the year he was exiled by the bankers, Buick's sales doubled and Cadillac's tripled. Durant's vision of burgeoning demand for motorcars appeared to be winning over the bankers' vision of a saturated market, despite the internal problems and politics of General Motors.

While the bankers' trust now in charge of Billy's baby was looking inward for fast fixes, the real story for the industry and the future of engineering, production, and pricing (not to mention the way Americans lived) was what Henry Ford was doing with his Model T. After introducing the Model T in the fall of 1908 and then quickly dropping all other models, Ford Motor's sales also doubled, from just over 10,000 cars in 1908 to more than 20,000 in 1910. That year, the Ford brand actually surpassed the Buick brand as the industry sales leader. While the General Motors bank trust focused on debt repayment and reorganization (with great success), Henry Ford focused on production efficiency and price reduction (with far greater success).

By 1915, when the bankers' control was scheduled to end, General Motors' market share had fallen from the 1910 level of 21 percent to less than 10 percent while Ford's soared to 28 percent. The actual sales numbers were even more staggering and a tribute to "Crazy Henry's" instinct. The four key General Motors brands showed wide variation, with Buick and Cadillac remaining the cornerstones after a sharp decline in 1911 and a remarkable comeback in 1912. Buick sales increased 300 percent between 1910 and 1915. During the same period, Cadillac sales doubled. Those numbers would appear to be good results by any standard, but they were anemic compared to Ford's. Thanks to the Model T, Ford Motor's sales increased by more than 1,800 percent, from 20,255 cars in 1910 to 394,788 in 1915.[7]

By 1915, Henry Ford, the unlikeliest of the early pioneers, was the man of the hour, a familiar voice on the political issues of the day as well as in the business world. The entire auto industry was thrust forward by the spectacular success of "Crazy Henry's" Model T, priced initially at $850 and down to $440 by 1915, thanks to Ford's mastery of mass production and the moving assembly line.

While no other brand could compete against the Ford Model T on price, other brands whose vehicles offered more features and power also saw their volume grow as buyers with only slightly more income than the typical Model T owner sought the status of a distinctive and superior set of wheels. In the 1920s, Alfred Sloan would become the master of this more segmented market, offering vehicles that made a statement about their owners' social status and aspirations.

As total vehicle sales in the United States grew from just 58,000 units in 1908 to more than 173,000 in 1910, and more than 1.4 million in 1915 (an increase of 2,300 percent, compared to Ford Motor's 1,800 percent increase),[8] the auto industry was also creating dozens of new ancillary industries and reinvigorating dozens of others whose markets had been thought by many (the investment banking community in particular) to have matured. These industries included petroleum, rubber, iron, and steel, all of which were critical materials for the automobile. They also included machine tools, road construction, shipping (with trucks rivaling horse-drawn wagons for local delivery), and automotive service and repair.

The automobile sparked not only the great oil boom that followed the discovery of the Spindletop gusher in 1901 (which launched the Texas oil industry), it also sparked innovations in petroleum refining and metal alloys that led to further innovation (and growth) in chemicals. It also spawned the motel industry as well as gasoline retailing. Thanks solely to the demand for gasoline to run the internal combustion engine automobile, crude oil production in the United States rose from 60 million barrels in 1900 to 250 million barrels in 1914. The first gasoline pump appeared in 1905. By 1915, Standard Oil had developed the first chain of gasoline service stations with standardized building design and signage.

Around the same time, the first family-owned campgrounds and motels appeared. With the passage of the Road Aid Act of 1916, the federal government began funding what has now become the interstate highway system. Ten years later, motels and roadhouse restaurants were common in every state. Thanks to Henry Ford's Model T, Billy Durant's vision of a nation transformed by the automobile had become a reality.

HEADY BUT PRECARIOUS DAYS FOR SLOAN THE SUPPLIER

The industry's fantastic growth after the Model T's launch also assured an abundance of work for the various manufacturers' suppliers, especially those who could demonstrate the ability to produce in large volume at consistent quality levels, the original criteria of Henry Leland.

One such supplier was Alfred Sloan's Hyatt Roller Bearing Company. Years later, Sloan looked back fondly on how the original New Jersey production complex had changed by 1915:

> During those years the business of the Hyatt Roller Bearing Company had grown as never before. The plant is on the main line of the Pennsylvania Railroad. The people I met used to comment that every time they traveled past our plant, they saw a new building rising. We were pouring profits into new buildings, new machines. It was a time of terrific growth in the industry.[9]

Alfred also remembered how the industry's growth was putting constant pressure on suppliers to expand their production capacity. Ford and General Motors were Sloan's two largest customers, with Ford's business outpacing the General's. The problem for Alfred and his peers was that, compared with the manufacturers, the suppliers' pockets were not nearly as deep. Expanding their production capacity meant investment in new plant and equipment, but there was no guarantee that the boom would continue once these commitments were made. Nor was there any guarantee from the manufacturers that they would not shift to a different supplier with lower cost at some point in the future, leaving Supplier A stuck with both excess capacity and the cost of the original expansion (usually financed through loans rather than Durant's favorite technique of stock issuance).

Sloan in particular faced a nightmarish worst-case scenario: His company's growth might actually end up bankrupting him. He understood both the power and the threat of Durant's original vision of the vertical integration of the manufacture of components and the assembly of vehicles. This concept, which Durant had proved in his original carriage business, was becoming part of the Henry Ford creed and was even being accepted by General Motors' conservative new management. If either General Motors or Ford Motor were to acquire its own cost-effective in-house source of bearings, Sloan would be left high and dry with excess production capacity and debt. As he described his predicament:

> Speed! Do what you have been doing, but do it faster. Double your capacity. Quadruple it. Double it again. At times it seemed like madness. Yet people clamored for the cars. There were never enough automobiles to meet the demand. The pressure on production men was desperate.
>
> However, I was not altogether happy about the increase in our business. The process of integration was raising a problem for me. Actually, we had two gigantic customers. One was Ford, and one was General Motors. Suppose one or the other or both decided to make their own bearings? The Hyatt Roller Bearing Company might find itself with a plant far bigger than it could use and nowhere to go for new business. I had put my whole life's energy into Hyatt. Everything I had earned was there in the bricks, machinery and materials. I was, I feared, out on a limb. But I was not alone. Other parts makers were out there, too.[10]

Of Sloan's two major customers, Ford Motor was (not surprisingly) the more difficult by far. When Henry Ford made his decision to put all bets on the Model T and then drive its price down through higher-volume production, he expected suppliers to reduce their own prices with neither comment nor question. It is not difficult to imagine the tension behind Sloan's face as he complied. In Sloan's own words:

> One day when I entered the Highland Park plant to discuss Hyatt production of bearings for the future, Mr. Wills [C. Harold Wills, Ford's production manager] interrupted me to say, "Maybe I'd better talk first." Then he proceeded to tell me that Mr. Ford had determined to make a

drastic reduction in the price of the Ford car. They were going to make only one chassis. It was the time of the famous decision: "The customer can have a car of any color he likes so long as it's black." Everything was being predicated upon the increased volume that Mr. Ford expected; this would justify the lowered price.

Hyatt was in a stronger position than most of Mr. Ford's suppliers. Our product was a patented article. We might have argued he could not easily dispense with us. Yet I knew we needed him more than he needed us.

I knew my cost system was sound. But Mr. Wills was telling me that a due proportion of lower costs of our bearings resulting from the increased volume of Ford cars ought to be reflected in reduced prices for bearings. . . .

A week or ten days later, after days and nights of figuring and planning, I went back to Detroit. I think we were getting sixty or seventy cents for our bearings. When I walked in, I proposed a substantial reduction.

Mr. Wills rubbed his hands together and said, "Thatta boy!"[11]

For the time being, Hyatt Roller Bearing continued to thrive and Sloan's reputation as an executive continued to grow, despite Henry Ford's pressure. Like Ford, Alfred Sloan was reinvesting nearly all his profits back into the company. When he and his friend Pete Steenstrup were given their six-month trial to turn Hyatt's fortunes around in 1898, the firm had employed a total of 25 people. By 1915, that number had grown to more than 3,800. Between 1913 and 1916 alone, Hyatt's production capacity was nearly doubled by the addition of new facilities. By 1916, it was generating $6 million a year in revenue.

Still, when the right offer finally came along, Alfred did not hesitate to sell his thriving business and put an end to his vulnerability.

THE BANKERS TURN TO JAMES STORROW, BRAHMIN

While Sloan, Ford, and the industry as a whole focused on growth, the team now in control of General Motors struggled to make sense (and profit) of the unique maze of more than twenty-five companies and brands that Billy Durant had strung together in just two years.

When the bank trust took charge of Billy's baby at the end of 1910, the rest of the industry (and their fellow bankers) had little confidence that General Motors could either be saved or turned around. As the early historian Arthur Pound described the situation:

> Many thought General Motors would never rise again. Saddled with what seemed at that time an unpayable debt, and all its property pledged as security, there remained only the intangibles of goodwill and a strong demand for cars to give the common stock any value whatever. To turn these factors to substantial account was the task of a new management inexperienced in automobile manufacturing and merchandising, though expert in finance and well-founded in business.[12]

The new team's plight and background hardly put it in position to focus on the coming sales boom that both Ford and Durant saw on the horizon. Their priorities were to (1) repair the balance sheet, fast; (2) install a more conservative, bottom-line-oriented management team; and (3) prune the operating units, either by selling or writing off those they deemed to be lemons and consolidating the staff functions and operations of the remaining units wherever it was feasible and made sense.

Overseeing the process was Boston Brahmin James Storrow, the Lee, Higginson partner who had led the coup against Billy Durant. Three years younger than Durant, Storrow was also the founder's opposite in all respects: a graduate of both Harvard College and Harvard Law School, a believer in thorough research rather than risk and speculation, distrustful of one-man rule, and driven by facts rather than intuition. Those were all, of course, traits that would cause Alfred Sloan to admire him and Durant to mistrust him.

Charles Nash, Durant's right hand in running the carriage business, was soon to become Storrow's own right hand. Nash described his new boss as follows:

> I doubt if a man ever lived who had a warmer, bigger heart than Mr. Storrow or who, on the other hand, was so unable to show it in his daily contact with men. A great many men felt that Mr. Storrow was of the "banker" type—rather cold-blooded—which was entirely contrary to his real makeup. He was the largest man I have ever met. . . . If he found he was wrong in his diagnosis of any problem, he did not hesi-

tate to immediately acknowledge that he was wrong and place the credit where it belonged—to the man who was right.[13]

Storrow was elected interim president of General Motors on November 23, 1910, but he relinquished the title just two months later to Thomas Neal, a local Detroit industrialist with no automotive manufacturing experience but who was well known in the industry as a paint supplier. Storrow was elected chairman of the company's finance committee and remained the nonexecutive head of the voting trust. He was in fact calling the shots at General Motors while retaining his duties as a partner in Lee, Higginson and a member of several other boards of directors.

Storrow's first act was to establish a temporary headquarters in a building directly across Woodward Avenue from the Pontchartrain Hotel, which continued to serve as the focal point of all wheeling and dealing among manufacturers and suppliers alike. (That site later became the headquarters of the National Bank of Detroit, which itself was created by General Motors during the Great Depression and is now known as Bank One.) From this base, Storrow began visiting and evaluating all of General Motors' operations. What he found made him even more dubious of what Durant had created. As Pound described it:

> Inventories were woefully out of balance; improper storage of supplies had caused great waste. In one plant thousands of tires were found exposed to heat and sunlight; in another valuable machinery lay rusting out of doors. Tons of unsalable merchandise had been built to faulty specifications.[14]

BILLY CHAMPIONS A FORMER PROTÉGÉ

Storrow proceeded to put together a new team of field managers to run the various operations at the same time he sold off several component operations that were clearly redundant—among them such long-forgotten names as Seager Engine, Michigan Auto Parts, and Ewing Motor Company. Remarkably, he turned to exiled Billy Durant for advice about who should run the most crucial operation, Buick. The widely respected Lelands were in no danger of getting the axe at Cadillac, but Buick needed a firm and steady hand to fill the vacuum left by the flamboyant Durant.

Even more remarkably, given what happened to him in 1910, Durant was eager to share his thoughts with Storrow. He still cared for his baby, and always would. In a private meeting, he recommended that his old friend and protégé from the carriage business, Charles Nash, be tapped to run Buick.

Nash was as different in background and temperament from Storrow as were Billy Durant and Henry Ford. Born in Michigan in 1864, the same year Storrow was born in Boston, he had been orphaned and "put out" to earn his keep as a farm laborer at the age of six. At twelve, he ran away and found employment on his own at a larger farm. There, he learned to read and write in his free time and somehow saved enough money to buy eighty sheep. Selling the sheep for a profit, he married and moved to Flint in 1884, when he was twenty. Durant hired him on the spot when he appeared at the main Durant-Dort Carriage plant in 1890. By the time Billy was ousted from General Motors in 1910, Nash was in charge of all Durant-Dort production, including its dozen plants beyond Flint.

Billy emphasized to Storrow that while Nash did not have any automotive experience, he knew how to deal with people and how to organize an efficient production line. His name was also universally respected in Flint.

Storrow went with the advice and appointed Nash general manager of Buick. There, Nash set out to do exactly what Storrow wanted him to do: cut costs and improve productivity. During Nash's first year at Buick, sales dropped more than 20 percent, but the following year, with major changes in place, they more than doubled. Profits followed the same pattern, and Nash was elected president of General Motors Company on November 19, 1912.

EVERY EXECUTIVE RECRUITER'S DREAM CANDIDATE: WALTER CHRYSLER

Even before taking on the added responsibilities of president of General Motors, Nash told Storrow he needed a strong manufacturing expert to run day-to-day production in Flint while he focused more on sales, logistics, and supplier relations. Storrow was sympathetic to the request. He also happened to be a member of the board of directors of the American Locomotive Company, the country's primary builder of railway locomotives. He told Nash he had heard about a candidate at American Locomotive who just might fit the bill. The candidate's name was Walter Chrysler, and he turned out to be eager to move to the automobile business, despite his stunning success in managing the complex process of manufacturing locomotive engines.

Like Nash and Ford, Chrysler was a classic American success story. Born in the town of Ellis, Kansas, in 1875, he spent much of his youth riding the rails across the western United States, earning his way doing various menial jobs for the various rail lines. His first full-time job was as a janitor for Union Pacific Railroad, at a wage of a dollar a day. When he was twenty-six, he married and began pursuing a machinist's career with the railroads. Again working for several different lines, he quickly stood out for his ability to organize tasks and break through bottlenecks in the assembly process. By the time Storrow approached him, he was in charge of American Locomotive's Allegheny Works in Pittsburgh, which was one of the industry's largest locomotive manufacturing centers.

He had also, on the side, become enamored with the mechanics and the components of the automobile. He had bought his first car in 1908 after attending the Chicago Auto Show, before he even knew how to drive. In the tradition of Henry Ford and other early tinkerers, he tore it down and reassembled it in his backyard before ever getting behind the wheel. Chrysler might well have been a spokesperson for all those early pioneers when he described his peculiar passion for the act of making things:

> There is in manufacturing a creative joy that only poets are supposed to know. Some day I'd like to show a poet how it feels to design and build a railroad locomotive.[15]

Under Chrysler's management, the Pittsburgh operation was taking in millions of dollars worth of new orders for locomotives every year and was one of the most profitable plants in the industry. Chrysler was seemingly at the top of his game, but when Storrow asked if he might consider a change, he didn't hesitate. Chrysler's own description of the two men's first meeting reveals both the charm and the self-confidence that he would be famous for throughout his life:

No. 43 Exchange Place was the New York address of Lee, Higginson and Company in 1911. I found it not without difficulties because I had never been in New York before that day. In my mind's eye I was still seeing fascinating visions of the fantastically high buildings when I was ushered into Mr. Storrow's office. He got up to greet me, saying, "So you're the fellow who transformed our Allegheny plant from a losing venture into a paying one?" Of course, it was not me; the best thing I had done in Pittsburgh had been to find the right kind of men for the right jobs. Actually, I had hired back a lot of good ones who had been fired before I came. But Mr. Storrow had not invited me down there to discuss the affairs of the American Locomotive Company. He wanted to know if I had given any thought to automobile manufacturing.

"Yes, sir. I've been thinking about it, off and on, for about five years."

"Well, then, if you are interested, I believe it could be arranged for you to go to work for the Buick Motor Company, of Flint, Michigan. It is the most important in the group of companies that make up General Motors. You know, I am now the chairman of the finance committee. For a few months last winter I was president of General Motors. The job I'd like to see you have is that of works manager for the Buick Motor Company."

"Sounds good to me."[16]

A week later, Chrysler received a telegram from Nash, asking if he would be available for lunch if Nash were to visit Pittsburgh. A date was set for the following week. Over cigars following the meal, Chrysler accepted Nash's invitation to tour the Buick complex in Flint and then get together in his Buick office.

Suspecting what was afoot, Chrysler's boss at American Locomotive raised his annual salary from $8,000 to $12,000 before Chrysler got on the train for Michigan. Chrysler later said he had never dreamed of that much pay; nonetheless, he boarded the train. His description of what he then saw in the Flint body shop was indicative of the broader chaos that Storrow and Nash were trying to rein in throughout General Motors. With his background in locomotives, which were all iron and steel, Chrysler saw opportunity rather than chaos—a chance to bring locomotive standards and practices to the more primitive way cars were built:

What I saw astonished me. Of course I was a machinist, and I was looking at workmen trained to handle wood. The bodies were being made of wood. In a big carpenter shop, long wide poplar boards were being bent and shaped in steam kilns. With wood they were admirably skillful, for most of them had been carriage builders, but wherever they were handling metal it seemed to me there was opportunity for big improvement. I saw a hundred such opportunities, so that I became excitedly eager, saying to myself, "What a job I could do here, if I were boss!"[17]

Meeting with Nash after his plant tour, Chrysler, who had never been in an automotive plant before, quickly began offering suggestions for improvement. One observation in particular struck a chord with the cost-minded Nash. Chrysler had noted that when the chassis was painted (by hand), the workers would paint the underbody as well as the visible panels. "I drive a car," Chrysler told his interviewer, "and I know that by the time you get a new car home, all the underpart of the chassis is splashed with mud; thereafter no one ever sees it."[18]

At that point, Nash was as eager to make a deal as Chrysler was. The issue of salary was the only question on the table. Nash was afraid that it would kill the deal, as it has in so many other recruitment interviews before and since.

Chrysler's own description of the rest of the interview makes him every recruiter's dream candidate, more interested in the challenge and opportunity of the assignment itself than in what it pays:

Finally he [Nash] said: "What salary do you want, Mr. Chrysler?"

"I've just had a raise, Mr. Nash. Over in Pittsburgh, when I told Mr. McNaughton that I was going to look at another job—well, they raised me from $8,000 to $12,000 a year."

I could see immediately that Charley Nash was getting ready to focus his attention on something else. His interest in me was gone; he just seemed to collapse, the way a tire does when its air is let out.

"In this business we don't pay such salaries." He was shaking his head from side to side. He was not bargaining; he was simply winding up an incident in his day. There was reason for that: $12,000 really was a big figure in Flint in 1911. He did not know me; I was an outsider. But I was not prepared to let this chance get away from me.

"Mr. Nash, what will you pay?"

He thought awhile and pursed his lips. He scratched his head. Underneath his hair, Mr. Nash was doing sums with pieces of my life. If I was getting $12,000, surely I would be expecting a larger sum to tempt me from a job with people who liked me. Suddenly he sat up straight and spoke.

"Mr. Chrysler, we can't afford to pay over $6,000."

"I accept, Mr. Nash." He looked bewildered. Before I had been with him three months we were the best, the warmest kind of friends. We became friends, in fact, for life. Charley is a grand man.[19]

Within a year, Chrysler had proven his mettle and his value in completely reorganizing not only the plant layout but making the Buick itself simpler to assemble. The audacious former janitor was by then well aware of his own worth—and not shy to express it. Again, Chrysler's own description of how he got his next raise reveals as much about his own character and confidence as it does the way Nash and Storrow operated together:

One day I walked into Nash's office and rested my knuckles on his table.

"Charley, I want $25,000 a year."

"Walter!" It was pretty nearly a scream, the way he uttered my name.

"Now, Charley, we've gotten along fine. We are making good. Here in Buick, we've got the one company that has been making money."

"Walter—"

"Just a minute until I have finished. I've waited a long time before saying this. When I came here I was getting $12,000; I took this job for $6,000, and you haven't given me a raise. I want $25,000 a year, or I'm going to leave you."

"Walter, this is something I'll have to talk about with Mr. Storrow." I walked out, smoking one of my own panatelas.

In a couple of days I learned that Storrow had arrived in town. Nash and Storrow were in conference. Then word was brought that they would like to see me down in Charley's office.

"What's this all about, Walter?"

"Not much to it. You know how I came here. You know I was getting $12,000, and now I'm getting $6,000; after three years of the hardest—I want $25,000 a year. By—"

"Don't get excited, Walter." Mr. Storrow did everything but pat me like a pet horse. "Don't get excited; you're going to get your $25,000."

"Yes? Well, thank you; and by the way: next year I want $50,000."
I was forty years old. When I got home, I really started to enjoy that
raise.[20]

By then, Chrysler had been on the Buick payroll for three years.
Like Walter Chrysler's salary, Buick's sales had quadrupled since he
was hired. Despite Nash's stinginess, Nash himself had recommended Chrysler to assume his duties as general manager of Buick
when he became president of General Motors in 1912. Storrow had
agreed wholeheartedly. In coming years, General Motors was to increase Chrysler's salary another sixteenfold.

THE BANKERS' BOTTOM LINE

With Nash and Chrysler getting Buick back in shape and with the
Lelands focused more than ever on making Cadillac the industry
standard for quality and prestige, Storrow was soon breathing easier. Although 1912 earnings were flat at $3 million (on revenues
of more than $40 million), they doubled in 1913 while revenues
increased just 30 percent. By 1915, the final year of the banker voting trust's control, net income had reached $15 million and General
Motors was financially sound on all measures.

The improvement shows most clearly in one of the most common measures of productivity: the amount of revenue generated per
employee. Using data from company annual reports, historian Arthur Pound made the following calculation: "In 1913 each employee of General Motors produced on the average $4,236 in net
sales value; in 1914, when there was a considerable drop in employment but only a small drop in sales, the average was $6,037."[21] This
increase was due primarily to improvements in products and production made under the operational watch of Nash, Chrysler, and
the Lelands while Storrow personally focused on debt repayment
and divestiture of marginal or redundant business units.

Three other developments during the bankers' watch would
prove to be crucial to General Motors' most rapid period of growth,
in the 1920s and the 1930s. The first was the establishment of the
General Motors Export Company in 1911. Before this unit was created, the various divisions handled their own limited export business. GM Export combined all export activity under one staff: the

first time any units of any kind had been consolidated within the company to create greater efficiency and clearer business focus. This was followed within a month by the establishment of the General Motors Truck Company (later renamed GMC) to combine the manufacturing and sales operations of the two truck makers, Rapid Motor Company and Reliance Truck, that Durant had purchased.

The third development occurred without any decision or intervention of the bankers but literally revolutionized the automobile itself. This was Cadillac's electric self-starter, introduced in 1911 on the 1912 model year Cadillac. Up to that time, all cars had manual ignition systems. The driver had to get out of the vehicle, insert a hand crank under the radiator, and pray that his arm or jaw would not be broken when the crank kicked back. It made great material for slapstick silent movie scenes but also detracted from the automobile's appeal to anyone who was muscularly challenged—women in particular.

ENTER KETTERING WITH HIS SELF-STARTER

Henry Leland was more focused on the problem of the hand crank than anyone else in the industry. Legend has it that a close friend had stopped to help a woman start her car and then been hit in the jaw by the back-kicking crank, with gangrene setting in and killing him. Whether the story is true or not, Leland commissioned an inventor unknown in Detroit to work on an electric self-starter to replace the hand crank.

That inventor, Charles "Boss" Kettering of Dayton, Ohio, would soon become a legend. Kettering had earlier been commissioned by the National Cash Register Company to develop a small electric motor that would apply power in short bursts rather than constant flow. This development led to the first electric cash register. With funding from Leland, Kettering formed his own company, called the Dayton Engineering Laboratories Company (Delco) and enlisted a handful of assistants to attempt to apply the same principle to a starter mechanism for the automobile.

Working from a small laboratory he had put together in his barn outside Dayton, Kettering's vision was a small battery-powered motor that would fit under the car's hood. It would apply the strong quick burst of power needed to spark ignition to the internal combustion engine and then automatically reduce its surge and divert its power to a generator that could also power electric headlamps and recharge the starter's battery while the car was in operation.

Fellow inventors who saw his drawings said it would never work, but on February 27, 1911, the first Delco self-starter was demonstrated on a Cadillac in Henry Leland's presence—and it worked.

Storrow and company were not convinced, however. When Leland announced his intent to make the Kettering self-starter standard on all 1912 Cadillacs, the bankers' voting trust argued that Kettering's device was unproven in real driving conditions, represented a huge financial risk, and could not be manufactured in sufficient quantity. Leland persisted, and Storrow appointed an independent committee of electrical engineers to evaluate the project. They ended up supporting Leland, and Storrow acceded. Kettering moved his operation from his barn to a leased factory in Dayton, hired his first team of full-time employees, and proceeded to build 4,000 self-starters within a period of months.

The 1912 Cadillac was marketed as "The Car That Has No Crank" and was an immediate hit. By 1916, Kettering had 1,600 employees producing self-starters in his own plant in Dayton. By the 1920s, all cars in America, even the Ford Model T, featured Kettering's self-starter. It was the industry's greatest single step forward in both safety and convenience. It also won Cadillac a second Dewar Trophy in 1912, a feat no other manufacturer has ever matched.

The Storrow team had yet another reason to feel good about itself and the company entrusted to it. Their greatest pride, however, was the balance sheet for 1915, which showed working capital of $31.1 million, cash on hand totaling $15.5 million, and net earnings for the year of $15 million.

THE BANKERS' PHILOSOPHY VS. HENRY FORD'S

That was the plus side of the ledger. On the minus side, General Motors' market share dropped from 21 percent in 1910, when the bankers took charge and threw Durant out, to less than 10 percent in 1915, when their own reign came to an end. By focusing almost exclusively on efficiency and profitability rather than growth, they failed to take full advantage of the boom under way in the industry.

Henry Ford's triumph, in contrast, was due to his obsession with both efficiency and growth. Ford would no doubt have sympathized with Billy Durant when Billy later recalled (with the benefit of hindsight, of course) his own view of what the bankers were doing to his baby:

> In a way, it was the same old story: "too many cooks;" a Board of Directors composed of bankers; action by committees; and the lack of knowledge that comes only with experience. I saw some of my cherished ideas laid aside for future action, never to be revived. Opportunities that should have been taken care of with quickness and decision were not considered. The things that counted so much in the past which gave General Motors its unique and powerful position were subordinated to "liquidate and pay." Pay whom for what? The people that took control of the business had received $9,350,000 in cash and securities as a commission for a five-year loan of $12,250,000.[22]

Rather than dwell on the past, Billy again put the bitterness behind him and focused on his comeback. While Storrow, Nash, and Chrysler continued to focus on efficiency and profits, he worked on creating another business he could call his baby, as well as the retaking of his first one. He approached the two objectives with even more zeal, energy, and confidence than he had demonstrated in the carriage business and in the Buick turnaround.

Billy saw the potential for a small, low-priced car as clearly as Henry Ford did. However, from 1909 to 1910, he had been too consumed with the thrill and the machinations of adding companies to General Motors to focus any of its people or assets on such a project. When Ford launched his Model T in 1908, Durant's way of getting his foot in the water was to invest his own money (rather than General Motors stock) in another start-up automaker that might one day compete head-on against the Model T.

CHAPTER | **TEN**

Beating the Odds
with Chevrolet

IRONICALLY, BILLY DURANT found his next start-up op-portunity in another former employee: Louis Chevrolet. Born in Switzerland in 1878 and uprooted to France when he was ten, Che-vrolet had immigrated to the United States in his early twenties. Six feet tall, weighing 210 pounds and sporting a thick mustache, Louis pined for adventure rather than manual labor. He ended up travel-ing the East Coast as a self-taught race car mechanic. By 1905, he was himself racing and developing a reputation as one of the cir-cuit's most daring and colorful racers. That year, he beat the legend-ary Barney Oldfield (Henry Ford's driver) three times. He also paid the passage for his brother Arthur to come to the United States, where he, too, became a race car driver.

With the Buick race team in first place on the racing circuit and the Buick brand leading the industry in sales, the Chevrolet brothers traveled to Flint in the spring of 1907. Unannounced, they appeared in Billy Durant's office and asked him to put them on his team. Always the admirer of chutzpah, Billy took them to a small dirt track near the Buick plant and had them race against each other. Although Louis won the race, Billy spoke first to Arthur, offering him the more lucrative job of being his personal chauffeur. When Louis asked why, given that *he* had won the race, Billy replied that Arthur had taken no chances—just the kind of man he wanted driving him. Louis, on the other hand, had shown no caution, and was immediately hired for the Buick racing team.

The Buick racers won half of all the automotive races in the United States, a total of more than 500 trophies, between 1908 and 1911. Louis became the scourge of all competing drivers, giving no quarter on the track and taking risks that no other drivers dared. During this period, it was standard practice for race drivers' chief mechanics to accompany them in their cars. No less than four of Louis's mechanics died in accidents while riding with him. Although he never won a race at the famed Indianapolis motor speedway, which opened in 1910, his bronze bust now sits at the entrance to the Speedway Hall of Fame Museum in tribute to his passion for winning at all costs.

With his victories and popularity making him a household name across the nation, Louis left the Buick team to become a free agent in 1909. Before parting with Durant to pursue more checkered flags and more money on his own, he mentioned his personal vision of a small but elegantly designed production car. Yet another self-taught mechanic and tinkerer was about to enter the auto-making business.

No records of their conversation have survived, but Billy clearly went away thinking that Louis wanted to build that small, low-priced car to go against the Model T. Ever on the lookout for opportunities big and small, he agreed to personally bankroll Chevrolet's part-time experimenting. With Billy buying established companies at the rate of more than one a month for his General Motors Company, and with no one foreseeing the pending problems of 1910, the Chevrolet experiment was just an aside.

TAKING ON THE MODEL T . . . SLOWLY

Durant did not step back from General Motors a poor man in 1910. He still had every share of stock he had purchased, and he had also played the stock market on his own during his tenure (as he would for the next twenty years), amassing a personal fortune worth millions.[1] However, as had always been his way, he did not plan to put up his own money to get back into the game.

With Louis Chevrolet still tinkering away in his free time, Durant quickly saw both the need and the opportunity to move faster and more boldly into the small-car market that Henry Ford had created and now ruled. Ironically, one of the General Motors bank trust's first cost-cutting decisions under James Storrow was to discontinue the Buick Model 10, which happened to be the only General Motors car that came close to Ford's Model T in size and price. Billy was appalled at the new management's conservatism and shortsightedness. As historian Pound put it:

> Few realized that General Motors' earning capacity far outran its debt commitments, and among those few was the man who had founded the company.[2]

As he continued to watch General Motors closely, Billy was convinced that a car offering the Buick Model 10's power at a slightly lower price could take away sales from the Model T. He was confident that he could even find the engineers and other employees required to build it in Flint, where the discontinuance of the Model 10 and the ensuing plunge in Buick sales had forced Buick to let go more than a third of its workforce before Walter Chrysler was hired.

Accordingly, Billy proceeded to create not one but four new companies to build and market automobiles. Naturally, all four were capitalized through stock offerings rather than cash.

First was the Mason Motor Company, named after another old friend and employee from the early Buick days, Arthur Mason, whose assignment now was to build motors for the new cars that had yet to be developed and tested. Mason Motor acquired the former Buick number 2 plant in Flint, which Storrow and company were eager to sell as part of General Motors' restructuring, and proceeded to configure and tool it for Billy's new cars.

Next came the appropriately named Little Motor Car Company. By coincidence, old friend and business associate James Whiting (who had enticed him into coming back to Flint to turn around Buick in 1904) was eager to liquidate his carriage business when Durant became a free agent in the fall of 1910. Billy immediately bought all of Whiting's Flint Wagon Works property and assets and set out to convert them to the production of cars. The new Little Motor Car Company was named after "Big" Bill Little, who had been Buick's general manager until Storrow replaced him with Charles Nash.

Three days after Little Motor Car was incorporated, Durant incorporated what proved to be the backbone of his new enterprise, Chevrolet Motor Company, with Louis providing his name but no money (and receiving 100 shares of Chevrolet common stock in return for the use of his name and expertise). Louis set up shop in rented space on Detroit's Grand Boulevard (where the General Motors Building would also eventually be built) and proceeded to develop a variety of prototypes.

A few months later, Billy incorporated the fourth and most forgotten of his new companies, Republic Motors. On paper, it was to encompass a network of regional assembly plants as well as dealerships to build and sell both the Chevrolet and the Little nationwide (even though neither brand had yet built a car). As he explained with typical confidence in an interview quoted in the *Flint Journal* on July 11, 1912:

> The motor car is rapidly nearing perfection. The problem today is not that of production, but of distribution. The enormous waste and extravagance in the marketing of automobiles, if continued, must result in the undoing of the industry. Regardless of high commissions, the majority of dealers are unable to make a profit. Under the plan outlined by us, the cost of distribution is materially reduced, and each district is given the type and style of car best suited to its local requirements. Our trademark will be, "Built on the Spot."[3]

Although Republic Motors never got off the ground because of problems at the three other new companies, Durant's vision for a new model of distribution was again ahead of its time.

None of the details of Billy's plans were widely known when Little and Chevrolet were incorporated in 1911, but everyone in Flint was certain that big things were to come. Although Billy and Catherine still lived in New York, they were again the toast of Flint society.

On November 28, three weeks after Chevrolet was incorporated, a banquet was held in Billy's honor at the city's Masonic Temple. It

Eyes on the Sky: Billy Durant in 1909, shortly after creating General Motors.

Young Dreamer:
Billy Durant
in his late teens.

The Good Life: Raymere, Durant's New Jersey estate, before it was auctioned off in the 1930s.

Proud Matron: Catherine Lederer Durant at ease on the estate.

Before the Fall:
Billy Durant in 1920,
shortly before losing control
of General Motors
for the last time.

The Guardian from Delaware:
Pierre S. du Pont,
Chairman of General Motors.

Alfred in Charge: Sloan at his desk in 1924, shortly after being elected president of General Motors.

The Old Master:
Henry Leland,
founder of Cadillac Motor.

The Most Tragic
of Pioneers:
David Dunbar Buick
created the company
that bore his name
but died in the pauper's ward
of a Detroit hospital.

The Original Chevrolet:
Race car driver Louis Chevrolet
gave Billy Durant
the use of his name
to create a new car brand.

𝒯he C A R
THAT HAS NO CRANK

Changing the Machine:
The 1912 Cadillac,
the first car to feature
Charles "Boss" Kettering's
electric self-starter.

Edifice of Dreams: Construction of the General Motors Building in Detroit, originally intended to be the Durant Building, in 1919.

Setting the Style: Legendary designer Harley Earl (at the wheel) and Cadillac President Lawrence Fisher show off the 1927 LaSalle.

Ruling in Japan: A 1928 Pontiac is demonstrated to dealers in Japan, where
General Motors dominated the market until World War II.

On Strike: Women march in support of workers "sitting in" at General Motors'
plants in Flint, Michigan, in 1937.

In the Pit: Workers adjust bolts on a 1940 Pontiac.

The Wizard in Winter:
Billy Durant's final portrait,
painted when he was
in his late sixties.

Putting the Past Aside: Founder Billy Durant (left) is led on stage by successor Alfred Sloan to celebrate the assembly of General Motors' 25-millionth car.

The General Goes to War:
A tank assembled at
the Detroit Fisher Body plant
in Detroit is lowered to a
rail freight car.

Defining an Era: The 1959 Cadillac Coupe de Ville symbolized the elegance
and prosperity that Americans saw within their reach in the 1950s.

Alfred Supreme: Sloan's last official portrait, painted in the mid-1950s, when he was hailed around the globe as the most brilliant CEO of the twentieth century.

was billed as "The Wizard's Banquet," and each guest was given a box of custom-made cigars. On the lid of each box was a portrait of Billy Durant, who had made his first reputation selling cigars in Flint after dropping out of high school. The band on each cigar inside read *El Capitan de la Industria* ("The Captain of the Industry"). The following morning, the *Flint Journal* reported that "while he [Durant] has declined thus far to disclose his plans, they appear to have been so framed as to take particularly good care of his hometown."

The plan was to build Chevrolet cars in both Detroit and Flint. Mason Motor would provide the engines for both Chevrolet and Little. The Little production complex, occupying the former Flint Wagon Works facilities, was to be the cornerstone, but it was still a mess. To straighten it out, Billy soon replaced "Big" Bill Little with his even closer old friend and manager from the carriage days, A. B. C. Hardy, and sent Little to Detroit to work with Louis Chevrolet. As Hardy described the situation:

As part of the deal [with Whiting], we were bound to pay off all debts of the Wagon Works, so the problem I faced was that of turning a set of old-fashioned carriage buildings into an automobile plant on only $265,000, getting the rest of the money out of the sales of horse-drawn vehicles and their parts. For the first year we were in several kinds of business at the same time.[4]

The plan's early fruits were bitter. The first Little car (called the Little Four—not the most appealing name for an automobile, even then) was launched in the spring of 1912 and priced at $650, only $50 more than that year's Model T. Its four-cylinder engine turned out to be far less powerful and reliable than the Model T's, however, and the car floundered in the market. Meanwhile, down in Detroit, Louis Chevrolet's first creation was hardly what Billy envisioned: called the Classic Six (for its six-cylinder engine), it was a large touring car priced at $2,500. Launched in early 1912 it, too, bombed in the market.

With debts again piling up and creditors knocking on the doors as sales faltered, Billy was still undaunted. He decided to drop the Little brand and concentrate on Chevrolet. Again proving himself "the wizard," he rolled all the assets of Little, Mason, and Republic into Chevrolet and then recapitalized Chevrolet through the issuance of more stock. After all the transactions were complete, Chevrolet ended up with nearly $3 million in new working capital.

In Detroit, Billy also bought a small plot of land directly across Woodward Avenue from Henry Ford's new Highland Park plant (which was soon to revolutionize mass production with its moving assembly line and $5-a-day wage). Thumbing his nose at both Ford Motor and General Motors, Billy put up a billboard on the site announcing that it would soon be home to a new plant that would build the Chevrolet. No plant was ever built, but the gesture was another example of Billy's flair.

To watch closer over Louis and try to guide him back toward the path of a smaller, lower-priced car, Billy and his wife Catherine also took up residence in Detroit, as did daughter Margery and her husband Dr. Edwin Campbell. Being closer to Louis only seemed to intensify Billy's impatience, however. Louis developed two more prototypes that Billy refused to put in production. Finally, in the summer of 1913, the two parted bitterly. According to Louis Chevrolet, the last straw was a personal jab, with the diminutive Durant ordering the hulking Chevrolet to stop smoking cigarettes and switch to cigars because cigarettes did not look manly in the mouth of an automobile executive.

The real issue, however, was the two men's disagreement over what kind of car the Chevrolet nameplate should be. Billy wanted more than ever to launch a car that could compete against the Model T but Louis Chevrolet still wanted a larger, more elegant (and European-like) design. Before the cigarette incident, Louis had taken a month off to return to Europe and contemplate his future (much as Alfred Sloan was to do in the summer of 1920). When he returned, he discovered that Billy—following the pattern he had established when he took the crosscut saw to a Buick body to create a new Oldsmobile—had completely redesigned Louis's latest prototype. Once again, Durant's voice was the only one that mattered when it came to his baby.

Louis Chevrolet ended up selling Durant his hundred shares of Chevrolet stock for $10,000 and returned to automobile racing. He also managed to get the backing of a fellow European, the French-speaking Albert Champion, to start a company called the Frontenac Motor Corporation. Frontenac built only race cars, one of which won the prestigious Indianapolis 500 race in 1920. Louis further dabbled in airplane engine development in the 1920s. Although that business collapsed with the Great Depression, Louis and his family lived in solid middle-class prosperity until his death in 1941. In the pattern of David Buick, however, Louis never reaped any of the fortune that the Chevrolet car brand generated for thousands of executives, dealers, and investors.

A DIFFERENT WAY TO BUILD BRAND AWARENESS AND COMMUNITY RELATIONS

Perhaps in part because of his own love of New York and his need to stay in touch with the movers and shakers of the stock market, Billy Durant decided to build his Chevrolet cars in New York City (of all places) as well as Flint. It was the first and only time automobiles would be built in Manhattan. It defied all logic even then, but he saw it from a totally different perspective. He thought (correctly) that the publicity generated by building Chevrolets in New York would offset the added costs. As he explained in his autobiographical notes:

> The next thing on our list was to do something unusual: to wit, bring the name Chevrolet prominently before the people of the United States. How could it be accomplished? New York had the greatest population of any city in the country and was destined to be the largest city in the world. It had no automobile plant and it occurred to us that a factory located in the heart of the great city of New York, if it could be worked out successfully, would be of great advertising value. . . .
>
> When our good friends heard of our plant, they, naturally, not knowing what we had in mind, took the position that we had lost our reason. "It can't be done, New York is the most expensive city in the world in which to conduct a large-scale manufacturing operation—labor conditions are dreadful, the surroundings impossible, etc., etc."
>
> Yes, we listened to the can'ts and don'ts, but we went right along with our well-advertised foolishness.[5]

The New York City plant was a leased building on Eleventh Avenue between Fifty-sixth and Fifty-seventh streets. While it immediately created brand awareness for Chevrolet in New York and among dealers and potential customers all along the East Coast, it also happened to be in a neighborhood known for criminal gangs and corrupt politicians, none of whom relished the idea of an automobile plant on their turf. After an engineer was beaten up for refusing to join one of the gangs, the local ward leader paid a surprise call on Billy. By the time the meeting ended, Billy the salesman and charmer had another ally. As the wizard himself recalled:

> On the northeast corner of 11th Avenue and 57th Street, directly across from our plant, a saloon, doing a tremendous business, was located. The proprietor was the boss of that district; and what he said in his forceful way, went. We had been operating but a short time when I was called upon by "his honor" with the blunt statement that he was giving a party the next week, and his organization was very much interested in its success. The tickets were $1 each, and he asked me how many we would take. I asked his name, how long he had been located at that place, how his business was; asked about the organization, and how many tickets he could reserve for us for "the great event." He said ten, and he had that number with him. I told him that our boys liked to have a good time and asked if he could let us have twenty, which surprised and evidently pleased him.
>
> After that meeting, there were no more beatings or intimidation from anyone in the neighborhood.[6]

FINALLY, THE LONG-AWAITED HIT

With his new Chevrolet prototype nearing production by the end of 1913, Billy's confidence was again soaring. That prototype actually led to the decision to build two separate cars and launch them at the same time. Both would be priced slightly above the Model T, but both would offer more size and power than the Tin Lizzie. One would be called the Royal Mail, a touring car priced at $750; the other, the Baby Grand, a roadster priced at $875.

As it turned out, the timing for both could not have been better. They were launched in the spring of 1914, when the U.S. economy and vehicle market were booming. Eager car buyers who had previously intended to go with the Model T flocked to the two larger, more powerful, and more distinctive Chevrolets. Unlike the Model T or any other car priced under $1,000, both the Royal Mail and the Baby Grand featured a self-starter and electric lights as well as a valve-in-head engine. They also featured the now legendary Chevrolet "bowtie" emblem, which Durant adopted after having seen a similar design in a newspaper advertisement for a coal company in Virginia.

Within months of the launch of the two Chevrolet models, Billy was faced with a shortage of production capacity rather than a car nobody wanted to buy. Ever the scrambler and hustler, he quickly put in motion his original vision for Republic Motors: the industry's first nationwide manufacturing network. Henry Ford, with all his Model T volume, had at that time concentrated his manufacturing in Detroit, Michigan.

Billy first leased plants as far away as Oakland, California, and St. Louis, Missouri, for conversion to automobile assembly. This was soon followed by construction of a new plant in Fort Worth, Texas; a licensing agreement with Colonel Sam McLaughlin to build Chevrolets in Canada; and the purchase of the Maxwell plant in Tarrytown, New York, to strengthen his presence in the high-volume East Coast market.

Within a year of the launch of the Baby Grand and Royal Mail, Chevrolet had surpassed all expectations (except, perhaps, those of Billy Durant). With typical bravado, Billy Durant boldly announced to the world that his next act would be to launch a car that would be called the 490. The name came from his planned price for the car: $490, the same price as the 1914 model year Model T. On January 2, 1915, Durant ran an advertisement in the major New York papers with a photograph of the prototype and a caption that read merely, "THE CAR." Superimposed over the photograph was the legend: "490—THE PRICE."

The public's appetite was whetted. The 490's actual price turned out to be $550, but both the car and the name struck another chord with consumers. No car offering as much power and as many features (including valve-in-head engine, self-starter, and electric headlights) had ever been priced so low. Billy proclaimed, "A little child can sell it," and he made that the car's advertising theme after it was launched. Chevrolet's sales rose from just under 2,000 cars in 1914 to 20,000 in 1915. More important for Durant's future plans, net earnings in 1915 exceeded $1.3 million.

At the top of his game again, Billy moved Catherine back to New York City in 1914. His mother and daughter Margery and her husband soon followed suit, all of them living on Park Avenue within a few blocks of Billy and Catherine. His first wife Clara was permanently settled in California and their son Cliff, now graduated from the Pennsylvania Military College (but more focused on partying than a career), had moved in with her for the time being. When Billy started a Chevrolet racing team in 1914, Cliff was hired as one of its first drivers. Clara, however, was history as far as Billy was concerned.

Margery described these early Chevrolet years as the happiest period of her father's life, even though he was on the road more than ever (often with Catherine at his side):

> One would imagine that he might be harassed by all the minute details of starting an entirely new line of automobiles; by the press of financial worries in getting started; by winning over new men to run his factories, his agencies, and so on.
>
> If anything, he seemed younger than ever. His slight spry figure was always on the alert. His bright eyes were, if anything, brighter. His color was good; his humor quick; his health perfect.
>
> He was almost boyish in the way he talked about the future of his new car. He felt from the very beginning that it was going to be a success. Men who doubted behind his back lost their doubts when they heard him talk.[7]

As the General Motors bankers' trust approached the end of its term in the fall of 1915, the men who had doubted Billy's ability to make a go of the enterprise were now listening closely to what he had to say. More and more of his words were being focused their way. His sights were set clearly and tightly on regaining control of his first baby, but he was going to do it in a way that the bankers would never expect or believe.

Meanwhile, two men from Delaware had quietly invested a good share of their personal fortunes in General Motors. They were watching the situation as closely as Billy. Their names were Pierre Samuel du Pont and John Jakob Raskob, and they were to become major players in the fates of both Billy Durant and Alfred Sloan, not to mention the transformation of General Motors into the world's largest enterprise.

HENRY AGAIN CHANGES THE GAME

For the auto industry, the biggest stories of 1914 had nothing to do with the ascendance of Chevrolet Motor or the appearance of Pierre du Pont and John Raskob on the automotive scene. The big head-lines of the year were Henry Ford's implementation of the moving assembly line at his Highland Park plant and his announcement of the unprecedented guaranteed minimum wage of five dollars a day for all the plant's workers. Both quickly changed the way the game was played by all competitors.

Ford had worked for years to improve his operation's productiv-ity through the adoption of more machine tools to perform the most laborious tasks and time-and-motion studies to tweak the way each worker's remaining tasks were performed. Although Ransom Olds, Charles Nash, and even Billy Durant had taken similar measures years before, "Crazy Henry" was obsessed with getting ever higher volume at ever higher speed at his new plant. He kept adding more and more specialized machine tools and changing the layout of each work station.

Henry Ford's breakthrough idea was to run a conveyor through the entire plant. The idea was as simple as it was revolutionary: have the vehicle itself move through each stage of the assembly process, rather than have the people move from one spot to the next to perform their assigned tasks. Legend has it that he got the inspira-tion from watching how cattle carcasses were moved through the various stages of processing by an overhead chain conveyor at a Chicago slaughterhouse, although both Nash and Chrysler used con-veyors in more limited applications in Flint.

The moving assembly line immediately increased the Highland Park plant's daily production by quantum leaps. By adjusting the speed of the line and the way each worker's job was done, daily production was constantly increased and Ford was able to con-stantly lower his prices and increase his sales numbers. In 1914, Ford Motor employed 13,000 people and built more than 260,000 Model T's. In contrast, the rest of the industry combined employed 66,000 people but built just under 287,000 cars for the year.

The assembly process began on the fourth floor of the four-story Highland Park plant with chassis assembly. From there, each vehicle-in-progress wove its way through hundreds of stations until it rolled off the line and out the door on the first floor. To keep the process simple, only cars were built: Ford made a deliberate decision to neglect the truck market, leaving it to independent regional body shops to alter the vehicle after purchasing it from Ford. To get maximum line speed, each worker's job was made as simple and repetitive as possible. As Henry Ford described it:

> The man who places a part does not fasten it. The man who puts in a bolt does not put on the nut; the man who puts on the nut does not tighten it.[8]

He went on:

> Every piece of work in the shop moves. It may move on hooks, or overhead chains . . . it may travel on a moving platform, or it may go by gravity, but the point is that there is no lifting or trucking. . . . No workman has anything to do with moving or lifting anything.[9]

It all brought a new definition to Eli Whitney's and Henry Leland's concepts of mass production and interchangeable parts. It also meant more monotony and physical strain for the workers, each of whom performed one and only one task and did not move from an assigned station except for lunch and bathroom breaks (both of which were monitored to the second by supervisors).

Not surprisingly, at the same time the plant's productivity increased, so did employee turnover. Yet when "Crazy Henry" announced that he would pay the unheard-of guaranteed minimum wage of $5 a day to all unskilled workers, there was a stampede to sign on. It was more than double what he had been paying. To sweeten it even more, he cut the workday from nine hours to eight.

For the workers, the money far outweighed the dreariness of the work. Ford's motive in paying so much (and suffering editorial ridicule from the business press for doing so, especially from the *Wall Street Journal*) was not to make the workers feel better about their jobs: It was to stabilize the workforce and, just as important, give his workers the wherewithal to add their names to the growing list of Model T purchasers.

There was also another catch to the five-dollars-a-day wage. Ford stipulated that all employees would have to meet his personal moral standards. To make sure everyone in the plant was of the right mold, he created what he called his sociological department, whose staffers made unannounced visits to employees' homes to make sure they had no liquor, bathed regularly, kept their dwellings clean, and didn't read the "wrong" kind of literature. The sociological department also initiated English-language instruction programs at the plant, with attendance mandatory for all immigrant workers after they had completed their daily eight-hour shift. The vast majority of these workers and their families would actually lavish praise and thanks on Ford for making it possible to learn English.

Henry Ford saw no contradiction in his patronization of his workers. As he claimed to have explained to his own church minister:

> There are thousands of men out there in the shop who are not living as they should. Their homes are crowded and unsanitary. Wives are going out to work because their husbands are unable to earn enough to support the family. They fill up their homes with roomers and boarders in order to help swell the income. It's all wrong—all wrong. It's especially hard for the children. . . .
>
> Now, these people are not living in this manner as a matter of choice. Give them a decent income and they will live decently—will be glad to do so. What they need is the opportunity to do better, and someone to take a little personal interest in them—someone who will show that he has faith in them.[10]

His faith in the people he proclaimed to be his personal wards lasted only as long as their values were a mirror of his own. The same would apply to their job security. When the Ford Motor Company eventually needed to tighten its belt, those workers whose jobs remained would be expected to tighten theirs. For his part, Henry Ford would see no obligation to those workers whose jobs were gone.

The workers would come to have a very different interpretation of the concept of company loyalty. The fast pace, monotony, and physical strain of work on the moving assembly line, combined with the lack of job security, inevitably fostered resentment rather than gratitude among the workforce. Neither Henry Ford nor Alfred Sloan ever understood this attitude, and the consequences had far more impact on the future of labor relations and business itself than did either of Ford's 1914 innovations. When the clash of values finally came to a head, in the 1930s, Ford dug in his heels while General Motors reluctantly accepted an accommodation that redefined the social contract not only for the General and Ford Motor but all American industry.

As he proceeded to maximize the Model T's production volume and efficiency, Ford also again put the squeeze on suppliers. Getting the price of the car down and the volume up were the two priorities, and suppliers were expected to contribute. For Alfred Sloan's Hyatt Roller Bearing Company, the pressure was especially acute because Ford was accounting for about half of its total business. Nonetheless, Sloan understood the logic of Ford's decisions and went on to articulate it far better than Henry ever did:

> Ford was growing as no other industrial enterprise had ever grown before. Hyatt Roller Bearing Company was obliged to grow with Ford, or else give way to some other supplier who would keep pace. The whole trick of that growth was to keep improving the technique of manufacture and to keep lowering the price of the car to reach an even bigger market. However, an even more amazing thing was the discovery that as the price of the car was reduced, wages could be raised. I well remember the consternation that spread through the industry when Mr. Ford made the dramatic announcement of a five-dollar-a-day minimum wage for his workmen. . . .
>
> At that time the industry's practice was to set wages low, the lower the better. Reduce them when you could, increase them when you must. The power of an economic wage rate to stimulate consumption had not been realized. The five-dollar rate made good, but only because the Ford worker was enabled to produce more. From 1909–10 to 1916–17 the price of Ford's Model T was lowered year by year as follows: $950, $780, $690, $600, $490, $440, $360. The magical result of that was a volume which justified the cost of the factory changes which preceded each cut in price. In those same years his production schedule grew as follows: 18,664; 34,528; 78,440; 168,220; 248,307; 308,213; 533,921; 785,432.[11]

Regardless of Henry Ford's own motives or logic, the moving assembly line made Ford Motor the most efficient manufacturer in the world, and the five-dollars-a-day wage further enhanced (for the time being) his popular image as a maverick in touch with the common man.

For the exiled Billy Durant and the players now in charge of General Motors, however, the highlight of 1914 was neither Henry Ford's innovations nor his publicity: It was that unheralded decision by Pierre du Pont and John Raskob to take a gamble on Billy's baby.

THE GUARDIAN FROM DELAWARE AND HIS RIGHT HAND

Unlike Billy Durant, Alfred Sloan, or Henry Ford, Pierre Samuel du Pont always knew where he would spend his working life: namely, in the family gunpowder and explosives business, which bore its name and was the biggest company in the state of Delaware.

Born on January 15, 1870, the first of eleven children (one of whom died as a child), Pierre was raised with the same Puritan values and work ethic as Henry Howland Crapo (Durant's maternal grandfather), receiving a monthly allowance of twenty-five cents despite the family's wealth. When he was fourteen years old, his father was killed in an explosion at the company's nitroglycerin facility. Pierre quickly became the shoulder the other children leaned on at their home in Wilmington, Delaware, while their legal guardian and uncle, Alfred Victor du Pont, proceeded to squander his health and a good deal of his fortune on liquor and women in Louisville, Kentucky. When Pierre enrolled in the Massachusetts Institute of Technology at the age of seventeen, he became an even stronger father figure for his brothers and sisters, who actually called him "Dad." When he was twenty-three years old (three years after graduating from MIT with a degree in chemistry and going to work as an assistant supervisor in one of the famous Brandywine Creek laboratories near home), Uncle Alfred died in a Louisville bordello and Pierre became the legal guardian of all nine children.

By all accounts, all these challenges made young Pierre mature beyond his years: He was shy, stern, totally consumed by his responsibilities at home and at work, and happy to be so. By the year 1900, however, thirty years old and still managing his siblings' affairs, Pierre had become frustrated with what he saw as poor management of the family business. Given an opportunity to run the day-to-day operations of the Johnson Company (an up-and-coming steelmaker in which Pierre happened to be a major investor), he gave his remaining uncles and cousins an ultimatum: Either they make him a partner and an executive, or he would go to the Johnson Company. The relatives refused to comply, and Pierre left Wilmington for Lorain, Ohio, where Johnson was based. There, he made the fateful decision to hire a brash twenty-one-year-old New Yorker as his bookkeeper.

The bookkeeper was John Jakob Raskob, and he would have seemed to have more in common with Charles Nash and Walter Chrysler than either Pierre du Pont or Alfred Sloan. Raskob had grown up poor in New York City's Hell's Kitchen neighborhood. He had worked his way through school as a newspaper carrier and office clerk, where the two traits that people always remembered about him were his charm and sense of humor. Although he was Pierre's opposite in personality and background, they immediately became friends.

In 1902, just two years after Pierre's move to Ohio, Eugene du Pont, president of the DuPont company (also another of Pierre's uncles), died suddenly. The family's initial reaction was that it was time to sell the business. Pierre quickly asserted himself again, joining forces with two cousins, Alfred and Coleman, to buy the company before anyone else could make a bid. He then returned to Wilmington as treasurer, with Raskob as his assistant. Within a year, the two of them had reorganized the company's finances and instituted a new system of financial controls and measures to monitor and guide the business, including the then-unknown profitability measure of return on assets.

In 1903, Pierre was named DuPont's president and chairman of the executive committee. With Raskob at his side, he proceeded to combine staff functions, establish a system of external auditing, require all business units to produce monthly consolidated balance sheets, and adopt a bonus and pension plan. All of these innovative policies would later be adopted by General Motors and in turn by virtually all large corporations.

By 1914, Raskob was a wealthy man thanks to DuPont's growth. He had replaced Pierre as treasurer and was Pierre's right arm and alter ego. More important, he alone had Pierre's blessing to implement new ideas. As biographer Alfred Chandler put it:

> Sure of Raskob's complete loyalty and respectful of his ingenuity and judgment, Pierre talked over his problems and ideas with Raskob in a way that he did not, or could not, or probably could not, with his subordinates in the departments or his colleagues on the executive committee. At the same time Raskob became an increasingly useful foil to

Pierre. He grew bolder and more innovative in financial matters as Pierre was becoming more cautious and conservative. Together they worked out successful complex schemes and programs which either might not have alone.[12]

Like Billy Durant, John Raskob was also a keen student and close observer of Wall Street. In 1914, he was following the rising sales figures of Ford Motor, General Motors, and the infant Chevrolet. The one company that especially caught his eye was General Motors. Not only did he understand that the bank trust had succeeded in remolding it into a financially sound enterprise; like Durant, he saw tremendous hidden value in its stock. General Motors had not paid a dividend to stockholders since its creation. Raskob and Durant both were convinced that a dividend would have to be declared once the voting trust ended; and when it did, the stock price would soar.

Although Pierre was not at all interested in the automobile business, Raskob told him he was absolutely confident that GM's stock price would double within a year as the bankers' trust ended. Both Pierre and his company happened to be reaping fantastic unexpected profits at the time as the result of the outbreak of World War I: The Allies and the Germans alike had turned to DuPont, the world's largest producer of explosives, to supply them with TNT and gunpowder.

With plenty of money available for investment in the stock market, Pierre took Raskob's advice. He bought 2,000 shares of General Motors and Raskob bought 500 shares. The price they paid was $70 a share. Within a year, the market value of their investment far exceeded Raskob's promise. In fact, General Motors' common stock price soared from $82 in January 1915 to $558 at year's end.

The twelve-month septupling of General Motors stock had actually been spurred in large part by Durant's strategy to regain the company and the bank trust's reaction to it (a reaction that included the largest stock dividend ever paid by any company up to that time). Billy was again the man everyone on Wall Street was watching, and Pierre du Pont and John Raskob (whose company would soon have tens of millions of dollars in idle cash as World War I and its consumption of powder and explosives wore on) were in his camp.

CHAPTER ELEVEN

A Boardroom Coup
Like None Before
or Since

BILLY DURANT had quietly held and continued to buy more General Motors stock from the day he was ousted in 1910. As Chevrolet became a going enterprise and the founder was again heralded as a genius for its creation and stewardship, he privately urged everyone he knew and trusted to do the same. Most of them, including Pierre du Pont and John Raskob, did not hesitate to take his advice. By the end of 1915, more than half of du Pont's personal investment portfolio was in General Motors stock.

With the bankers' voting trust due to expire on October 1, 1915, a meeting of the General Motors board of directors was scheduled for September 16, which was also, coincidentally, the seventh anniversary of the birth of the company. Although Durant had been stripped of an active voice in General Motors, he had retained the title of director (but did not attend any meetings until this one). The main item on the agenda was nomination of members of the board of directors for election at the annual stockholders' meeting scheduled for November 16. James Storrow and company fully expected the board to approve its slate of candidates, in effect leaving the same people in control after the bankers' trust expired. None of the bankers' camp was prepared for what Durant had in store.

Not surprisingly, there are several differing accounts of what actually transpired at the September 16 showdown. One urban legend has Billy, ever the showman, showing up with bushel baskets of stock certificates to make his point. Another has him proudly parading key investors and supporters into his New York office to show them piles of stock certificates. While several enthusiastic stockholders did indeed deliver hundreds of certificates at a time to his office, Billy stored them all in his walk-in safe: He did not need to bring any props to the showdown.

The board meeting was scheduled to begin at 2:00 P.M. at New York's Belmont Hotel but was delayed because of another private meeting under way a few blocks from the Belmont. Billy showed up for this private pre-board meeting with Pierre du Pont and Jacob Raskob at his side. He also brought his personal adviser and investment banker Louis Kaufman, of Chatham and Phoenix Bank. Kaufman had gained Durant's absolute trust, much the way Raskob had du Pont's. As it happened, Kaufman was also handling all New York transactions for the DuPont company and had put Pierre on his bank's board of directors.

Storrow knew instantly that it was not going to be an easy day.

Kaufman had actually been the one to invite Pierre to the meeting. Months earlier, he had also been Durant's point man in his strategy to regain control of General Motors. Unbeknownst to Storrow, Kaufman had been dispatched to win support from major GM stockholders for putting Billy back in charge. The proxies he sought included thousands of shares bought by citizens of Flint, Michigan, back in 1908 in exchange for Buick shares. They also included shares of the heads of many of the companies that Durant had brought into General Motors during the 1909–1910 expansion. None of those individuals had sold a single share of their GM stock, and all were still believers in Billy's genius.

Billy wasted no time announcing that he controlled the majority of General Motors shares. He is said to have looked Storrow straight in the eye and told him, "There won't be any trouble, Mr. Storrow. I'm in control of General Motors today."[1]

Storrow, in turn, called Billy's bluff. With Billy unable to prove his claim at that moment, the private meeting dragged on in deadlock. Storrow finally came up with a surprising compromise: He proposed that the number of directors be expanded from eleven to seventeen and that each faction (Durant's and his) name seven candidates. The remaining three candidates would be neutral. Remarkably, Storrow proposed that Pierre du Pont, whose name was already on Durant's list of nominees, be the one to nominate the three neutral candidates.

Why did Storrow propose the compromise, and why did he turn to du Pont? Did he not think that du Pont and Raskob's connections with Kaufman and Durant would influence his decisions? Was he simply ready to throw in the towel, tired of the burdens of overseeing General Motors while maintaining his duties at the investment bank of Lee, Higginson and Company?

No remaining documents or anecdotes reflect Storrow's private thinking, but he may have in fact thought that Pierre du Pont would remain neutral in the battle. The du Pont name now commanded almost as much awe as Morgan, with Pierre's enterprise making millions of dollars every month from the rising sale of explosives to the governments and armies fighting each other in Europe. Despite his ties to Durant and Kaufman, Pierre was also universally respected in the Wall Street community for his integrity and fairness. No one would have thought him capable of doing anything contrary to the interest of the stockholders, regardless of internal board politics.

Durant, on the other hand, was absolutely confident that du Pont would stay on his side. At the off-site meeting on September 16, he did not hesitate to accept Storrow's compromise proposal.

At 6:00 P.M., the group finally moved to the Belmont Hotel, where the other directors were waiting, and the formal meeting of the board of directors commenced. The afternoon's showdown was not discussed. Charles Nash announced that all of General Motors' debt had been paid and proposed that a dividend in the sum of fifty dollars be paid on every share of common stock outstanding. The board immediately approved. The market price of the stock at the time was $100, making it by all measures the largest dividend yet paid by any company.

After the dividend was approved, Storrow explained the proposed new structure of the board of directors. Pierre du Pont's three nominees were Raskob; J. A. Haskell (another DuPont executive, who later became General Motors' vice president in charge of personnel and administration); and Lammot Belin, Pierre's brother-in-law. By all accounts, there was no show of the rancor and mistrust that had come forth that afternoon. The compromise slate was endorsed unanimously, with final approval to be made by the stockholders at their November meeting.

Durant, however, was not through yet. He knew he had the momentum, and he was confident that he could soon produce concrete proof that he controlled the majority of General Motors stock.

THE MOTHER OF ALL PROXY BATTLES

One week after the September showdown with Storrow and company, Billy called a meeting of his Chevrolet board of directors. At that meeting, on September 23, Chevrolet was restructured as the Chevrolet Motor Company of Delaware and the issuance of an additional $20 million in new stock was authorized. When the new Chevrolet stock actually went on sale, it was oversubscribed by a factor of ten. On Wall Street, this was seen as a tremendous vote of confidence in the future of Chevrolet Motor. Few people outside Durant and Kaufman's inner circle suspected that it was linked to Billy Durant's other plans.

With the fifty dollar dividend, General Motors' stock price reached $400 within a week after the Chevrolet board meeting. Many Wall Streeters actually linked the run-up with rumors of a new plan by the Storrow camp to oust Durant for good by purchasing control of Chevrolet. A story run in the *Flint Journal* on September 29 quoted Billy's rebuttal to that rumor: "There is not enough money in this country to buy Chevrolet or take from our little crowd control of Chevrolet. The Chevrolet is my newest, latest, and best-prized baby, dedicated to, and controlled by, the men who built it up against terrible odds."[2]

That story, like all others at the time, failed to speculate that Billy and his friends, not to mention the recapitalized Chevrolet, might be the real force behind the run-up in General Motors' stock.

The compromise slate of directors was approved at the stockholders' meeting on November 16. Pierre du Pont, who had named the three "neutral" directors in September, was nominated and elected chairman of the board. He accepted the position reluctantly, preferring to devote all his time to his own company as it expanded at an unprecedented rate with the wartime business. However, with most of his personal fortune now tied to General Motors, and not wanting that enterprise to be paralyzed by the ongoing rift between the Storrow and Durant camps, he saw no other choice than to accept the job.

On December 23, Billy's Chevrolet board met again, and Chevrolet was again recapitalized—this time with another $80 million in authorized stock. With this new war chest, Billy announced publicly that he was offering all holders of General Motors common stock the opportunity to trade each share of GM for five shares of Chevrolet. If his plan worked, Chevrolet, still a fraction of the size of General Motors, would in effect own General Motors.

Again, there was no shortage of takers for his offer. Combined with the proxies Billy had already won in advance of the September GM board meeting, the Chevrolet proxies finally swung the balance his way. On December 23, 1915, just one day after the latest Chevrolet restructuring, the *New York Times* announced: "Durant Again Holds Control of General Motors." The following day, the *Flint Journal* ran the same news and quoted Durant's reaction:

> "No greater compliment could be paid me than the placing in my hands, as syndicate manager, to be handled for the account of my friends and associates with and as my own, securities valued at more than $40 million," Mr. Durant said. "It is unnecessary to say that I will not betray this great trust."

The Storrow camp was also not through, however. A publicity campaign was launched immediately to persuade General Motors stockholders to rise up against the Durant camp. The campaign included newspaper articles written by "friendly" reporters. One such article in particular so incensed Billy that he had it retyped and filed in his personal papers. The story appeared in the December 31, 1915, edition of the *Detroit Times*. In a patently biased style worthy of today's Internet bloggers, the reporter wrote:

> Those who are in a position to know of the affairs of the big company blame Durant for "pulling a bone" on the Chevrolet consolidation deal.

Even when he announced that he had enough stock to control the company, they did not show any feeling over it, and they did not believe he had as much stock as he claimed. They met him halfway and elected a new board which had on it a number of men of his choosing, making it practically a compromise board.

But instead of accepting this treatment as it was intended, Durant has felt it necessary to go out of his way to humiliate the men who made the company what it is today, by proposing a consolidation deal that is ridiculous on its face. They will probably go out and "get him" now.[3]

In his personal papers, Durant added the following unpublished note with his own reaction to the story:

The matter of humiliating anybody was farthest from my thoughts. The bankers responsible for this publicity were annoyed because they thought they might lose control of "the biggest plum" they had ever captured and wanted a few more years of trust control. They did not know it, but the control was "in the bag."[4]

A few weeks after this *Detroit Times* story appeared, Storrow and the directors who had been nominated by him boldly sent a letter to all General Motors stockholders. Written in the obtuse, legalistic style still typical of many such communications, the letter denied reports that Billy Durant or Chevrolet were in control of General Motors and urged the investors not to trust Billy or let General Motors fall into his hands. It also endorsed Nash as president and urged establishment of a new three-year voting trust to replace the recently elected board of directors.

More incensed than ever, Billy wrote his old protégé and friend Nash a series of blistering letters and cables demanding to know if he had anything to do with Storrow's letter. Nash denied any involvement or endorsement, but both men knew their relationship could never be the way it had been before Billy had recommended that Storrow make Nash president of the company back in 1910.

Billy's offer to exchange GM shares for Chevrolet was closed on January 25, 1916. The Storrow campaign was having no impact on General Motors stockholders, who had jumped at the chance to trade. While Pierre du Pont quietly educated himself with both the way the company's day-to-day operations were being run and the way different executives viewed each other, the issue of formal control remained in limbo until the May 1916, board meeting. Putting an end to what arguably remains the most bizarre proxy fight in the annals of business, Billy Durant rose at that meeting to officially report to the board that the Chevrolet Motor Company now controlled 450,000 of the 825,589 shares outstanding. General Motors, with sales of more than 102,000 cars in 1915, was now under the wing of Chevrolet, which sold just 20,000 cars that year.

The fight between the Storrow and Durant camps had been waged in the news media as well as the boardroom and the trading houses of Wall Street. The tactics used by both sides, especially the manipulation of reporters and the issuance of new stock to fill war chests, were the precedents of similar tactics still employed (on a much larger scale) today.

Billy's audacity and unlikely underdog victory kept him in the headlines across the country for months and further cemented his reputation as a voice to be listened to on Wall Street. In her version of the triumph, daughter Margery included a quote from an undated New York *Evening Mail* story:

> W. C. Durant has won out. That's no surprise, though. It is a way he has had in life ever since he started years ago building wagons there in Flint. The surprise in the big General Motors–Chevrolet deal, which is by far the most stupendous that has yet been put over in the history of the automobile industry, is that Chevrolet gets control of General Motors instead of General Motors absorbing Chevrolet. In a word, it is the tail that is to wag the dog.[5]

The battle to regain the baby was over and Billy had been again vindicated: for the time being.

ANOTHER CLASH OF PHILOSOPHIES: PIERRE VS. BILLY ON CORPORATE GOVERNANCE

Billy made it a point to express his thanks for Pierre du Pont's support and board leadership on several occasions, going back to the September 16, 1915, meeting of the board of directors. Pierre, meanwhile, was quietly using his own eyes and ears to appraise Billy's leadership and protect his own interest as well as that of other

stockholders. Just one day after that fateful board meeting, he declared in a letter to Haskell that he had "no intention of being a
dummy director."[6]

In the first half of 1916, with the DuPont company running
smoothly (for the moment) under the day-to-day oversight of his
cousin Coleman du Pont, Pierre and Raskob made several unannounced field trips to Detroit and Flint. They also met privately
with Nash, Walter Chrysler, Henry Leland, and dozens of other General Motors executives. Not surprisingly, they were warned by all
(even Billy's admirers) that Durant's genius could prove the downfall of General Motors if he were given free rein. All acknowledged
Billy's drive and his absolute passion for General Motors, but they
were also concerned that his triumphs since the humiliation of 1910
may have made him overly confident and ambitious. Henry Leland
warned especially of the dangers of Billy's knack and love for stock
manipulation and speculation.

Pierre and John Raskob kept what they had heard and observed
to themselves as they also met several times with Billy in New York
City. Expressing their support for his vision of a larger and more
aggressive General Motors, they also consistently urged that he
adopt many of the policies Pierre had instituted at DuPont, especially in the areas of finance and procurement.

For his part, Billy was attentive, gracious, but noncommittal to
Pierre and Raskob. Despite his sincere gratitude for both men's support, he had no intention of giving any real power to any chairman
of the board of directors or any adviser. Like many later CEOs in all
kinds of industries who ultimately lost control of their companies
in boardroom clashes, Durant believed that directors were to be informed, not involved. In his mind, the board's role was to approve
policy rather than help set it.

Pierre began to suspect as much shortly after the board formally
elected Durant president of General Motors on June 1, 1916. At that
same meeting, all seven of the bankers' slate of board members were
replaced with general managers of the four key car divisions and
various other operating units of the company. Billy in effect threw
out the most independent of his directors (save Pierre du Pont and
John Raskob) and replaced them with his own operating executives,
all of whom owed their position and their jobs to him. Although
Pierre also volunteered to resign from the board, Billy immediately
asked him to stay on as chairman and Raskob to stay on as a direc-

tor. No doubt concerned about the future of their investment, both agreed.

Billy was well aware of the value of now having at his side a man of Pierre's reputation and influence. After the June board meeting, however, weeks went by with Billy not even bothering to communicate with the chairman of the board. Finally, in a letter dated August 25, Pierre expressed his frustration directly to Durant:

> Am I wrong in waiting for advice from you relative to General Motors matters? It is my understanding that you wish to talk to me on the subject. As I have not heard from you, I fear that through misunderstanding I have failed to communicate with you as to a convenient date of meeting.[7]

Billy was again unresponsive. In September, he went so far as to try to restructure the board itself, proposing that its members be cut to five and the finance committee eliminated. Pierre and Raskob were able to kill the idea, but the board and the concept of corporate governance itself remained secondary priorities at best on Billy's agenda. He had no time to waste explaining his decisions to the board or asking its blessing before making the next big move: a mistake that would prove fatal to his reign at General Motors during the crisis of 1920.

CEMENTING THE BASE: STEP ONE, LOCKING IN CHRYSLER

Billy's ouster from power in 1910 had done nothing to alter his one-man, informal, shoot-from-the-hip style of leadership. On the contrary, his ensuing triumphs only seemed to reinforce it. Margery recalled his reaction to the very concept of planning when she tried to assist with his travel schedule:

> "If I plan ahead," he argued when I tried to make his trips a little easier, "I may be able to get away sooner and then I'd waste time waiting. Or it might be that I should wait a day longer and then I'd neglect something that I ought to attend here."[8]

Again, Billy's philosophy was the antithesis to that of Pierre du Pont, not to mention Walter Chrysler and Alfred Sloan. Rather than move back to Detroit or Flint, the center of the company's operations, he chose to stay in New York with a staff of only three officers: the treasurer, Herbert Rice; the comptroller, Meyer Prensky; and legal counsel, John T. Smith. As Pierre du Pont's biographer, Alfred Chandler, succinctly put it:

> Durant not only expected to run his own show but to do so with very little help. He saw little need for the type of systematic group management that Pierre had done so much to create at the DuPont Company.[9]

Nonetheless, Billy was well aware that he needed capable and loyal lieutenants to run his empire while he focused on expanding it further. He had known as early as January of 1916, when victory in the Storrow proxy battle was clear, that Nash would have to go (as did Nash himself). To counter the void left by Nash, Billy also knew he would have to do whatever it took to keep the man responsible for General Motors' highest-volume and most profitable division: Walter Chrysler at Buick.

Even before Billy made the formal, painful announcement that he was replacing Nash as president in June 1916, Storrow had approached both Nash and Chrysler with a proposal to take over one of Cadillac's chief rivals in the large car market: Packard Motor Company. Nash and Chrysler were interested, but the deal fell through. With Storrow's financial backing, Nash ended up taking over a smaller operation called the Thomas Jeffrey Company, located in Kenosha, Wisconsin. Nash renamed it after himself and turned it around in a matter of months, but he never managed to make it grow the way Billy Durant did his enterprises. That was, in part, because Nash had neither the drive nor skill to put together capital the way Billy did through the stock market.[10]

Chrysler owed his automotive career to both Nash and Storrow, and he did not have any relationship with Durant. Although he did not relish uprooting his family again, he was ready to join Nash in Kenosha. When he actually submitted his resignation from Buick, however, Billy pounced with another offer that Chrysler could not refuse. As Billy recalled it:

> Upon receiving his letter of resignation, I took the first train to Flint and went to his office unannounced. I had occupied this office for a number of years and felt perfectly at home. When Chrysler came in, I told him

I had received his letter and had come immediately from New York to see if we could work out a solution.[11]

Walter Chrysler's own version (told through his ghostwriter) is more detailed and revealing of why and how the two men would soon clash:

I dropped into my swivel chair between my rolltop desk and my wide table; Durant seated himself on the opposite side of the table. I was going to ask him for a raise.

"I'll pay you $500,000 a year to stay here as president of Buick." He just sprang it on me that way; he did not bat an eye. I couldn't think for a few seconds.

"Mr. Durant, the salary you offer is, of course, far and away beyond anything I expected, but—"

"Now, Walter"—we were getting acquainted fast—"you just put aside, for the time being, all your plans of getting into business for yourself. I don't blame you for the ambition, but I ask you to give me just three years of yourself."

"There's one thing—"

"You shouldn't run away from this proposition, Walter. Nash is going. But the boys here stood by you, and now—"

"They have stood by me, as you say, but I'm standing by them when I say that I can accept only if I'm to have full authority. With their help, I can run this property. I don't want interference. I don't want any other boss but you. If you feel that anything is going wrong, if you don't like some action of mine, you come to me; don't go to anybody else and don't try to split up my authority. Just have one channel between Flint and Detroit: from me to you. Full authority is what I want."

He was beaming at me then. I saw him touch his fingers lightly to the table for emphasis. "It's a deal," he said.[12]

Chrysler had been granted the largest raise and the largest salary ever given to anyone in the auto industry up to that time. In the end, it proved to be far more than the $500,000 he had agreed to: He was allowed to draw $10,000 in cash each month, with the remainder paid in the form of General Motors stock. He was a millionaire several times over by the time he finally resigned for good in 1919.

Billy, in turn, had made a promise not to interfere with the way Chrysler ran his operation. That promise would have required a complete change of character, and Billy Durant was the last man on the planet capable of such change.

As Billy resumed his hunt for more companies to add to the retaken General Motors, especially companies that manufactured vehicle components, he also resumed his maddening ways of dropping in unannounced on busy managers and making decisions and changes that affected their operations without bothering to inform them. Not seeing his own management style as a problem, he focused on luring capable managers as well as companies that would add to General Motors' growth potential. In some cases, the value of the managers ultimately far outweighed the value of the companies.

Two such men in particular, Alfred Sloan and Charles Kettering, would end up playing key roles in redefining General Motors itself.

STEP TWO, LURING ALFRED INTO THE FOLD

As the battle for control of General Motors played itself out through the fall, winter, and spring of 1915–1916, Alfred Sloan's stature and his Hyatt Roller Bearing Company's sales and profits continued to grow in line with the growth of Ford Motor and General Motors' vehicle sales. Hyatt's payroll had grown to 4,000 employees; its main plant had been expanded to 750,000 square feet; and its sales staff had expanded to three offices (one in Newark, one in Chicago, and one in Detroit). Each sales office had its own staff of chemists and metallurgists to assist customers with problems or special product development needs.

Eighty percent of all this growth had occurred during the years 1913–1916, thanks largely to the Model T business. However, the higher volume and expansion also meant higher vulnerability should either Ford Motor or General Motors, Hyatt's two largest customers, decide to source its bearings in-house or with another supplier. Sloan saw insourcing as the bigger threat. As he described it:

> The Dodge brothers had started to make Dodge cars only a year or so before. In the trade world we believed they had changed from parts manufacturers into automobile makers because they believed their biggest customers contemplated making parts previously bought from Dodge. The same uncertainties that troubled makers of parts were valid worries of those who bought our parts. Suppose Buick or Willys-

> Overland or Ford suddenly got the idea it might be cut off from an
> important source of supply? Lack of one tiny part might hold up their
> assembly line. That fear was the nightmare of the business.[13]

Adding to the suppliers' nightmare was the possibility that if a major automaker began making parts in-house, it could also sell those parts to other automakers, putting further pressures on all independent suppliers.

This was precisely the strategy Billy Durant now had in mind. He had pioneered and mastered vertical integration back in the carriage business, and several companies (including Ford Motor) had since copied the idea. In contrast to Henry Ford, who was focused only on making his Model T production faster and more cost-efficient, Billy was now on the lookout for a core group of suppliers whose capabilities and vision went beyond the immediate requirements of General Motors' own production network. His plan was to combine them into a new holding company to be called United Motors.

Hyatt was a perfect fit for this new enterprise. Although smaller than most of Billy's other acquisitions, its numbers were rare: growth in net sales from $1.3 million in 1912 to $3.2 million in 1915 and projected at $6 million in 1916, with net income for that year projected in excess of $2.3 million (a profit margin in excess of 30 percent). Well aware of Billy's shrewdness and his earlier business innovations, Alfred Sloan was not surprised when he received an invitation to join Durant for lunch on a warm spring day in 1916.

Alfred couldn't make it for lunch but reshuffled his schedule to meet Billy later in the afternoon. It was the first time the two had ever met. Like all others who came into contact with Durant, he was immediately impressed. As he recalled more than forty years later:

> I found Mr. Durant a very persuasive man, soft spoken and ingratiating.
> He was short, conservatively and immaculately dressed, and had an
> air of being permanently calm.[14]

Alfred was also certain that Billy was going to make him an offer—and he was prepared to sell. Again, in Sloan's words:

> Durant's luncheon invitation was like an alarming knock on the door in
> the middle of the night. It might be a sign I would have to make a

decision about the future of the Hyatt Roller Bearing Company. The integration of General Motors was proceeding. What should I do? I saw no way to place the business under the wing of the giant Ford Motor Company. Could I wisely remain in the same status of apparent independence? Willys-Overland, third largest grouping in the field, then appeared unstable—at least many thought so. So there was small room for choice in the future. In my heart I felt I would be acting soundly for our business if I made a deal with Durant.[15]

Alfred's premonition was on the money. At that fateful first meeting, in Durant's Chevrolet office at Fifty-seventh Street and Eleventh Avenue, Alfred played coy, just as Billy undoubtedly knew he would.

When Billy asked whether he'd ever considered selling Hyatt, Sloan answered no. Billy then asked if he had a lot of stockholders. Alfred again answered no, describing the business as "kind of a family affair."

Finally, Billy asked if he would now consider selling. Sloan answered, "Why not? Provided, of course . . ."

Billy interrupted and asked what price he had in mind. Sloan answered that he would have to consult with his board.

Sloan did not tell Billy that his "board" consisted of himself, his father, and their two attorneys. Nor did he tell him that between them, the four men owned all of Hyatt (with Alfred holding majority interest). Recalling his parting with Billy that afternoon, Sloan noted:

He [Durant] betrayed no impatience as I rose to go. His was the manner of a gentleman striving to be harmonious with the world. Besides, he had found out what he wished to know: Hyatt could be bought.[16]

ALFRED MOVES UP WITH BILLY

When Durant and Sloan got together again a few days after that first meeting, Sloan wasted no time in offering an asking price of $15 million for Hyatt. His father and the other "board members" had told him that such a sum was astronomical, but they had also authorized him to negotiate the best deal he could. As Sloan recalled this second meeting:

Mr. Durant never batted an eye or ceased to smile, and his teeth were very white.

"I'm still interested, Mr. Sloan."

Then he told me a little more about his plans; his great promoting talent was about to be exercised in arranging a combination of the most successful of the parts-manufacturing companies. He was acting for the Durant-Kaufman syndicate.[17]

Sloan's point that Billy was acting for the Durant-Kaufman syndicate is especially important. At this time, late spring of 1916, Billy was about to be officially named president of General Motors, but he intended to put together United Motors on his own rather than through General Motors, thus enhancing his own clout and avoiding the hassle of getting approval from the General's board of directors.

At the same time he was courting Alfred Sloan, Billy was courting four other suppliers to fill out United Motors: New Departure Manufacturing Company, based in Bristol, Connecticut, which produced horns as well as heavier ball bearings than Hyatt; Charles "Boss" Kettering's highly respected Dayton Engineering Laboratories Company (Delco) of Dayton, Ohio, now the leading supplier of self-starters and automotive electrical systems; Remy Electric, based in Anderson, Indiana, which also produced starters and electrical components but used a different technology than Delco; and Perlman Rim of Jackson, Michigan, which supplied wheel rims and steering wheels to General Motors and a few smaller automakers. All four suppliers were in the same boat as Alfred, vulnerable to any sourcing shift by their major customers.

When Alfred and Billy got together for a third session, Durant brought his lawyer, John Thomas Smith (who was now also General Motors' counsel) and his financial adviser, Louis Kaufman (also a director of General Motors). This time, Billy had Smith and Kaufman take the lead. They quickly explained to Sloan that $15 million was out of the question. Sloan countered with the figure of $13.5 million, adding: "I'm finished. It's that, or nothing."[18]

Durant then stepped in and agreed to the new figure, with no argument from his aides.

Alfred was thrilled, though he never would have used that word himself. In a rare revelation of emotion, he described how especially rewarding it was to see much of the money go to his father:

The transaction did not cause excitement in our family, because neither my father nor I discussed business affairs at home. I felt I had
escaped a cause for worry, that everything I had earned since leaving
college was no longer exposed to such complete risk. There was
deeper satisfaction because my father had been put on Easy Street.
He had worked hard. Yet year after year the tea-and-coffee business
had lost ground. Finally he had merged with a wholesale grocery. This
had not turned out well. I think he might have lost everything, had it not
been for his courageous support of Hyatt. His comparatively small investment had brought him millions. Yet it was characteristic of him to
keep silent at home about the wonderful return. He was determined
that his younger children should not be spoiled by wealth. He scarcely
changed his way of living. My father conservatively invested the bulk
of his share, but I was led to invest much more than I had intended in
this new company, United Motors.[19]

Within the next few weeks, Billy made deals to buy all four of
the other targeted companies. All were eager to be combined with
Hyatt into United Motors. All saw the growth potential of the new
enterprise, especially with its links to General Motors. And all knew
Billy's track record in making a go of such ventures.

In the pattern of most of Billy's previous deals, the sellers of the
combined firms were expected to take a large portion of the sale
price of their own babies in United Motors stock rather than cash.
In the case of Kettering's Dayton Engineering Laboratories, the total
price was $5 million in cash and $3 million in stock, divided
equally between Kettering and his partner, Edward A. Deeds. At
Hyatt, Sloan agreed to take half of his lion's share of the selling price
of $13.5 million in United Motors stock, but his father and their two
lawyers wanted cash only. To save the deal, Alfred bought all three
out with his own money and took on even more United Motors
stock. While this was a great expression of Alfred's confidence in
Billy Durant and the new company, it also left him, in his own
words, "with rather little cash and a devil of a lot of stock."[20]

With the creation of United Motors, Billy had not only put together the auto industry's first integrated supplier network (which
the Japanese industry later copied and called *keiretsu*), he had also
laid the foundation for the final and complete vertical integration of
General Motors, with enough parts-making capacity to ensure an
uninterrupted flow of parts for GM and, at the same time, to sell to

other manufacturers and the retail replacement-parts market. More important for the General's future, he had secured the service of Alfred Sloan, who would soon catch the eye of Chairman Pierre du Pont with his concept of a coordinated team of managers while Billy continued to run his one-man show.

As soon as United Motors was incorporated, Billy asked Alfred to serve as its president and chief operating officer. He also pledged not to interfere with Alfred's management: the same pledge he had made to Walter Chrysler and to Henry Leland. Alfred would also serve as chairman of United Motors' board of directors, and the other directors would be the heads of the units that had been brought into the new enterprise.

Alfred Sloan accepted the job offer with no hesitation. At the age of forty-one, more confident than ever in his own capability as an executive, he was eager for the challenge. He would later credit the experience of integrating and expanding the varied operating units of United Motors as the learning laboratory that blossomed into his own concepts for reorganizing General Motors, which were in turn soon adopted by all corporations:

> In United Motors I met for the first time the problems of operating a multiple-unit organization with different products made by separate divisions. All that held United Motors together in its beginning was the concept of automotive parts and accessories. We made horns, radiators, bearings, rims, and the like, and we sold them to both automobile producers and the public. Certain limited areas of possible coordination presented themselves; for example, the servicing of the numerous small products made by the different divisions. Separate service agencies for such small items were uneconomic. I therefore set up a single nationwide organization called United Motors Service, Inc., on October 14, 1916, to represent the divisions, with stations in twenty-odd large cities and several hundred dealers at other points. The divisions naturally resisted this move for awhile, but I persuaded them of the need for it, and for the first time learned something about getting decentralized management to yield some of its functions for the common good.[21]

During his first year at United Motors, Sloan brought in several other small companies on his own, without interference from Billy. They included Harrison Radiator, which would eventually become a pioneer and leader in automotive heating and air-conditioning systems, and the Klaxon Company, which made horns. In its first year of existence, United Motors reported revenues of $33,638,956. Alfred's quick, decisive moves and his solid results were already turning heads in Detroit and in the General Motors boardroom.

Billy Durant, however, was still the Man. His track record was unrivaled in all of American business: He had built the world's largest carriage empire from an investment of $1,500; he had brought Buick up from the ashes with initial capital of $75,000 and leveraged it to create General Motors; and when others thought he was ruined, he had created the Chevrolet Motor Company from scratch and leveraged its success to regain control of the larger General Motors from the bankers who still scoffed at his risk-taking. Although even the boldest of entrepreneurs may have been content with such a record, Billy Durant was still dreaming of bigger things. Wealthier and more confident than ever, he was still restless.

CHAPTER | **TWELVE**

The Founder's Grip
Slips Again

WHILE BILLY PROCEEDED with grander dreams, the automobile industry and the nation remained more fascinated with Ford Motor and its founder than with General Motors and the wizard from Flint. The drama unfolding at General Motors during the crucial period of 1916–1920 was a footnote to what was happening in Henry Ford's life and his company. More important for the future, the way Ford captivated the public during this period was a stark contrast to the way the fundamental business issues of corporate governance and organizational structure were coming to the fore at General Motors.

The country was enthralled with Ford's every word and act, and with reason. While total U.S. car sales more than doubled during World War I, the Ford Model T accounted for an astounding 87 percent of that growth. "Crazy Henry" was hailed around the globe as the real guiding genius behind American industry in general and its ever-expanding auto industry in particular.

Henry's extracurricular activities were also drawing attention. His unrivaled business success and his self-styled common man, anti-intellectual, country-boy image gave him a unique platform for promoting his personal philosophies, which were crafted and accepted quite differently than his car.

Like Alfred Sloan, Henry Ford had a passion for controlling the message. Unlike Sloan, however, he relished personal adulation and failed to distinguish his own image from that of his company. Worse, he was not bothered when the facts conflicted with the claims he wanted communicated to further either of the two.

HENRY FORD'S PLUNGE INTO PACIFISM, POLITICS, AND PREJUDICE

While most American companies and business leaders avoided making political statements about the war in Europe before the United States entered it in April 1917, Henry Ford jumped into the fray early on, in 1915. He made headlines across the country with charges that the war had been started by greedy bankers and munitions makers. He also boldly declared that he would never build war goods of any kind in any of his plants. When he followed this with an announcement that he was willing to personally finance an antiwar campaign (without defining it), pacifist groups of every ilk came knocking on his door with proposals.

By November 1915, his personal peace campaign had received so much attention that he was granted a private meeting with President Woodrow Wilson at the White House. At that meeting, Ford invited the president to join him on a "mission" to Europe to end the war. Wilson wisely declined the invitation, but Ford proceeded to charter a Norwegian liner called the *Oscar II*. He set sail from New York to Europe on December 4, taking with him (at his own expense) fifty-five self-proclaimed peace delegates from around the world.

He also brought along forty-four reporters but no agenda. No appointments with any official government leaders of any country had been made in advance of the trip. During the journey of the "Peace Ship" across the Atlantic, Henry was bombarded with lectures from the "delegates" and questions from the reporters. Mercifully, he took ill just as the *Oscar II* docked at its first stop in Norway. True to form, he turned the illness into opportunity, using it as an excuse to abandon the entire mission and return home alone the very next morning, leaving the pesky delegates and reporters to fend for themselves.

Privately, Ford blamed his mission's failure on the head delegate, whom he claimed had charmed him and his wife Clara into organizing the trip. That delegate was Rosika Schwimmer, a firebrand Hungarian pacifist who also happened to be Jewish.

Within months of the *Oscar II*'s ill-fated voyage, Henry felt himself even more abused when a reporter from the *Chicago Tribune* quoted his latest administrative chief, Frank Klingensmith, as saying that it was the Ford Motor Company's policy *not* to continue the salary or reinstate the job of any employee who was a member of the National Guard and was called to active duty. At the time, in the summer of 1916, guardsmen and reservists had been sent to Mexico with General John J. "Black Jack" Pershing to chase down the Mexican revolutionary Pancho Villa after his infamous raids into U.S. territory on the Arizona–New Mexico border.

Klingensmith had actually misstated the company's policy: Ford Motor in fact continued to pay the salaries and hold open the positions of all eighty-nine of its employees who were called up to service on the border. The company's sociological department even visited the soldiers' families to make sure they were holding up during the breadwinners' absence. Before a clarification was issued, however, the *Tribune* followed up its initial story with an editorial attacking Henry Ford's own character, calling him an "ignorant idealist" and "an anarchistic enemy of the nation which protects him in his wealth."[1] A livid Henry Ford filed suit against the *Tribune* for libel and defamation of character.

Meanwhile, Henry's pacifism proved to be a temporary passion. When the United States entered World War I in April 1917, he immediately (and very publicly) pledged to build any item he could, including weapons, to help America win. Because of his unique track record in fast mass production of the Model T, he was awarded a contract to build a new kind of boat, the submarine chaser. Called the Eagle boat, it was to be produced exclusively by Ford Motor Company.

As part of this contract, the U.S. government also agreed to provide the financing to build a new plant and drain the marshland site where it was erected, at the mouth of the Rouge River in Dearborn, Michigan. The Rouge site happened to have been purchased by Ford Motor in 1915, at the height of Henry's avowed pacifism. He bought the land with no publicity, intending to stun the world with the largest and most vertically integrated manufacturing complex ever built. By the mid-1920s, after the government had paid for the first phase (and after the Eagle boat was history), that vision was a reality.

While building the very profitable Eagle boats, Henry also ran in Michigan's 1918 U.S. Senate election. Losing by fewer than 5,000 votes, he demanded a recount but still fell short. To his great satisfaction, his victorious opponent was later found guilty of illegal campaign contributions. Henry was not as pleased, however, when the governor filled the seat with Henry's own former right hand, James Couzens. Couzens, who staunchly supported his native Canada's entry into the war, had finally turned in his resignation to Henry (but not his shares of Ford Motor stock) in October 1915, a month before Ford's meeting with President Wilson.

After the 1918 election, with the *Tribune* trial still pending, a frustrated Henry Ford bought his own newspaper to make sure America heard exactly what the father of the Model T wanted to say. It was called the *Dearborn Independent* and it soon became synonymous with anti-Semitism. When the *Tribune* lawsuit finally went to court in the summer of 1919, in Mount Clemens, Michigan, less than fifty miles from Ford's home, the *Independent* assigned a team of fifty reporters to the courthouse to dispatch daily stories to rural and weekly newspapers across the country under the guise of "the Mount Clemens News Bureau." The stories were completely sympathetic to Henry, of course, and nearly 3,000 publications agreed to run them as written.

Nonetheless, Henry's own testimony was what the urban dailies reported, and the image it cast was not what he had in mind. To substantiate the charge that Ford was "an ignorant idealist," the *Tribune*'s lawyers grilled him on American history and government:

Q. Have there been any revolutions in this country?
A. Yes.
Q. When?
A. In 1812.

Q. One in 1812, eh? Any other time?
A. I don't know of any others.
Q. Do you know that this country was born in a revolution?
A. I guess I do. . . .
Q. Do you know what forced us into the Revolutionary War?
A. No, I do not. . . .
Q. Mr. Ford, I have some hesitation, but in justice to yourself I shall ask this question: I think the impression has been created by your failure to read some of these things that have been presented to you, that you could not read. Do you want to leave it that way?
A. Yes, you can leave it that way. I am not a fast reader and I have the hay fever and I would make a botch of it.[2]

In the end, the *Chicago Tribune* was found guilty of libel. However, in what the urban media (and Henry himself) saw as another humiliating slap at Ford's character, the jury awarded Henry a total of six cents in damages.

The tone of the *Dearborn Independent* proceeded to grow even more paranoid, with detailed portrayals of "the Jewish conspiracy" as the cause of all the world's political, social, and economic problems. The central headline of its May 22, 1920, issue made clear its editorial slant (and that of its owner). The lead story was entitled, "The International Jew: The World's Problem."

Yet, reflecting the climate of the time, Henry's popularity continued to soar. In 1923, his ghostwritten autobiography, *My Life and Work,* became a bestseller. The book and collected reprints of back issues of the *Independent* were also big hits in Germany, where a rising politician named Adolf Hitler became one of Ford's greatest admirers. In the fall of 1922, shortly before the autobiography was published, there was even a movement to draft Ford to run for president of the United States against Warren G. Harding, whose administration had been rocked by scandal and corruption after less than two years in office. When Harding died unexpectedly in the summer of 1923, however, Henry's political star was overshadowed by "Silent" Calvin Coolidge, who had been Harding's vice president and now moved into the White House.

Coolidge's image as the shy, soft-spoken country boy ill-at-ease in public was precisely what Henry saw in himself: precisely what Middle America wanted, without all the baggage of Ford's public relations gaffs. That winter, Henry visited Coolidge at the White House and pledged to endorse him in 1924.

Remarkably, none of these personal crusades, contradictions, or public relations disasters affected sales of the Model T. Ford Motor's car sales more than doubled between the years 1915 and 1917. By 1923, when Henry's book was published, they had risen another 50 percent.[3]

BILLY DURANT VS. THE LELANDS

While Henry Ford's views and ideas splashed across the headlines, Billy Durant remained focused more quietly on expanding his regained empire. World War I actually had little impact on demand for automobiles in the United States, even though it forced manufacturers to divert some of their production to war materiel. As General Motors' historian Arthur Pound noted:

> Although millions of young men, the best potential buyers in the light-car field, were mobilized, and savings were being drawn on for war loans, nevertheless automobiles continued to sell. The purchasing power of the country was high as a result of war inflation and the consequent rise in wages. While automobile prices rose somewhat in answer to increased costs, they did not rise in proportion to food and clothing. The people had money to buy cars, and the automobile fitted into the high-speed picture of the war years, when time was the most important element in a life-and-death struggle and economy was a forgotten word. With millions of men withdrawn from employment, those at home increased their activities by using motor cars more freely.[4]

Although this strong domestic vehicle market was Billy's priority, his baby actually ended up providing more to the Allied war effort than Ford Motor. Eighteen of General Motors' twenty-three U.S. facilities had wartime contracts of one kind or another. The General produced war goods with gross value of $35 million, including 5,000 ambulances and trucks; 2,350 officers' cars; 1,157 artillery tractor engines; and 2,528 Liberty aircraft engines (which were also built by Ford Motor).[5]

Ironically, the issue of war production was manipulated by two of Billy Durant's own executives to smear him in the press. The executives were Henry Leland (Sloan's hero) and his son Wilfred. Billy's relationship with the Lelands had been strained ever since their protracted haggling over the sale of Cadillac back in 1909 and Billy's promise to leave Cadillac's management in their hands. With America's support for the war effort at its peak in the summer of 1917, the Lelands abruptly "resigned" from General Motors that August. The stately Henry, who had been deeply affected by the loss of his brother in the Civil War and by his own inability to enlist in the Union Army, claimed that he wanted to devote more of Cadillac Motor's production capacity to Liberty aircraft engines and that Durant didn't.

In testimony before a U.S. Senate committee, son Wilfred went as far as to charge that Billy Durant was "not in sympathy with the war." The headline in the August 27, 1918, edition of the *Detroit Free Press* read: "Head of G.M.C. Opposed War: Durant Unwilling to Take Any Part in Work, Leland Tells Committee." The story went on to claim:

> William C. Durant, president of the General Motors company, which is filling war orders at many of its plants throughout the country, was not in sympathy with the war at the time it was declared, Wilfred C. Leland, of Detroit, told the Senate aircraft committee when it visited Detroit some months ago.
>
> Mr. Leland and his father, Henry M. Leland, as a result of this attitude on the part of Durant, withdrew from the Cadillac Motor Car company, a part of the General Motors company.[6]

The real story of the Lelands' departure from Cadillac and General Motors was more about business strategy and conflicting personalities than patriotism. The Lelands were in fact fired by Durant, despite what they told the Senate committee.

With the independent-minded Pierre du Pont watching over his shoulder as chairman of General Motors' board of directors, Billy needed an executive team that was undivided in its loyalty to him. He was eager to consolidate his own control at General Motors and to expand Cadillac sales. The stubborn Lelands, more concerned with maintaining their product's prestigious image than with increasing the mother company's sales, did not share his urgency. They clearly had to go.

When the *Detroit Free Press* story appeared, Billy sent the father and son four separate telegrams over a period of four days, demanding that they substantiate their claims. They refused to comply, and Billy finally issued his own public response:

> Under these circumstances, I regret that I am no longer able, out of consideration for the Lelands, to withhold the facts of their compulsory retirement. They did not resign voluntarily but were discharged from the management of the Cadillac Company. Their discharge had nothing to do with patriotism or the war. It was brought about by prudential business reasons, and they were so notified by me before war was even declared.
>
> On March 10, 1917, I sent to W. C. Leland and H. M. Leland the following letter of dismissal, to take effect at the close of the fiscal year:
>
> Dear Mr. Leland:
>
> I take this opportunity of advising you that the present arrangement will not be continued after the 1st of August 1917, and that a change in management of the Cadillac Motor Car Company is contemplated.
>
> I trust that you will cooperate with me in any attempt to build up an organization capable of meeting the problems of the future.
>
> Yours truly,
>
> W.C. Durant, President
>
> War was not declared until April 6, some twenty-six days after the notice.
>
> In due course the discharge referred to in the letter of March 10 was effected in July 1917. It had nothing to do with the war or contracts for aircraft engines. It was purely routine business for the good of the Cadillac company.
>
> Of course it is superfluous to add that the Cadillac Company and all the companies connected with the General Motors Corporation are very busy on Liberty motors and other war work and their entire organization is out to win the war at all hazards, cost what it may.[7]

Billy's response was probably intended more for the eyes of Pierre S. du Pont and his own executive team than the newspapers. Perhaps in deference to the senior Leland, or perhaps because he wished the entire episode to go away, he never again publicly mentioned the rift. It was more important that he could now put a trusted ally in charge of Cadillac. The man he chose was Richard

Collins, whom he had met during his carriage days and hired as a sales manager at Buick. Collins was by now in charge of the entire Buick sales system and was known throughout the car business as "Trainload Collins" because of his success in managing Buick's sales— filling orders by the trainload.

As for the Lelands, their subsequent story falls just short of the tragedy of David Dunbar Buick's. After their 1917 exit from General Motors and Cadillac, they immediately organized a new company called Lincoln Motor Company (named in honor of Henry Leland's eternal hero, Abraham Lincoln). Leveraging their reputation for precision manufacturing, they secured a government contract to build 6,000 Liberty aircraft engines and found no trouble in putting together the capital to purchase an existing plant in Detroit, which they updated and expanded.

When the war ended on November 11, 1918, the Lelands went on to design another large car intended to be the most luxurious (and most expensive) on the market. Again, they had no trouble finding financial backers. However, when the first Lincoln automobile was launched in 1920, it was immediately ridiculed as an expensive clone of the previous model year's Cadillac. Adding further insult to this injury, the federal government began investigating the Lelands for failure to pay taxes and overcharging for Liberty engine production. By November 1921, their new company was in bankruptcy and Henry Leland (like Billy Durant eleven years earlier) was scrambling to find loans to keep his baby afloat.

As a last resort, Henry Leland called on Henry Ford, the man whose operations he had taken over and renamed Cadillac in 1902. The shrewd Ford stalled Leland's request for help until the bankruptcy judge put all of the Lincoln Motor Company's assets up for auction on February 4, 1922. He then made the sole bid to purchase all of the company.

Ford's offer was $5 million, far less than the appraised value of Lincoln's assets. In deference to the Lelands' creditors, the judge pushed the minimum bid to $8 million, and "Crazy Henry" agreed. Despite an initial personal pledge to let the Lelands continue to manage their baby as Ford Motor employees, he then dispatched his own executives to redesign the Lincoln plant's production techniques on the lines of his own concept of mass production (as opposed to the Leland philosophy of lower volume production).

Less than four months after the auction, the Lelands found

themselves totally removed from the automobile business, never to return. Henry Leland, the man who had made Ford's moving assembly line possible with his mastery of interchangeable parts, died at his Detroit home in 1932; he was eighty-nine. His Lincoln brand lives on today under the Ford Motor umbrella, as does Cadillac under that of General Motors.

GOOD TIMES ON THE NEW JERSEY SHORE, BUT NOT ON WALL STREET

With the Lelands' firing in 1917, all of the executives now running General Motors' operations (including Walter Chrysler) were personally indebted to Billy Durant for their success. The same still could not be said of the chairman of his board of directors, however. Pierre du Pont continued to take note of Billy's style and strategy as his own proconsul, John Jakob Raskob, assumed more responsibility at General Motors. At Pierre's suggestion, Raskob was put on General Motors' finance committee and began devoting himself full-time to the General's affairs.

Pierre's own priority at General Motors was to reorganize both its financial controls and its operating structure along the lines of the DuPont company's. Raskob, however, soon became a fervent Durant cheerleader and did not push hard to overcome Billy's resistance to such controls. Raskob fully endorsed Billy's ambitions for the company, even if they meant taking risks on acquisitions whose balance sheets showed more debt than assets and even if they required the issuance of more stock and debt by General Motors itself. Indeed, Raskob had as much if not more to do with the General's overreach in the 1919 expansion program as did Billy Durant.

As his baby thrived, Billy finally began to enjoy the wealth he had amassed during its roller-coaster ride. In 1917, he and his second wife, Catherine, bought an apartment overlooking New York City's Central Park, at 907 Fifth Avenue (on the corner of Seventy-second Street). The same year, they bought an estate called Raymere in Deal, New Jersey, on the Atlantic coast. Raymere had been built by the global financier Jacob Rothschild; the Durants bought it at a bargain price from the heirs of Jacob's widow.

As if Raymere's white marble façade and thirty-seven rooms on Ocean Boulevard didn't make a bold-enough statement, Billy also bought several surrounding properties. Walter Chrysler recalled never having seen such a luxurious residence or such gracious hosts.[8] Raymere became Catherine's domain and her husband's retreat from New York City and General Motors. Billy spent weekends there and stayed at the Fifth Avenue apartment when not traveling on General Motors business.

Even at Raymere, however, he was never far from a telephone. Business associates were still at his beck and call for unscheduled queries, suggestions, or meetings. Incredibly, all the units in the General Motors empire were still structured and managed the way they had been before Billy bought them, and the heads of each unit all reported directly to him.

As long as profits and the vehicle market itself continued to grow (as Durant and Raskob fully expected them to), the matter of delegating more of his own authority and improving coordination and financial controls among the units didn't appear to be an urgent issue. Thanks to a fickle stock market, however, Billy soon was forced to bow to du Pont's demands for a more systematic and institutional management structure.

While the country's entry into World War I in April 1917 did not have a major effect on automobile sales, it created unforeseen uncertainty in the stock market, with no one able to guess how long the conflict would last or what its impact would be on commodity prices and availability. Automotive stock prices in particular plummeted throughout the summer and fall before recovering late in the winter. In January 1917, General Motors common stock was selling in the range of $200 a share. By June, it was down to $115; by September, $86; and, by October, $75.

Billy proposed to Pierre and Raskob that they form a buying syndicate to stabilize and strengthen the stock price, but they turned him down, arguing that paying solid dividends was a better way than market manipulation to stimulate interest in the stock. The rebuff was hardly enough to keep Billy on the sidelines, however.

THE WIZARD GAMBLES AGAIN . . . AND DILUTES HIS POWER

Still absolutely convinced of General Motors' growth potential and its underestimated value, Billy began buying large blocks of GM stock on his own in the summer of 1917 in a one-man campaign to stabilize the share price and the company's market capitalization. Adding to the risk (and to the adrenaline rush), he bought the shares on margin, using the shares of General Motors he already owned as collateral with his brokers.

Then as now, the margin was the difference between the deposit the purchaser put down (in Billy's case, usually 10 percent) and the purchase price of the stock. When the market price of General Motors stock fell below Billy's purchase price, brokers began "calling" the margin, demanding full payment of the money that they had in effect loaned him to buy the shares.

Billy's back was again to the wall. In what would prove to be just the first of a series of moves that weakened his influence and control over his baby, he went to Raskob, explained his situation, and asked if the corporation could extend him a loan of $1 million. He explained that he had been acting in the interest of the corporation and did not want to sell any of his shares to cover his own margin calls.

A sympathetic Raskob took Billy's request to the board of directors. On November 9, 1917, with Billy absent from the meeting, the board decided against the loan because of potential legal liabilities. However, partly out of fear of embarrassment to General Motors if Billy's game became publicly known and partly in deference to all that the founder had done for the company and its investors, they agreed to a more creative proposal from Raskob. The only salary Billy had drawn since his return to General Motors was seventy dollars a month, which was the fee he received as a director. Raskob proposed that Billy be given an annual salary of $500,000 retroactive to the year 1916.

The directors concurred. Billy was given a check for $1 million, and the incident never hit the newspapers.

General Motors' need for capital did not abate, however, and the company's low and unstable market valuation continued to worry both the du Pont interests and Billy Durant as the holidays approached. Raskob saw the solution in E. I. du Pont de Nemours & Company (the new name the family business had assumed after a 1915 restructuring), which now had an unanticipated cash surplus of $50 million as the result of mushrooming wartime sales of its chemicals and explosives.

From the DuPont perspective, General Motors offered not only a sound investment for the surplus cash but an opportunity to acquire a stake in a growing business that also happened to be a consumer of chemicals, especially paints (a point that seemed to make good business sense at the time but was later used by the federal government to force E. I. du Pont de Nemours & Company to divest itself of all interest in General Motors on antitrust grounds). On top of this, Raskob saw investment by the DuPont company as a buttress to the personal stake both he and Pierre now had in General Motors.

From Billy's perspective, a major investment by the DuPont company would mean a weakening of his own position, even if it buttressed the stock price. Through his shares of Chevrolet as well as General Motors, he was GM's largest stockholder. If the du Pont family interests acquired enough equity and leverage to force him to merge Chevrolet and United Motors with General Motors, as Pierre and Raskob wanted him to, he would be forced to share power to an extent that he never had in any of his many enterprises.

Pierre told Raskob that he would take the investment proposal to the DuPont board of directors on two conditions: first, that Durant agree to merge Chevrolet and United Motors into General Motors as part of the recapitalization; and second, that Durant agree that the General Motors finance and executive committees be patterned after those of DuPont, with Billy allowed to chair the executive committee but with Raskob chairing the restructured finance committee.

In exchange for the capital to maintain General Motors' stock price and the company's expansion, Billy Durant was in effect being asked to cede financial control of his baby. Pierre's 1915 vow not to be a "dummy director" was being thrown in the founder's face, as were Billy's many earlier snubs at Pierre's efforts to improve communications and financial controls within the company. After two days of spirited discussion, on December 20 and 21, the E. I. du Pont de Nemours & Company's finance committee and board of directors voted to purchase 97,875 shares of General Motors stock, nearly 25 percent of the shares outstanding, plus 133,000 shares of Chevrolet Motor Company. The total investment was $25 million, half of the DuPont company's wartime cash surplus.

In February 1918, shortly after all the legal requirements surrounding the Chevrolet merger transactions had been completed, Pierre threw a black-tie dinner at New York's Metropolitan Club. The official intent was to formally announce the DuPont company's stake in General Motors and "introduce" Billy Durant to the most influential bankers in the East. As Billy recalled the evening:

> It was a swell affair. . . . I was asked to give a brief history of General Motors, which I did, concluding my remarks with the statement that the corporation was eleven years old, that the automobile field was fairly well covered, and that the corporation was becoming interested in other lines. . . .[9]

By "other lines," he was referring to Frigidaire, a company he had bought on his own for its pioneering work in electric refrigeration. He went on:

> I was confident and did not hesitate to make the statement that when the public recognized its [the electric refrigerator's] importance and value as a household unit, the earnings of that division alone would be sufficient to pay the dividends on the entire issue of General Motors preferred stock.[10]

Although no one acknowledged it that evening, the wizard's words were prescient once again. In 1928, nine years after Durant sold Frigidaire to General Motors for $100,000, the Frigidaire division contributed more than $15 million in net earnings to General Motors' coffers. As the elite guests filed out of the Metropolitan Club that evening in 1918, however, the message they took with them was not the growth potential of Frigidaire: It was that General Motors, unlike Ford Motor and unlike any other enterprise ever created and run by Billy Durant, was no longer a one-man show. The fortunes of Billy's baby were now tied to those of the DuPont business empire—an empire managed by firm policies and controls rather than instinct and whim.

Despite the DuPont cash infusion, General Motors' need for capital continued to grow in line with its confidence and ambitions. Durant's personal ownership and influence, in turn, continued to be diluted. In January 1918, the company's authorized capital stock was increased to $200 million to complete the merging of Chevrolet into GM's operations and the acquisition of all outstanding shares of Chevrolet stock. In June, an additional $44 million in new GM preferred shares was issued to bring United Motors under the General Motors umbrella.

Alfred Sloan, who had accepted United Motors stock rather than cash in payment for the sale of his Hyatt Roller Bearing Company to Billy back in 1916, received the biggest block of this second issuance of GM stock. In recognition of his stake and his value as a manager, he was also elected to the company's board of directors and appointed to its executive committee (chaired by Durant).

In November 1918, the authorized capitalization was again increased, this time to $370 million. A month later, E. I. du Pont de Nemours & Company invested another $28 million, further solidifying Pierre du Pont's power and the two companies' business ties. General Motors' stock price continued to recover even as the number of shares outstanding grew, giving the DuPont interests a most handsome return on their investment. In his annual letter to DuPont stockholders that year, Pierre noted:

> We feel fortunate in our partnership with Mr. William C. Durant, president of the General Motors Corporation and the father and leader of the motor industry not only in the United States but in the world today.[11]

In June 1919, with the expansion program proceeding at full speed, Billy Durant proposed the largest recapitalization of all, and his board of directors again supported him all the way. This time, new issues of common and preferred stock increased the General's authorized capitalization to slightly more than $1 billion, making it the second company (behind U.S. Steel) to reach that milestone. Caught up in the postwar economic recovery and the automobile market's fantastic growth, investors and stockbrokers were more enthusiastic than ever about the company's future: There was no shortage of buyers for the new shares.

CHAPTER | **THIRTEEN**

A Last Good-Bye to the Baby

FLUSH WITH CAPITAL, General Motors proceeded with its ambitious expansion program (discussed in Chapter 1) throughout the year 1919. The plan called for a doubling of current vehicle production capacity and gave virtually every operating unit a green light for expansion of existing plants plus the acquisition or construction of others. During the year, Buick alone spent more than $5 million on bricks and mortar; Cadillac, just under $5 million; Chevrolet, more than $7 million; Olds, more than $2 million.

The largely uncoordinated spending did not end there, however. To ensure an uninterrupted supply of car bodies as vehicle production expanded, the company paid $27.6 million for a 60 percent interest in Fisher Body, the industry's largest and most prestigious supplier of automobile bodies. In addition, $17 million was paid out in common stock dividends for the year. Finally, at the insistence of John Raskob rather than Billy Durant, construction of the world's largest office building was begun in Detroit, with more than $4 million spent on this project by the end of the year (a sum that would ultimately exceed $20 million).

While these obligations far exceeded the previous year's earnings of $13 million, there was no immediate concern over cash flow or debt. The expansion plan was drafted by Raskob and approved by both the executive and finance committees. Everyone was outwardly confident that expanding sales would offset any risk of insufficient cash flow in particular.

By the end of 1919, Billy Durant's General Motors Corporation included the following principal operating divisions and dozens of other minor parts-making subsidiaries:

- Buick Motor Division

- Cadillac Motor Car Division

- Chevrolet Group (the umbrella for four separate Chevrolet units)

- Oakland Motor Car Division

- Olds Motor Works Division

- General Motors Truck Division (GMC)

- Scripps-Booth Corporation (experimental car builder)

- General Motors of Canada

- General Motors Acceptance Corporation (GMAC, responsible for dealer and retail financing)

- Samson Tractor Division

- United Motors Group (umbrella for nine separate accessory subsidiaries)

- Champion Ignition Company

- Dayton-Wright Company (builder of airplanes)

- Delco-Light Company (lighting manufacturer)

- Frigidaire Corporation

- General Motors Europe, Ltd.

- General Motors Export Company[1]

PRELUDE TO THE CRISIS

Incredibly, the empire was still largely run and coordinated on a day-to-day basis by Billy himself. By the end of the year, he was overseeing more than seventy factories in forty cities in the United States alone, with no fewer than fifty senior operating executives reporting directly to him. Only a leader of his boundless energy (and minimal need of sleep) would have even dared accept such broad responsibility. Billy not only accepted it, he thrived on it. When Alfred Sloan approached him with his proposal for a reorganization that just might make life simpler for all, Billy did little more than thank him politely. As Sloan recalled:

> In late 1919 and early 1920 I developed a plan of organization and presented it to Mr. Durant. He appeared to accept it favorably, though he did nothing about it. I think this was due in part to the fact that he was not prepared then to take up organizational matters; he was over-burdened with all manner of immediate operating and personal financial problems which made it extremely difficult for him to consider a broad plan of this kind.[2]

Not surprisingly, Pierre du Pont also began to lose patience with the founder's failure to impose a semblance of structure on the empire. Without consulting Billy, he asked the DuPont company's engineering staff to send an "observer" to evaluate the efficiency of General Motors' management. The resulting report stopped short of proposing a new structure but made clear that one was needed. One can only imagine Billy's body language when he read its many criticisms, which included the following:

> Mr. Durant apparently has complete charge of all the planning and dictates largely the policies to be followed. His opinion is consulted for final decisions in a great many cases as there seems no one else in the organization who is the final arbitrator for the various plants or for the new [expansion] developments. . . . There is also a certain lack of cooperative spirit between the different plants. These plants are practically independent as regards the purchasing, accounting, and other organizations, and as they were independent organizations before the General Motors was formed, and have been more or less functioning ever since as independent organizations, it is very easy to understand

a feeling of this kind as there is no central organization directing them, except in the most general way.[3]

After reviewing this report with Pierre, Billy agreed to allow the various staffs of E. I. du Pont de Nemours & Company (DuPont) to advise his division managers, but he again refused to consider a more formal organizational structure. Throughout the boom year of 1919, the operating divisions continued to spend more and more, not only on bricks and mortar but on parts inventories, with no coordination or control from the central office. When a surprise shock to the U.S. economy shattered the central premise of the entire expansion strategy, the founder of General Motors found himself unable to rein in his independent-minded field lieutenants.

While inflation had been on the rise and prices for all goods were driven artificially high by postwar boom and demand in 1919, no one expected the sky to fall as fast and hard as it did in the summer of 1920. By the end of the year, the nation's confidence was again supplanted with doubt as the gross national product fell 6 percent, stocks traded on the New York Stock Exchange lost an average 25 percent of their value, manufacturers cut employment by 25 percent, a half million farmers lost their homesteads, and 100,000 businesses went bankrupt.[4]

General Motors was hit harder than any corporation in the country. All of the elements of catastrophe abruptly came together: the cost of the 1919 expansion program, the accumulation of huge inventories in anticipation of more demand, the end of cash flow as dealers stopped ordering vehicles, the fall of the stock price, and the lack of an internal structure or mechanism to force the divisions to cut production and costs in a timely or orderly manner.

GENERAL MOTORS' RESPONSE VS. FORD MOTOR'S

While Billy Durant and Henry Ford had both based their business strategies on the premise of constant growth in the American automobile market, Ford did not have a Pierre du Pont or an Alfred Sloan looking over his shoulder when the market for vehicles and all other noncommodity goods abruptly disappeared in the spring of 1920. By then, he had taken his company private. Also unlike

Durant, Ford generated his working capital from reinvestment of profits rather than the issuance of stock. He was in a position to ride out the storm and emerge stronger than ever: Billy Durant was not.

As sales declined in the spring and summer, Ford repeatedly lowered his prices to keep inventory moving and preserve a semblance of cash flow. When this failed to support production, he didn't hesitate to bite the bullet. Within twenty-four hours of an edict from Henry himself, all Ford Motor production was shut down and all workers were sent home. With absolute confidence and will, Henry Ford then personally cajoled his dealers to buy his remaining vehicle inventory. The dealers knew the cars could not be sold at retail without a loss, but they complied in order to remain in Ford's good grace when the good times returned. Ford also demanded price concessions from suppliers, and got them. In short, the pain was spread and shared among all Ford's constituents.

General Motors, on the other hand, was in no position to move quickly or forcefully on any front. With the plant expansion program, Billy Durant's plants (like Ford's) were running at full capacity when the vehicle market dried up in the spring. Edicts went out for the car divisions to cut production and even write off parts inventories, but they went unheeded, thanks largely to the culture and attitude of independence and shooting from the hip that Billy had done nothing to discourage. In the end, the General's divisions were forced to stop production without having moved any of their inventory.

Throughout the late summer and fall, General Motors' inventories and debt continued to soar while Ford Motor's actually declined. Henry Ford's decisiveness caused Ford Motor to take a severe hit in sales in 1920, but it also put the company in position for a far more dramatic comeback the following year. General Motors' total vehicle sales for 1920 actually slightly exceeded the 1919 level, thanks to strong sales in the first five months of the year, but the crisis forced a drastic restructuring the following year that killed the General's momentum while Ford Motor moved into high gear.

As Sloan described the crisis some forty years later:

> Total [General Motors] corporation inventories in January 1920 had stood at $137 million; in April at $168 million; in June at $185 million; in October at $209 million . . . and the worst was yet to come.
>   In September the bottom dropped out of the automobile market.

To meet the situation, Mr. Ford cut his prices on September 21 by 20
to 30 percent. Mr. Durant, supported by the division sales managers,
attempted for a time to maintain prices and to guarantee dealers and
customers against any reduction. By October the situation had become
so serious for General Motors that many managers were having difficulty in locating cash to pay invoices and payrolls. In that month we
borrowed about $83 million from banks on short-term notes. In Novem-
ber all the major car-producing divisions, except Buick and Cadillac,
had virtually shut down their plants, and those two were operating at
reduced rates.[5]

Sloan's new mentor, Chairman Pierre du Pont, waited two years
after the crisis (when the company was reorganized and back in the
black) to give an official explanation to General Motors' stockholders. He went out of his way to lay the blame not with the national
economic downturn or the 1919 expansion program, but rather the
lack of clear policies and controls at the hands of Billy Durant.
There were no flies on Pierre or any of his close associates. After a
detailed discussion of the problems of inventory control and cash
flow, he concluded:

The purpose of the above recital is to show definitely that the troubles
of past years were not related to an ill-financed expansion program or
to delay in receiving the proceeds of financing. It is quite certain that
the funds provided before the close of the year 1920 were sufficient to
carry out the whole program and also to finance new business offered
during the year 1921 and the first half of the year 1922. It is equally
certain that disregard for control of inventories and purchase commitments cost the Corporation a very large sum of money, of which the
greater part might have been saved by proper safeguards in Divisions
now differently managed. Further, it is important to the stockholders to
know that the financial misfortunes of the Corporation in the past two
years were only slightly related to the manufacture and sale of its products, but that these misfortunes were directly related to loose and un-
controlled methods which are now corrected.[6]

In the chairman's mind, all fault lay at the feet of Billy Durant,
the man he had helped take control of General Motors in 1915.

Yet the chairman also separated the company's performance
from Durant's own fate. According to Pierre, Billy's downfall was

again his own personal finances and his attempt (again) to manipulate the stock market to prop up his baby's stock price at the peak of the crisis.

THE FOUNDER HAS HIS OWN DOUBTS AS HIS LEADERSHIP TEAM REMAINS MUTE

As in the past, Billy Durant did not sit idly by as he watched his baby slip into peril. Ironically, even before the 1920 recession, it was Billy alone who voiced concern about how the General's expansion was being financed. He wrote to finance committee chairman Raskob:

> I do not wish to annoy you, but I feel that I should call your attention to the enormous expenditures and capital commitments which are being authorized by the Finance Committee against prospective earnings—a method of financing which I do not think is either safe or sound and which, in the event of industrial disturbance or paralysis, might seriously impair our position. Frankly, I am very much worried and I know that many members of our organization in the managerial and operating divisions are much concerned.[7]

That letter was written in January 1920 but was apparently ignored by Raskob and the finance committee: There is no record of any response or discussion.

Billy also expressed doubts about the new office building in Detroit, to be named the Durant Building, which was also a Raskob (not a Durant) idea. However, in this instance, he expressed his concerns verbally (as he usually did) rather than in writing. After the crisis was history, he wrote identical letters to several sympathetic executive committee members asking them to verify his recollection of opposing the office building project. These letters demonstrate that the committee members all concurred that Durant had opposed the office building.[8] Yet the impression conveyed by Pierre du Pont and Alfred Sloan at the time was that Billy was on board with the project. Indeed, Sloan took pride in claiming that he persuaded Billy (not Raskob) to move the site from downtown Detroit to an undeveloped area a few miles north, where land was much cheaper.[9]

Significantly, not one of the members of the board, the finance committee, or the executive committee went on record opposing Billy Durant's leadership even as the business situation and Billy's own power base declined throughout the spring, summer, and fall of 1920.

Even when one of his seemingly whimsical acquisitions proved to be a dog, the brilliance of Durant's other acquisitions seemed to outweigh the mistake. The dog was a company called Samson Sieve-Grip Tractor, based in California, which Billy saw as a counter to Henry Ford's plunge into the mechanized farm-implement business. Billy paid far more than its market value and falsely assumed that the company could come up with a more practical and reliable tractor than Ford's. He also bought another tractor operation in Janesville, Wisconsin, and put it under Samson. The entire business was disbanded within two years of its creation and written off after having incurred a total loss of more than $33 million. The only thing that survived was the Janesville plant, which was converted to build Chevrolet cars.

DONE IN BY THE STREET . . . AGAIN

While Billy's executives and directors alike remained officially mute, the weakening of his credibility and control that began with the resignation of Walter Chrysler continued inexorably as his baby's revenues plummeted in the summer of 1920. The General's monthly sales declined from more than 42,000 cars and trucks in March to fewer than 13,000 in November.

The most severe decline, however, was in the value of General Motors itself. The company's stock price and its market capitalization went into near free fall. In March 1920, just before the economy hit the skids, E. I. du Pont de Nemours & Company purchased another $60 million in General Motors common stock. The street price of the shares purchased by DuPont that month was $200 a share. Within weeks, it reached a high of $420. By the end of July, however, General Motors common stock was trading on the New York Stock Exchange at $20. By November, it was down to $12 a share.

With the expansion program plus mounting debt and dwindling cash flow, the Wall Street situation was far more critical than in

1917, when Billy had intervened to try to support the stock price and ended up only diluting his control of the company.

This time, John Raskob and Pierre du Pont intervened directly. They ended up securing $80 million in short-term loans from various banks and forming two new syndicates to buy General Motors shares: one led by the Nobel Company in England (a company with close informal ties to DuPont through its chemical and explosives sales) and one led by Billy Durant's eternal nemesis, J. P. Morgan and Company. Part of the deal with the Morgan bankers was that they would be allowed to add their own representative to the General's board of directors. It was another slap at Billy, but he was again helpless to resist.

When the syndicates were formed, it was also agreed that neither the DuPont business interests nor Billy himself would do anything on their own to try to prop up the stock. The House of Morgan in particular was not to be interfered with by any speculating that might undermine its own efforts. Yet Billy once again proceeded secretly to start buying on his own, on margin, just as he had in 1917.

Once again, Billy's margin calls soon exceeded his cash and forced him to pledge shares of his own General Motors stock as collateral. Before the spiral began in the spring, those shares had given him a personal fortune in excess of $90 million. By Thanksgiving, it was all gone and he again found himself at the mercy of Pierre du Pont for a bailout.

What could have driven Billy to play the fool's game again, especially with his promise not to countermand the Morgan syndicate's effort? Had all the pressures, adrenaline, and lost sleep of all his razor's-edge rides finally forced something to snap in his psyche? Had the ghost of his father's failures on Wall Street come back with a vengeance? Had he become a gambling addict long before the term was coined? Or had his eternal optimism led him to believe that comeback and greater glory were again just around the corner, no matter how bad the situation might appear at its worst moment?

Perhaps the only mystery greater than his own motive is how he managed to keep his gamble secret for several months, until he was in a far worse position than in 1917.

Billy did not leave behind any notes or letters explaining his motivation. He did, however, give an exclusive interview to one of the most popular automotive journalists of the day, a now-forgotten writer named W. A. P. John. Durant even read and approved John's manuscript before it was published: a fact that John went out of his way to mention in the article, which appeared in the January 1923 issue of *Motor* magazine. Though the article is written in the third person, the voice is clearly that of Billy himself:

> Knowing the value of General Motors stock, spurred by his sublime faith in the Corporation he had conceived and created . . . and holding uppermost in his thoughts the trust that had been placed in him by thousands of stockholders who had invested in General Motors because of their faith in him, Durant's conception of his responsibility made him feel that it was his duty to protect against the slaughter of General Motors stock. For the manipulators were kicking it about relentlessly, since the market was favorable for such buccaneering operations.
>
> So whenever large blocks of General Motors were offered for sale, he, knowing their value and the earning power of the company, purchased them privately.[10]

The article's underlying premise was that other forces were deliberately dumping the stock to undermine its price and force Billy out of General Motors. Many of Billy's later defenders blamed a vengeful House of Morgan, but there is no hard evidence of such a conspiracy. Both the Morgan bankers and Pierre du Pont claimed they were ignorant of Billy's own buying until he had already dug himself into a hole far deeper than the one he had burrowed in 1917.

Not surprisingly, daughter Margery was even more passionate than the *Motor* article in Billy's defense. She put the entire affair in the context of principle and loyalty on her father's part and vengeance and conspiracy on the part of his enemies:

> Thousands of people had put their faith in him and had invested in General Motors. He had felt for some time that professional traders on the stock exchange were forcing the stock below its proper value. It was his duty, as he saw it, therefore, to protect the corporation of which he was president and whose stockholders had entrusted him with their funds.[11]

Regardless of which side may or may not have been out to do the other in (Durant or the House of Morgan), Billy kept on buying, even as the price continued to fall and his own financial position became untenable. As recounted by W. A. P. John:

> One day—it was July 27, 1920—one hundred thousand shares of General Motors stock were suddenly dumped into the market. The market was demoralized. General Motors stock broke to twenty-and-one-half. Durant—caring not one whit for money, and caring everything for the thousands who believed in him—bought that stock. More came into the market, at a lower price. He bought that, too. Then more and more—always at decreasing prices, which made all his previously acquired holdings worth just so much less. Alone, unsupported, single-handed, and smiling—he fought the battle, purchasing the stock down to $12 a share, endeavoring to save General Motors for those who had made it possible more than ten years previous.[12]

Unlike Billy, who used the journalist as a surrogate, Pierre du Pont carefully recorded his own recollection of the entire chain of events in a 2,500-word letter to his cousin Irénée du Pont (then president of E. I. du Pont de Nemours & Company). It offered a detailed explanation of Pierre's self-proclaimed ignorance of both Billy's personal speculation and any possible speculation against Billy by the Morgan camp or anyone else.

According to Pierre, a meeting was held on November 10 between Billy, Raskob, Pierre, and Morgan partner Dwight Morrow (who later became U.S. ambassador to Mexico and whose daughter Anne married Charles Lindbergh, who in turn became close friends with Margery Durant's next husband, Fitzhugh Green). Morrow asked bluntly if any of them were buying General Motors shares in violation of the agreement with the Morgan syndicate. In his letter, Pierre pleads ignorance:

> I stated that so far as I knew, none of the individuals in the DuPont group were borrowers on General Motors stock or operating in any way. Mr. Morrow stated that the shares purchased by Morgan & Company and their friends were still held and that there was no intention to sell. I do not remember that Mr. Durant made as positive a statement on his part, but he did not give any intimation that he was a borrower on the stock or operating in the market in any way. Mr. Morrow asked him the direct question whether he knew of any weak accounts in the market, to which Durant replied "no."[13]

The next day, Billy invited Pierre and Raskob to lunch and told them that "the bankers" were trying to force him out of General Motors. Pierre's letter claims that he reassured Billy that this was not the case but adds that as the discussion continued, Billy mentioned that he was worried about his "personal accounts." When Raskob asked Billy outright how much he owed, Billy's answer (according to Pierre) was, "I will have to look it up."

Five days later, after a long weekend, Pierre and Raskob called on Billy in his New York office to see what the numbers were. Incredibly, he kept them waiting outside several hours. He then stunned them with his report. Again, as recalled by Pierre:

> Mr. Durant was very busy that day, seeing people, rushing to the telephone, and in and out of his room, so that although we waited patiently for several hours, interrupted only by lunch time, it was not until four o'clock that afternoon that Mr. Durant began to give us figures indicating his situation. He had pencil memoranda of the number of loans at banks. The total memoranda, as written down by us from what he said, showed an indebtedness of twenty million dollars, all presumably on brokers' accounts and supported by 1,300,000 shares of stock owned by others and by an unknown amount of collateral belonging to Durant; also $14,190,000 which Durant estimated he owed personally to banks and brokers, against which he held three million shares of General Motors stock, this, of course, exclusive of the 1,300,000 shares owned by others. Mr. Durant stated that he had no personal books or accounts and was wholly unable to give definite statements as to the total indebtedness; what part of it was his personal and what part was the indebtedness of others on which he had lent collateral without other commitment.[14]

Billy had finally boxed himself into a corner from which even he knew there was no escape.

However, du Pont and Raskob were also in a corner of their own. If Billy were allowed to go under, the ensuing publicity and the further decline in value of those 4.3 million-plus shares could be the final blow to General Motors. There was no alternative but to bail Billy out, again.

The DuPont interests and the Morgan partners joined forces to form yet another new syndicate to pay off all of Durant's debt to all his bankers and brokers. When all the calls were added up, it came to more than $30 million.

In accepting the bailout, Billy Durant also submitted his resignation from General Motors. It was accepted with no comment. Billy never returned to the General's offices. While Pierre du Pont claimed the resignation was Billy's own decision, all parties knew the founder's credibility and influence with the board of directors were gone no matter what he did. For his part, Billy claimed that the resignation was part of the bailout deal.

As the surrogate voice W. A. P. John described Billy's farewell:

> On December 1, 1920, he appeared in his office for the last time as president of General Motors. About him his men were working with tears welling in their eyes and their throats filled with a strange thickness. He entered—quiet, unperturbed, and smiling. He signed a few papers, attended to a few details, and then put on his hat and coat.
>
> "Well," he said, without a trace of rancor or regret, as he glanced about the room, "May first is usually national moving day. But we seem to be moving on December first." This was the exit line of the man who has been called the "soul of General Motors." [Playwright Eugene] O'Neill has never written a finer line.[15]

When he left his office that day, Billy Durant was one week short of his fifty-ninth birthday. Wife Catherine, the belle of Raymere, was thirty-two. Both still saw great opportunities ahead.

BILLY DOES RIGHT BY HIS BABY

After Billy's resignation, Pierre S. du Pont was the unanimous choice to serve as president as well as chairman of General Motors. As much as Pierre wanted to implement reform and reorganization, he neither relished nor enjoyed the new responsibilities. Eager to retire to his 200-acre country estate just across the Delaware state line in Pennsylvania, he saw himself as a transitional caretaker. In that role, he immediately gave the key job of vice president of operations to Alfred P. Sloan, Jr., the one member of the previous management team who was furthest from Durant and closest to himself in style and character.

Pierre was well aware that the company's culture and identity had been shaped by the founder's own personality and style. He was just as aware that Billy's charm and his reputation as the "wizard" had made him a hero to nearly all employees.

At the same time, Pierre knew that his own persona was an unknown factor: He was a name without a face as far as most of the organization was concerned. The new president's first challenge was thus to make himself known and reassure employees of the company's stability and direction. As the official history puts it:

> To his old employees Mr. Durant had been both boss and friend, and while thousands of the later comers in his labor ranks had never seen him in the flesh, they knew him by hearsay. Years ago he had taken on for them the attributes of myth and story. He was their hero, their superman, doing the things they would like to do if they could. Particularly they had rejoiced when, like Lochinvar out of the West [hero of Sir Walter Scott's epic poem], he had stolen the General Motors bride from the Eastern bankers in 1915. Now they began to grumble about absentee ownership and Eastern control, and whether their jobs and houses would be worth anything a year hence.[16]

As in 1910, Billy Durant stepped up to help the cause, despite his own ouster. Rather than fire broadsides, he called the closest members of his former leadership team together and told them they should stay with General Motors rather than jump ship. To those who said they wanted to leave and help him in whatever he wanted to do next, he replied that they could best help him by helping General Motors, where his vastly diminished personal fortune still lay in the form of shares of common stock. Finally, he told them that Pierre du Pont and his new team were "good people" and had only the company's best interests in mind.[17]

Billy had reason to be gracious to his successor. After the du Pont and Morgan syndicates paid off the $30-million-plus that he had accumulated in debt, they allowed him to keep 230,000 shares of General Motors common stock, with total market value of $3 million as of January 1921. While this final compensation paled in comparison to future "golden parachutes" granted to executives whose sins and the damage they inflicted on their companies were far worse, it was extraordinary for that era. Alfred Sloan later went out of his way to portray it as more than generous, noting in *My Years with General Motors* that the value of those shares would have risen to more than $25 million, and that Billy would have received an additional $27 million in dividends if he had held onto all the shares until his death in 1947.

Alas, Billy was not able to hold onto all of those shares: He still had other dreams.

THE END OF AN ERA

While Billy refrained from public comment about the crisis of 1920, more criticism of his management shortcomings inevitably sprouted inside and outside of General Motors.

Yet no one could deny that Billy Durant alone was the man who had seen and nurtured the original vision of the enterprise. He alone had shown the audacity, persistence, and creativity to pull it off. Alfred Sloan's summary comment about the founder is perhaps the most fitting epitaph to the affair and to Billy's corporate legacy:

> Mr. Durant was a great man with a great weakness—he could create but not administer—and he had, first in carriages and then in automobiles, more than a quarter of a century of the glory and creation before he fell. That he should have conceived a General Motors and been unable himself in the long run to bring it off or to sustain his personal, once dominating position in it is a tragedy of American industrial history.[18]

The General's official history strikes a similar note in its brief account of the founder's departure, noting: "He always hoped for the best, and never prepared for the worst in time to ward it off."[19]

Could General Motors have survived if Billy Durant had somehow held on through the crisis, as Henry Ford did?

Did du Pont, Raskob, Sloan, and all the other executives and board members serve the company and its employees poorly by not confronting Billy directly and openly before the company was in crisis?

What did their actions (and lack thereof) say to employees, all of whom either adored or at the very least admired Billy, but had no clear image of the character of du Pont and Sloan?

Apart from what Billy's downfall says about the importance of clear, honest, and open communication, it also marks the dawn of a new awareness throughout the business world of how complex and unpredictable the economy and the consumer can be. It also marks a new appreciation that capital investment, cash flow, and debt must be managed hand-in-hand with corporate vision and growth. The day of the tinkerer and dreamer was gone: The day of the manager had dawned.

While Billy went on to even higher highs and lower lows throughout the 1920s, his name and what he had stood for quickly became irrelevant to the General's mission. With speed and efficiency unprecedented in the history of private enterprise, Pierre du Pont and Alfred Sloan proceeded to reshape the loosely coordinated empire into a machine capable of adapting to any change in its environment and poised to grind down any obstacle or competitor in the way of its objective.

With the founder gone, General Motors was transformed almost overnight into the model for all other corporations and even non-profit organizations. Under that model, the balance sheet rather than one man's vision became the compass and the rule book. Performance and effectiveness were measured by targets established by committees that were guided by data rather than instinct. Those who didn't meet the targets were held accountable, with the employees under them also often suffering the consequences, regardless of their individual performance.

Henceforth, any new Oldsmobile (or any other product change) would come from joint decisions among executives rather than one man with a crosscut saw. Acquisitions would be made after careful study of the potential return on investment rather than after one man's being captivated with a product demonstration (as Billy had been in the case of Buick, AC Spark Plug, and Frigidaire). Individuals would still be allowed and encouraged to offer new ideas on their own, but the concepts would be thoroughly vetted before being acted on. Spontaneity and impulse belonged to the preceding era of the pioneer, not the era of the corporation as defined by Alfred Sloan.

Sloan went on to be credited with coining the term "professional manager," and he viewed all key members of his leadership team as just that, professional managers, dedicated and indebted to the perpetuation of the enterprise itself rather than to any one dream or individual. Neither Billy's baby nor corporate America would ever be the same.

CHAPTER FOURTEEN

Alfred Pulls the Ranks Together

FROM THE YEAR 1921 until Sloan's retirement in 1956, General Motors' growth was unparalleled and virtually uninterrupted, even during the Great Depression. In his letters to stockholders, Sloan even referred to General Motors as an institution rather than a company.

The institution's culture was one of methodical, logical, results-oriented teamwork and accountability: a culture typified by the way Sloan and his private research/writing team structured *My Years with General Motors,* which became the bible not only for the General Motors team but thousands of companies and thousands more would-be CEOs. The book was written as a management primer rather than a memoir or history (despite the misleading title). Its core chapters have such titles as "Co-ordination by Committee," "The Development of Financial Controls," "Policy Creation," "Personnel and Labor Relations," "Incentive Compensation," and "The Management: How It Works."

My Years with General Motors remains the only detailed and documented record of the transformation of Billy Durant's undisciplined baby into an industrial icon: just as Alfred Sloan would have preferred. Durant's own autobiographical sketch ends before the crisis of 1920. He made it far enough into the writing to have a proposed title page and table of contents set in type, but there is no record of him ever sharing it with anyone other than his daughter Margery. Nor is there any indication that anyone in General Motors ever knew or cared that he had put pen to paper.

PIERRE COMES OUT FROM BEHIND THE CURTAIN

As Billy proceeded to again chase new dreams, forming a new company called Durant Motors within a month of his last good-bye to his baby and managing to drum up $5 million in capital through the issuance of stock before he even had a plant or a single dealer lined up, Pierre du Pont took to the road in a whirlwind tour of General Motors plants and the communities where they were located. His purpose was to let them see him in person and let them judge for themselves what kind of "Eastern control" was now at the helm.

The new president's message was that tough measures were in the offing to right the course, but that General Motors would not turn its back on any of its constituents, especially the employees and civic leaders of Flint. According to the official history, he succeeded quickly and handily:

> He visited plants and talked to groups of employees and associations of citizens. Everywhere he went he had the benefit of what the diplomats call "a good press." Local interests, from banks down to laborers, were reassured when they beheld this kindly, steady man and heard him tell them to be of good cheer. General Motors, he said, would stand by its investments in their communities as long as those communities stood by General Motors. There would be changes, of course, since not to change at the challenge of events was to risk corporate dry-rot, but the changes would benefit rather than injure the workers and the communities sustained by General Motors payrolls. Opinion in Michi-

gan completely reversed itself as soon as it heard that message: Real estate values began to regain their buoyancy; labor, its morale; and plant executives, their stamina.[1]

Pierre had been granted a honeymoon period of trust and good-will: Now, he had to cement the relationship—and build on it—with deeds, not words. He saw the answer in a revolutionary new engine that promised (falsely) to redefine the automobile itself.

KETTERING'S COPPER-COOLED ENGINE

As both a chemistry major at MIT and a former supervisor at the family's Brandywine laboratories, Pierre du Pont was as firm a believer in scientific research and advancement as he was in financial controls. Not surprisingly, when the burden of General Motors' leadership fell to him in December 1920, the one person inside the company he felt comfortable with, apart from Sloan, was Charles "Boss" Kettering, who had been elevated that summer to the official title of president of General Motors Research (which included advanced engineering activities). While Pierre was immediately reassured by Sloan's detailed plans for a new organizational structure, he was even more captivated by Kettering's vision of a radical new engine that Kettering claimed would give General Motors an edge over Ford Motor.

Kettering's new engine, which even stern Alfred Sloan called revolutionary, was actually not new in theory. It was a traditional gasoline internal combustion engine with a cooling system that used air rather than water. The air-cooled engine (to be produced commercially decades later in the Volkswagen Beetle and the Chevrolet Corvair) used air blown through fins welded to the engine walls rather than the water-cooled engine's more complex radiator and plumbing system to cool the engine while it was operating. It had been previously demonstrated in a few automobiles but never produced in volume because of its weight and unreliability.

Kettering proposed to make the air-cooled engine commercially feasible by using copper for the fins that cooled the engine. Copper had ten times the heat conductivity of iron (the only material used in previous air-cooled engines) and was far lighter and more malleable. However, it contracted and expanded at different temperatures than iron. The key challenge was getting the metals to bond and remain intact during real-world temperature and driving conditions.

"Boss" Kettering had actually begun experimental work on the concept in 1918 at the Delco laboratories in Dayton, Ohio. On December 2, 1920, only a day after Durant's exit, he told Pierre du Pont that it was near commercialization. The engine's advantages, he proclaimed, were clear: It was 200 pounds lighter and used 25 percent fewer moving parts than the traditional engine. In addition, it was more fuel efficient and would neither freeze in winter nor overheat in summer, regardless of how severe the conditions. Kettering suggested that a small number of pilot cars be built and tested. If the testing went well, he assured the new president, 1,500 to 2,000 cars with the engine (soon called "the copper-cooled engine" because of the copper fins) could be on the market by summer of 1921.

Pierre, well aware that 1921 was going to be a disastrous year for sales and earnings, was excited. As Sloan later noted, "If it fulfilled all these promises, it would revolutionize the industry."[2] Pierre du Pont gave Kettering the green light with no hesitation.

In du Pont's eyes, Kettering's engine was the magic bullet for regaining market momentum. Chevrolet in particular was in need of a serious upgrade to its aging 490 model if it were ever to have a chance at eating away the Model T's sales lead. On December 7, just five days after Kettering's report, Pierre took Sloan and several other executives to Dayton to see the engine's progress firsthand. According to Sloan, enthusiasm was so high that it was agreed informally during the trip that if Kettering's engine worked, it should become the standard engine for the Chevrolet 490's replacement next year.

Chevrolet field management, however, was not informed of the discussion. As development work continued in Dayton, the Chevrolet team grew dubious of the cost and complexity of retooling for production of the experimental new engine. Chevrolet proceeded on its own to develop an improved version of the 490's traditional water-cooled engine.

In January 1921, a formal study was ordered of the merits of the 490's water-cooled engine versus the copper-cooled engine. To Kettering's chagrin and Chevrolet management's delight, it concluded that the copper-cooled engine could *not* be commercialized for more than another year.

Kettering and du Pont remained enthusiastic, however. Just two weeks after the study team's report, the executive committee approved development of a six-cylinder version of the Chevrolet copper-cooled engine for the Oakland car line. This time, Sloan expressed doubts on the record but developmental work proceeded. Meanwhile, Chevrolet management voiced concern that while the copper-cooled engine was being shoved down their throat by the executive committee, Buick and Cadillac were being left alone to do their own design and engineering. The absent voice of Billy Durant and his insistence on operational independence was already echoing through the halls.

Kettering was actually conducting his pilot test program independently of Chevrolet. Meanwhile, Pierre du Pont ruled that as soon as the staggering inventory of 150,000 Chevrolet 490s was sold, Chevrolet was to convert completely to the copper-cooled engine (even though testing was still not validated). Chevrolet was ordered to be ready for production by May 1922.

As it turned out, Pierre had made a near-fatal mistake common to hundreds of other seemingly brilliant CEOs: He let his own confidence in the project (plus his own strategy's reliance on it) to deafen him to others' doubts and blind him to the possibility of failure. As he wrote in a letter to Kettering while work proceeded in Dayton:

> Now that we are at the point of planning production of the new cars I am beginning to feel like a small boy when the long-expected circus posters begin to appear on the fence, and to wonder how each part of the circus is to appear and what act I will like best.[3]

The Oakland version of the copper-cooled engine was scheduled to be launched in January 1922, but Kettering did not send the first pilot car to the Oakland engineering team in Pontiac, Michigan, for its own testing and validation until October 1921. The report from the Oakland team was devastating:

> With the changes that are necessary to make this a real job, it is going to be impossible to get into production in the time specified; in fact, to get this car to the point where, after all tests are complete and we are ready to put our OK on same, it will take at least six months.
>
> To bridge the time when the present allotment of the old models are completed, which will be about Dec. 15th, and the time we bring in

the Air Cooled car, we are planning on bringing in a complete new water-cooled line . . .[4]

This was another slap from the operating side at both Kettering and the president of the corporation. Within days, the management of the other car divisions chimed in to defend Oakland's position.

Kettering stated openly that he was under personal attack. On at least one score he was right: Pierre was the only colleague outside of Dayton, Ohio, to reassure him that the project and his position were still sound.

FROM STANDOFF TO NEAR MELTDOWN

Alfred Sloan also continued to grow more and more frustrated, just as he had the previous summer when he saw Billy Durant's management style leading General Motors to disaster. While Alfred dared not defy Pierre, and while he respected Kettering and valued his talent, he knew that Chevrolet desperately needed to get a new car ready for market, fast. Finally, in December 1921, he emerged as the peacemaker and compromiser, proposing simultaneous development of the Chevrolet division's own "new" water-cooled replacement for the 490 alongside development of the copper-cooled car.

All parties agreed to the Sloan compromise. However, three months later, Chevrolet's general manager, Karl W. Zimmershied, resigned as bickering and backstabbing continued behind the scenes. Zimmershied had worked tirelessly to develop an improved version of the water-cooled 409 while dealing with the copper-cooled challenge, to the point where colleagues at the time reported him collapsing from exhaustion. He was replaced by Pierre du Pont himself, who now had three separate titles (chairman and president of General Motors and general manager of Chevrolet).

Pierre already knew who would really run Chevrolet, however: William K. Knudsen, who had become a legend in the industry after organizing the production layout of all of Ford Motor Company's regional assembly plants. Knudsen (like so many others) had finally had one rift too many with Henry Ford and resigned in the spring of 1921. Within days, he was hired by Alfred Sloan. Pierre quickly became Knudsen's biggest fan after Knudsen toured the Dayton facilities and announced his confidence in the copper-cooled engine. He made Knudsen vice president of operations for Chevrolet (for the time being) and made it clear that the launch of the copper-cooled Chevrolet was his top priority.

Even Knudsen was soon disillusioned, however. As he began ramping up production, beginning with ten cars a day with a target of fifty a day by year-end, the U.S. vehicle market began a strong recovery from the 1920 recession. With even the aging Chevrolet 490 suddenly selling again, a great marketing opportunity was being missed. Accordingly, it was decided to continue on Sloan's compromise of parallel water-cooled and copper-cooled production programs. When Knudsen emphasized the need to proceed with more caution on the copper-cooled version, Kettering only became more convinced that the Chevrolet team was deliberately dragging its feet.

The copper-cooled Chevrolet was finally unveiled at the New York Automobile Show on January 23, 1923. The press marveled at the technology, but Knudsen and his team were finding the car much more difficult to assemble in volume than anyone had anticipated. Early customers also soon filed dozens of complaints about the engine's reliability and performance. Meanwhile, car sales in general soared to new records.

By the end of spring, not even Pierre du Pont could deny that the copper-cooled car had become an irreversible disaster. On May 10, Pierre resigned as president of General Motors (but stayed on as chairman of the board) and was replaced by his own candidate, Alfred P. Sloan, Jr. Less than a month later, all copper-cooled Chevrolet cars were recalled by the company: the industry's first official recall. In the end, a total of just 759 copper-cooled Chevrolets were produced. Of these, 239 were scrapped before they ever reached dealerships. Only 300 were actually sold to retail customers.

With the recall, Kettering wrote Sloan a personal letter expressing his desire to take his copper-cooled engine design to another manufacturer and blaming all its problems on the vehicle divisions. Four days later, he submitted his resignation from General Motors.

Sloan, however, was still eager to keep Kettering's talent, despite the fiasco. He appeased him by offering to allow him to continue development work on the engine under a new and separate organization headed and run by Kettering himself. Kettering would also retain his position as head of all corporate research and advanced engineering.

Assured of a free hand, Kettering agreed to stay on. To everyone's relief, his own focus quickly shifted from the copper-cooled engine to other projects that would prove to be truly revolutionary in the areas of paint, fuel, and diesel engine technology.

In his typical style, Sloan quickly put the episode behind him to focus on more urgent issues. As he wrote in *My Years with General Motors*:

> The copper-cooled car never came up again in a big way. It just died out, I don't know why. The great boom was on, and meeting the demand for cars and meeting the competition with improved water-cooled car designs absorbed our attentions and energies.[5]

DEFYING THE CONSULTANTS TO SAVE CHEVROLET

Shortly after giving Kettering the green light to proceed with the doomed copper-cooled engine in December 1920, Pierre du Pont also authorized what he thought would be a thorough and objective evaluation of the corporation's operations. Like many chief executive officers thrust into the Big Job without having prepared for it (and with no operating experience in the auto industry), he turned to outside consultants as well as a few trusted insiders for new ideas.

As would also be the case with so many other CEOs, what the consultants suggested was hardly what the troops wanted to hear. As Alfred Sloan recounted it, "someone" commissioned an outside study at the end of 1920 that concluded with the recommendation to *kill* the Chevrolet brand and operating division, the company's only presence in the low end of the market. Sloan vigorously led the opposition, taking his case directly to du Pont.

In the end, Alfred's view held sway over the advice of the consultants. His own description of the episode remains a fitting admonition to those who would turn to outside "experts" in time of crisis:

> At the time Mr. du Pont became president, someone had the idea of having a survey made of the General Motors properties, with recommendations as to what might be done in the way of a reconstruction program. The job was entrusted to a firm of consulting engineers of

high standing. The most illuminating recommendation was that the whole Chevrolet operation should be liquidated. There was no chance to make it a profitable business. We could not hope to compete. I was much upset because I feared the prestige of the authors might overcome our arguments to the contrary. So I went to Mr. du Pont and told him what we thought we might accomplish if we built a good product and sold it aggressively. We urged upon him the fact that many more people always could buy low-priced cars than Cadillacs and even Buicks. That it was an insult to say we could not compete with anyone. It was a case of ability and hard work. "Forget the report. We will go ahead and see what we can do." Mr. du Pont was always that way. He had the courage of his convictions. Facts were the only things that counted. So Chevrolet was saved and General Motors avoided what would have been a catastrophe.[6]

Chevrolet in fact went on to transform itself into the company's largest division and the one that ultimately beat Henry Ford. Under the leadership of William Knudsen, the man who had quit Ford only to be hired by Sloan, Chevrolet overtook the Ford brand as the U.S. sales leader in 1927. One can only speculate on how General Motors would have competed had the recommendation of those outside experts been accepted.

DECENTRALIZED OPERATIONS WITH COORDINATED CONTROL

The decision to stick with Chevrolet demonstrated to all insiders that Alfred Sloan had Pierre's confidence when it came to operations, despite Pierre's commitment to the copper-cooled engine over the divisions' objections. Sloan also knew that Pierre shared his view regarding the need for a new organizational structure and set of controls to make Billy's baby function. On December 30, 1920, less than a month after the copper-cooled engine project was approved, the board of directors unanimously approved Sloan's reorganization plan, which was basically the same one he had presented to Durant more than a year earlier.

An entire chapter of *My Years with General Motors* is devoted to the Sloan concept of corporate organization, which came to be known as "decentralized operations with coordinated control." As simple as it sounds today, it was unprecedented at the time. As its merit was demonstrated by the success of Sloan's management team, it was soon copied not only by companies of all sizes in all kinds of industries but by nonprofit organizations and even some government agencies.

At the concept's heart was the delegation of decision making to operating divisions and field managers while at the same time holding them to clear and distinct performance objectives. Functional staffs were established under the central office to assist the divisions and remove administrative burden to the greatest extent possible. Finally, a group of policy committees was created whose membership included both division management and top members of the corporate executive and finance committees (as appropriate) to resolve turf issues, establish priorities and targets, and coordinate the allocation of resources.

Alfred's network of policy committees dealt primarily with technological, manufacturing, sales, purchasing, and advertising issues. Top leadership of the operating units was represented on each committee, and each one's monthly agenda was determined by current issues that required immediate decision and emerging issues that warranted analysis before the decision point was reached. Each committee was also provided a staff whose function was to gather input from the business units in setting the agenda and setting the analysis in motion. This policy committee structure endured at General Motors until the 1990s.

Sloan's description of the decentralization-and-coordination concept in *Adventures of a White Collar Man,* published in 1941, remains a litmus test for all kinds of organizations today that are struggling to remain agile, efficient, and effective in a world of constant technological change and globalization. Despite the current emphasis on "flat" and "matrixed" organizations rather than the "silos" of the Sloan organization chart, the key elements of Sloan's model are still followed across the globe: Indeed, many companies have ended up either returning to it or borrowing from it.

Sloan's starting point is decentralized business units:

> The first step was to determine whether we would operate under a centralized or decentralized form of administration. Decentralization was analogous to free enterprise. By that is meant that we would set

up each of our various operations as an integral unit, complete unto itself.[7]

The key advantage of decentralization, in Sloan's view, was that it encouraged initiative and creativity at the local level while limiting the individual power and control of central office executives:

> We realized that in an institution as big as General Motors was even then, to say nothing of what we hoped to make it, any plan that involved too great a concentration of problems upon a limited number of executives would limit initiative, would involve delay, would increase expense, and would reduce efficiency and development. Further, it would mean an autocracy, which is just as dangerous in a great industrial organization as it is in a government; aside from the question as to whether any limited number of executives could deal with so many diversified problems, in so many places, promptly and efficiently.[8]

From there, the core question was how to define and divide the units. After that came the mechanism for coordination:

> I would say that my concept of the management scheme of a great industrial organization, simply expressed, is to divide it into as many parts as consistently can be done, place in charge of each part the most capable executive that can be found, develop a system of coordination so that each part may strengthen and support each other part; thus not only welding all parts together in the common interests of a joint enterprise, but importantly developing ability and initiative through the instrumentalities of responsibility and ambition—developing men and giving them an opportunity to exercise their talents, both in their own interests as well as in that of the business.
>
> To formalize this scheme, I worked out what we speak of in industry as an organization chart. It shows how the business functions from the standpoint of the relationship of the different units, one to another, as well as the authority delegated to the executives, also in relation to one another. I grouped together those operations which had a common relationship, and I placed over each such group for coordinating purposes what I termed a Group Executive. These group executives were the only ones that reported to me. Then I developed a General Staff similar in name and purpose to what exists in the army. The general staff was on a functional basis: engineering, distribution, legal, financial

affairs, and so on. Each of these functions was presided over by a vice president, the purpose being two-fold: first, to perform those functions that could be done more effectively by one activity in the interests of the whole; and, second, to coordinate the functional activities of the different operating units as well as to promote their effectiveness.[9]

Again, none of it sounds radical or revolutionary today, but it was all untested theory back in 1920 (except for the control and staff structures that the DuPont company had adopted during wartime on a much smaller scale). General Motors' weakened financial and competitive position at the time provided the perfect laboratory for testing and validating Sloan's concepts and repudiating everything about the way the company had run under Billy Durant.

In the end, however, Sloan (like Billy Durant) knew that General Motors' success or failure would be determined by the caliber of his leadership team, regardless of how ingenious his organization chart and road map might prove to be. Unlike Billy, however, Alfred had the genius for knowing when to give his lieutenants free rein, when to push them harder, and when to rein them in: all without making them jealous of one another and without offending them or damaging their egos the way Billy had Walter Chrysler's.

While it was crucial to give executives clear lines of responsibility and accountability, it was also crucial to consult and involve them in the decisions that affected their business (another point that Billy Durant so often ignored). In Sloan's mind, that was the real lesson of the copper-cooled engine. Part of the art of being CEO was to make sure that the cooperation, agreement, and integration that were implied between the neat lines of the organization chart were in fact a way of life. It was an art that Sloan mastered; but for succeeding generations in all industries, decentralization with coordination would be more difficult to adhere to as the competitive environment and the definition of self-fulfillment changed among customers as well as employees.

HENRY FORD MISSES A SEA CHANGE IN THE MARKET

As the Sloan leadership team struggled in the market while dealing with the copper-cooled engine and a corporate reorganization, Henry

Ford was riding high. With General Motors selling only one Chevrolet for every thirteen Model Ts that Ford Motor sold in 1923, Henry saw no threat. In his mind, there was absolutely no need to alter the Model T, which was essentially the same car as the one launched in 1908. Nor was there any need for more Ford models in the market. Anyone who dared suggest differently was inviting Henry's wrath.

William Knudsen, who went on to lead Chevrolet in its sales triumph over Ford, was one of the few who dared speak up to Henry Ford and take his anger. Having left his native Denmark for America alone and in his teens, Knudsen had learned to use his fists to survive on the streets of New York. He had gone on to use both his size (six feet tall, 200 pounds) and his reputation as a fighter to master the art of employee relations as a foreman in a steel mill in Buffalo, New York. When Henry Ford bought that company, he insisted that Knudsen come with the deal because of his skill at "handling" men and organizing production. After rising to the position of head of Ford manufacturing in less than seven years, Knudsen was more respected by Henry than any other Ford Motor executive.

When Knudsen dared suggest the Model T may have seen its day, however, he immediately lost his place on Henry's A-list. Knudsen, like Sloan and Durant, saw a need for a variety of models, despite the Model T's continued dominance of the low end of the market. He was also concerned about the inefficiency of the large manufacturing plant Ford built (with the help of a federal contract) near Dearborn's Rouge River. By then, the Rouge complex employed more than 80,000 people. It was so huge that some of the engineering and production functions were separated by miles of walkways, defeating the purpose of centralizing all steps of production in one place.

Early in 1921, Knudsen boldly presented Ford with a design for a new car to replace the Model T. It was summarily rejected by Ford, and Knudsen never brought up the subject with him again. Henry did not express any hint of doubt in Knudsen's abilities, but Knudsen soon found his own orders and directions on the production floor being altered and even remanded behind his back by Ford Motor's founder and owner.

This was the last straw for Knudsen. When he resigned from Ford Motor Company on April 1, 1921, he had no idea where he would go next.[10] Less than a month later, he was hired by Alfred Sloan (whom he had met and done business with when Hyatt Roller

Bearing was a major Ford supplier); less than two years after that, he was in charge of all Chevrolet operations.

Not surprisingly, Henry Ford's own version of Knudsen's departure from Ford Motor Company indirectly validated Knudsen's frustration. Blaming the resignation on Knudsen's own need for control rather than differences over product philosophy and policy, Henry was not shy to declare that he would tolerate no second-guessing from anyone. At a business dinner just a few weeks after Knudsen's resignation, he relayed the following story to a friend seated at his table:

> Mr. Knudsen was too strong for me to handle. You see, this is my business. I built it and, as long as I live, I propose to run it the way I want it run. I woke up one morning to the realization that I was exhausting my energy fighting Mr. Knudsen to get things done the way I wanted them done, instead of fighting the opposition. I let him go, not because he wasn't good, but because he was too good—for me. Now I can concentrate my energies.[11]

While Sloan and company (including Knudsen) worked to coordinate and differentiate the maze of brands, car models, and operations that Billy Durant had brought under the General Motors umbrella, Henry Ford's energies became concentrated even more on the Model T and the Rouge production complex, which was by now the world's largest and most vertically integrated manufacturing operation of any kind.

Ford's goal was nothing less than to control all raw materials and components himself, even if they could be attained at lower price from outside suppliers. He bought coal mines in Kentucky and rubber forests in Brazil, where he built a jungle community that he envisioned as a utopia and called Fordlandia. With his Rouge complex, where he boasted that coal and iron ore entered from ships at one end of the plant and left as automobiles at the other, he drove the concept of vertical integration to the point of absurdity, eventually making it a cost burden rather than a competitive advantage when demand for the Model T finally tapered off because of the rising popularity of what Alfred Sloan and company offered the consumer.

Ford didn't see that engineering improvements and innovations among his competition were inevitably eroding the Model T's appeal, regardless of how low he drove the price through mass production. Nor did he understand the way the industry's growth was restructuring the market. Alfred Sloan did.

By 1923, most people buying a new car had already owned one and were looking for more convenience, comfort, and performance in the new purchase. For those people looking for the bare-bones basic transportation that was the essence of the Model T, there was a new alternative: the used-car market. Dealers were also now accepting trade-ins of used cars toward the purchase of new ones, which added to the used-car pool and put more price pressure on the Model T, at the same time it made all types of new cars easier to buy.

On top of this, more and more buyers were choosing to purchase new cars through the retail financing plan that General Motors had pioneered with the General Motors Acceptance Corporation (GMAC) in 1919. Before then, only a few small manufacturers and regional dealer groups had offered automobile financing. Yet Henry Ford still refused to assist his dealers with a financing arm the way General Motors did. Ford buyers had to either pay cash or get a bank loan, which meant more red tape as well as a higher interest rate than GMAC offered. By 1926, thanks largely to GMAC, three out of every four cars in the United States were bought through financing rather than hard cash. That year, only thirteen of the more than 130,000 banks in the country had more money available to lend than GMAC.

A CAR FOR EVERY PURSE AND PURPOSE

Henry Ford's blindness to the changing consumer and the changing market played right into the hand of Alfred Sloan as he worked through the process of weeding out the losers from the potential winners in the mix of brands Billy Durant had acquired for the General. Alfred, like Billy before him, understood that people viewed the automobile as more than a transportation machine. They viewed it as a statement and reflection of their own status and aspirations. The kind of car they owned made a clear statement about who they were and where they were going on the social and economic ladder. They also expected the experience of driving and riding in that car to be comfortable and enjoyable: two criteria not high on Henry Ford's list of priorities.

Sloan developed a product strategy targeted at buyers' specific aspirations. Its essence was to divide the market into price segments and offer cars with the most appeal and value in each segment. Sloan called it "a car for every purse and purpose," a phrase he coined in the 1924 annual report's letter to stockholders. No General Motors vehicle division or brand would compete against any other in any of the segments; each was to have a distinct identity and appeal to a distinct buyer. And, as buyers' purchasing power and aspirations changed, General Motors would keep them as customers by offering what they wanted on the next rung of the price ladder.

While Henry Ford stuck with his Model T, General Motors proceeded to develop and offer a full range of products to appeal to the aspirations and pocketbooks of all buyers. With Chevrolet covering the low end of the market, the divisional price ladder ascended to Cadillac at the high end, with Pontiac (which replaced Oakland in 1925), Oldsmobile, and Buick filling out the price ladder.

In the 1920s, General Motors (and Chevrolet in particular) built so much momentum under Sloan's "car for every purse and purpose" strategy that Henry Ford was finally forced to acknowledge that the Model T had outlived its time. His engineers developed a new car (only one) called the Model A to replace it. Design, engineering, and retooling began in 1927 for a 1928 product launch. However, because so much of Ford's production capacity was concentrated at the massive Rouge complex, Henry had to shut down the entire operation while machinery was retooled for the new car.

With Ford out of production, General Motors had a unique window of opportunity: a virtually open market, which it eagerly seized. Once again, the numbers tell the story. In 1925, the Chevrolet division sold 341,000 cars in the United States, compared to more than 1,250,000 sold by Ford Motor Company. In 1927, when the Rouge plant shut down, Chevrolet dramatically took the lead, selling 647,810 cars compared to Ford's 393,424. General Motors' total sales that year, including trucks, were more than double those of Ford Motor Company.[12]

CHAPTER FIFTEEN

From Transformation to Domination

SLOAN'S GENERAL MOTORS continued to pull steadily ahead of both Ford Motor and the Chrysler Corporation, which had emerged by the end of the 1920s as the only other strong competitor in the low- and mid-priced market segments. Along the way, the General pioneered several costly innovations that Ford resisted but which customers proved eager to pay for, even during the Great Depression. Among them were:

- Duco paint (developed in cooperation with DuPont), which greatly reduced the drying time of traditional automotive paint and expanded the range of possible colors and shades

- Leaded gasoline (sold under the Ethyl brand, developed in cooperation with DuPont and marketed through a subsidiary created in cooperation with Standard Oil), which eliminated engine knock and enabled development of far more powerful and efficient high-compression engines

- Independent front-wheel suspension, which drastically reduced the impact on a driver or passenger's derriere when a wheel hit a bump or hole in the road

- Crankshaft ventilation, which expanded the time between engine oil changes from 500 miles to 2,000 miles of driving

- Electric turn signals

- Electric windshield wipers

- Fully automatic transmissions, which eliminated the challenge of coordinating hand and foot with clutch, brake, and accelerator

While Charles Kettering and his research laboratories shifted their focus to these kinds of innovations that enhanced the entire lineup's convenience, comfort, and performance (as opposed to revolutionizing the internal combustion engine, as Kettering had thought he had with the copper-cooled adventure), the General also pioneered and mastered the art of automotive design.

A NEW PARADIGM FOR PRODUCT DESIGN

Prior to 1926, the look of volume-production cars had taken second seat to their function (as Henry Ford wanted it to). Bodies were created and altered by engineers with no training or interest in design or aesthetics and who viewed the car's body as the cover to put on top of its mechanics. If buyers wanted more in the look of their cars, they could special-order it without the body and have a body custom-made to their likes.

One of these custom body shops in Los Angeles, California, whose customers were (not surprisingly) primarily Hollywood stars, was run by a Stanford University design graduate named Harley Earl. In 1926, the Cadillac division's general manager, Lawrence Fisher (one of the seven Fisher brothers who founded Fisher Body), hired Earl on contract to design the body for a new model, called the LaSalle, scheduled to be launched the following year.

The LaSalle was the first volume-produced American automobile to be designed from the ground up by a designer rather than a team of engineers. It was also the first developed from a "clean sheet of paper" rather than through incremental changes to models already on the market. It was longer and lower to the ground than any preceding model and featured "flying wing" fenders that flowed gracefully into the running boards. Most strikingly, all its corners were rounded, in contrast to previous models' sharp edges.

Launched in March 1927, the LaSalle was a market hit. More important to the future of the entire industry, Alfred Sloan was so impressed with the LaSalle's distinctive look that he hired Earl full-time, enticing him to Detroit with an offer to let him create his own staff and design the full General Motors lineup. Initially called the Art and Colour Section, Earl's staff was the first of its kind in the industry.

Not surprisingly, there was initial resistance from the vehicle brands and divisions to having the design of their products dictated by a staff that reported to the CEO rather than to them. Sloan was well aware of the natural tension and went out of his way to ensure that Harley Earl worked directly with each division's engineering teams as designs were developed, in sharp contrast to the way Kettering had developed the copper-cooled engine.

For his part, Harley Earl was just as stubborn as Kettering when it came to defending his ideas. Fortunately, what his team came up with easily won division approval once personal relationships and informal networks between the two teams were established at lower levels. By the end of the 1920s, all General Motors brands and models were not only distinct from each other, they stood out immediately from the competition. For the next thirty years, General Motors was the undisputed leader in automotive design.

THE ANNUAL MODEL CHANGE

Along with the concepts of distinctive brands and design, Sloan added the annual model change to the mix. This concept had greater impact on the auto industry and General Motors' own momentum than his organizational concept.

Traditionally, technical advances that were not visible to the customer or did not require radical redesign of the chassis or power train were introduced without fanfare as they were developed. In line with his vision of buyers who wanted their cars to make a statement about personal status and aspirations, Sloan introduced the idea of not only launching technical innovations on a regular cadence but also changing the look of each model at the same time.

There was again initial opposition from the vehicle divisions, but Sloan allowed the differences to be aired openly through the executive committee and the product policy and general sales committees, which had been established as part of the 1921 reorganization. Rather than dictate a specific deadline for each division to adopt the annual model change, he allowed it to evolve into consensus over a period of three years as the pace of technical improvement accelerated and as Earl's styling changes won support in the marketplace as well as within the company.

The annual model policy was adopted by Chevrolet in 1928, when Ford Motor was finally on the defensive. After that, it soon became official corporate policy without Sloan ever issuing a formal mandate. As Sloan later described it:

> When we did formulate it [the annual model change] I cannot say. It was a matter of evolution. Eventually the fact that we made yearly changes, and the recognition of the necessity of the change, forced us into regularizing change. When change became regularized, sometime in the 1930s, we began to speak of annual models. I do not believe the elder Mr. Ford ever really cared for the idea. Anyway his Model A, which he brought out in 1928, as fine a little car as it was in its time, it seems to me was another expression of his concept of a static-model utility car.[1]

By the end of the 1930s, not only General Motors customers but people who still only dreamed of owning a car (especially adolescent boys) looked forward to the official unveiling of the General's new models as a major event. When Alfred Sloan finally stepped down as chairman of the board in 1956, dealerships all across the country were hyping each year's new model launch event as if it were a country fair, with free hot dogs and other giveaways.

By then, the concept of the annual model change had been adopted even by Ford Motor and the much smaller and more resource-strapped Chrysler Corporation. The concept endured until the late 1970s, when there were so many competing models

that the costs of annual retooling and reengineering were prohibi-
tive even for General Motors.

BEYOND THE UNITED STATES

While forging an entirely new structure and strategy in the United
States, Alfred quietly yet aggressively expanded General Motors'
overseas network far beyond the founder's vision, shifting the focus
from exports to local manufacture in key markets, particularly Europe and Asia.

General Motors had begun exporting vehicles from the United
States in 1911 from an operation called GM Export. GM Export
began in an office in New York City staffed by three people with a
working budget of $10,000. In its first year, it sold 1,200 vehicles.
Next year, that number tripled. By 1920, Billy Durant's last year
with General Motors, it had grown to 30,000.

By 1923, the year Alfred Sloan became president of General Motors, the General's cars and trucks were being sold in 125 different
countries, including many that were to throw General Motors out
during World War II and the Cold War years only to later welcome
the General back in the 1990s (e.g., China, Indonesia, India, Russia,
and all of Central Europe). Between the years 1923 and 1928, Sloan
opened nineteen new assembly plants in fifteen different countries
in Europe, South America, mainland Asia, Australia, and Africa.

In 1924, Sloan made a run at acquiring the British automaker
Austin, then balked because he felt GM's management was
stretched thin and he was not impressed with the Austin management team (which later built the famous Austin Healey line of
sports cars). In 1925, General Motors bought the U.K. automaker
Vauxhall, which at the time was a leader in larger cars, but allowed
it to continue operating as an independent brand and manufacturer.

In 1926, General Motors Japan was established in the city of
Kobe. From the late 1920s right up until Japan's attack on Pearl Harbor on December 7, 1941, GM Japan was the number-one automotive manufacturer and seller in Japan. During the period 1927–1939,
it consistently accounted for more than 42 percent of Japan's vehicle
market. This was a greater share than General Motors had in the
U.S. market at the time: a situation that was to dramatically flip-flop
by the end of the twentieth century, in part because of the prohibi-

tion of U.S. companies from manufacturing automobiles in Japan after World War II and in part because of the lack of import restrictions in the States.

In 1929, the General acquired a car company in Germany that traced its roots to sewing machines: Adam Opel. Led by the five sons of its colorful founder, Opel was stretched for capital at the same time the five brothers faced the impending payment of enormous inheritance taxes. Their answer was to sell to the hungry General. Under General Motors' ownership, Opel was left largely on its own to adapt its manufacturing and marketing as local conditions required. It was soon one of Europe's largest automakers. Opel's series of transformations from sewing-machine maker to bicycle maker to carmaker had made it an icon in Germany. All Europeans came to identify the Opel name with engineering innovation, but few identified it with General Motors.

Sloan also instituted a global policy of hiring and promoting managers and executives from the country where operations were based, rather than assigning Americans to all key positions. As explained in GM Export's 1927 annual report, it was a precursor of the global hiring and staffing policies many companies now espouse:

> In many countries General Motors is coming to be looked upon as an integral part of the basic industrial life of those countries. There is not one American in the entire organization of Vauxhall Motors, Ltd., in London. The daily business of the office in Osaka is conducted by Japanese, and the native workers are carrying on their jobs under native foremen. The tendency to employ local personnel, and to promote this personnel into a position of responsibility and authority as far as it qualifies, is present everywhere. It is definitely General Motors' policy to award the job to the man who merits it, whatever his nationality.

NONAUTOMOTIVE FORAYS AND LEGACIES

While Sloan's primary focus was always the automobile business, he was also willing (like Billy Durant) to take limited risks in other businesses that were young and promising. One of these was aviation.

In the early 1920s, Alfred integrated a string of small acquisitions into a subsidiary called North American Aviation Corporation, which not only built airframes and engines but included several airline routes. Those holdings included operations that eventually became the core of both Trans World Airlines (TWA) and Eastern Airlines, which were among America's largest, most efficient, and most profitable airlines in the 1970s but are largely forgotten today. By the late 1940s, the General had (wisely) sold most of its aviation assets at a profit. Sloan saw the specter of government regulation and the huge capital requirements for commercial airplanes and routes as unwarranted diversions of both capital and management talent from the core car and truck business.

He also saw potential in one of the industries that the automobile was actually displacing: railway locomotives. General Motors almost stumbled into the locomotive business because of yet another of "Boss" Kettering's new ideas, but it ended up dominating the industry. In 1928, Sloan gave Kettering the green light to proceed with development of what Kettering described as a revolutionary two-stroke diesel engine (shades of the copper-cooled engine adventure). Within two years, Kettering's team had perfected a new diesel engine that weighed one-fifth as much as commercial diesels of that time but produced the same amount of power.

General Motors demonstrated the new technology at the 1933 Chicago World's Fair, using it to operate a full-scale Chevrolet assembly line displayed on the exhibit floor. The president of the Burlington Railroad, Ralph Budd, saw the display and immediately placed an order for a 600-horsepower GM diesel to power his latest locomotive, the streamlined, futuristic Pioneer Zephyr. Union Pacific followed suit and by the end of the 1930s, General Motors was the leading producer of locomotive engines. The GM two-stroke diesel sealed the end of the steam era for railroading and also opened up fuel-miserly diesel technology to dozens of applications (including large trucks and boats) that had been unthinkable because of the bulk and weight of earlier diesels.

FINANCIAL (AND OTHER) CONTROLS

Further repudiating Billy Durant's business philosophy and management style, Sloan also established a system of direct and indirect financial controls in the core U.S. market to ensure that his executives would have a vested interest in the performance of both their own business units and the corporation.

First came the concept of "standard volume," a phrase coined by Donaldson Brown, a DuPont finance executive dispatched by Pierre du Pont in 1921 to serve as General Motors' finance vice president (reporting to John Raskob, who was elevated to treasurer). Brown's definition of standard volume was the optimum production capacity utilization needed to guarantee an acceptable profit and return on investment in both up cycles and down cycles. It was an elaborate formula predicated on accurate sales projections: one more exercise that no one else in the industry had ever done.

One of the key lessons of the 1920 crisis was that the company needed clearer and more accurate data on actual and projected retail sales to manage its production and inventories and avoid a similar crisis in the future. Before 1921, all U.S. car manufacturers had relied on their own wholesale sales to dealers and the dealers' own less-than-rigorous retail sales forecasts to determine production volume. That year, at Brown's suggestion, General Motors began instituting a system of ten-day sales reports from the field. Brown and his staff also devised their own system of sales forecasts based on the data as well as the staff's own analysis of a myriad of other indicators, including the federal government's economic reports and the company's own consumer research.

Rather than rely on vehicle-division sales executives or the dealers, who had a vested interest in making things look better than an objective researcher might, Brown approached the highly respected independent research firm R. L. Polk and Company to compile the data. In an unprecedented show of magnanimity, General Motors agreed to pay R. L. Polk to gather all data on its own sales and issue ten-day reports that were then made available at no charge to the rest of the industry. Over time, the same ten-day reporting system was adopted by all other manufacturers and was incorporated into the federal government's own index of key economic indicators.

The General's ten-day sales reports were also distributed to division management and dealers to let them know how they were doing compared to each other and the rest of the corporation. More important, Brown and his staff used the ten-day sales data in compiling detailed forecasts. These forecasts in turn were used to determine production levels at each plant under the standard-volume production formula.

According to the standard-volume theory, if General Motors knew where the market was going and constantly adjusted production to maintain a predetermined overall capacity utilization target, it could generate a constant profit and return on investment regardless of how the market fluctuated. Brown knew that his formula would mean loss of potential incremental sales during boom times and that it would add stress and uncertainty to daily life in the plants, with monthly production quotas constantly fluctuating in line with the sales forecasts. However, he was also certain that if the General stuck to the formula, it would not be caught with excess inventory and would remain profitable during even the worst downturns.

To the delight of stockholders, Brown's theory proved correct. Plant managers and production workers were not as thrilled, however. Uncertainty as to when people would be laid off or pressured to increase their output led to a work environment at the plants that was, to say the least, far more tense than the one Billy Durant had created in Flint.

To keep all division executives and managers on their toes, Brown's staff also compiled monthly competitive analyses of each business unit's performance. Each unit received a summary report ranking it against all others on such measures as product quality, revenue, and return on investment. Those executives and managers who wanted to climb the corporate ladder had a clear incentive to keep their return-on-investment numbers moving higher. Those whose numbers were near the bottom knew they had best not let them stay there long if they valued their own careers. The reports enhanced the efficiency of the entire corporation (while adding another element of stress to the daily work environment) and continued to be issued by the central office to all units until the 1960s.

To put even more fire in the bellies of his field leadership, Sloan always carried what he called his "little black book," which listed each unit's latest forecast as well as its historical performance and its competitive position vis-à-vis other units of the corporation. Whenever he visited the units, he would refer to the little black book at least once during his conversation with local management.

In the case of dealers, Alfred did not flash the little black book, but he loved to grill them about their business. He also used the dealers as another gauge not only of the market but the competency of his executive team and its decisions. As Sloan put it:

I made it a practice throughout the 1920s and early thirties to make personal visits to dealers. I fitted up a private railroad car as an office and in the company of several associates went into almost every city in the United States, visiting from five to ten dealers a day. I would meet them in their own places of business, talk with them across their own desks in their "closing rooms" and ask them for suggestions and criticism concerning their relations with the corporation, the character of the product, the corporation's policies, the trend of consumer demand, their view of the future, and many other things of interest in the business. I made careful notes of all the points that came up, and when I got back home I studied them.[2]

ATTRACTING, DEVELOPING, AND HOLDING THE BEST TALENT AT ALL LEVELS

While Sloan's own attention was focused on the management team and the dealer network, he was also aware of the need to attract and develop talent at all levels, especially in technical and supervisory areas. With the company's employment roster growing from 80,612 people in 1920 to 175,666 in 1927 and 233,286 in 1929, the need was especially acute for plant supervisors and engineers who were in tune with the latest technology and techniques and capable of taking on further responsibilities.

To meet the need, the General Motors Institute (GMI) was established in Flint in 1926. Both day and evening courses were offered for employees living in the Flint area, with extension courses designed by GMI faculty made available to all others at no cost to the employees. In addition, a co-op program was started for entry-level employees seeking a career in engineering. GMI technical students and engineering graduates immediately developed a special sense of loyalty to the organization. Over time, GMI became an accredited university. Its engineering graduates were unique in the industry because of their hands-on training with real-world equipment and problems as well as theory.

To instill loyalty in the top executive ranks, where Alfred was focused most, a special block of 2,250,000 shares of GM common stock was sold by Pierre du Pont and John Jakob Raskob to the corporation in 1923 for resale at market price to its top eighty executives. The amount of stock each executive bought was determined by Sloan. Payment was made partly in cash and partly in "contributions" from their compensation. While the program was technically voluntary, no one declined to participate after Alfred met privately with each executive to explain how many shares he would be entitled to and why it was a great deal.

Sloan's real intent was to make the executives feel and *act* like owners rather than employees, with their own personal fortunes tied directly to the company's performance. Unlike later executive stock option bonus plans, the shares were bought with each person's own money rather than awarded by the corporation in the form of option grants. If the General's performance and its stock price declined, so did the executive's wealth, regardless of salary and bonus. Again, the concept worked: Within seven years, the corporation's net income had increased from $72 million to $248.2 million and the market value of every thousand dollars invested in the original shares was $61,218.

In a company pamphlet sent to all employees and stockholders in March 1927, Alfred spelled out his philosophy that the top leadership team should be the principal owners of the enterprise:

> Ten years ago General Motors had 1,927 stockholders. Today, while a large part of its stock is in the hands of over 50,000 stockholders, the remainder is actually owned by a small group in whom lies the executive management and upon whom may be fairly placed the full responsibility for the success or failure of the institution.[3]

For those managers and potential leaders below the top eighty, an annual performance bonus in the form of stock rather than cash and a policy of promotion from within, combined with the company's continuing growth prospects, provided the incentive for them to work hard and stay with the General. Once talent and outstanding performance were singled out by the Sloan leadership group, those individuals were offered a series of rotating assignments at different operations to both test them and broaden their experience. Many high-potential up-and-comers came out of GMI, where they were thoroughly schooled in the General's culture.

For all other employees, there was the employee savings and investment plan, which had been created under Billy Durant in 1919. All employees, even the most junior plant worker, were allowed to contribute up to 20 percent of their annual wages toward the purchase of General Motors stock. The company matched each dollar with an amount that was tied to the company's annual net earnings: a precursor of today's 401(k) plans.

Although wages and working conditions at the General's plants were considered the best in the industry during the 1920s (a fact that Sloan reminded shareholders of in his written communications to them), the distinction between "white collar" and "blue collar" grew sharper as the company and its executives' pocketbooks continued to grow under Sloan. When Social Security became law in 1935, the employee savings and investment plan was ended but the executive bonus plan was not. An attitude of resentment rather than respect toward management eventually pervaded the ranks: an attitude that Sloan never comprehended. In the 1930s, it led to an institutionalized adversarial relationship between labor and management. Most American manufacturing companies are still trying to move beyond that relationship today.

Nonetheless, Sloan's controls and incentives made General Motors the most successful industrial enterprise of the 1920s in the United States, the one that anyone seeking a job or career in automobiles aspired to work for. The head of Chevrolet, William Knudsen, vividly recalled the difference in atmosphere between General Motors and Ford Motor:

> Having come from what was considered an efficient plant [the Rouge complex], this is what I saw. I saw no great difference in equipment or in buildings. I saw no difference in tools, or in quality of the work that was produced; but I saw an awful difference in the way people received me when I came to the plant. Everybody said "How do you do." I had not seen anything like that for a long while. If I went over to a workman and said "What are you doing?" he explained in detail what he was working on.
>
> There was a great feeling of security over the whole outfit that I hadn't noticed before.[4]

Such attitudes were to change radically with the dawn of a new decade and the era of the Great Depression.

UNREST IN THE RANKS

As the 1920s came to a close, Alfred Sloan was at the top of his game and the General was setting the pace in all areas of business in general and automobiles in particular. Sloan's numbers spoke for themselves. Net sales had grown from $304.5 million in 1921, the first full year after Billy Durant's ouster, to $1.5 billion in 1929. During the same period, net income had grown from a loss of $38.7 million in 1921 to a net profit of $248.3 million in 1929.

It was the largest turnaround and the most thorough transformation in business history. Billy's baby had come of age, and Alfred was the business world's Man of the Hour. Yet life in the General's plants was not as rosy as its balance sheet.

All the confidence that had been built up within the General's workforce since Billy Durant's sad departure seemed to evaporate with the shock of the Great Depression, as it did for most large organizations. Across the nation, trust and confidence in all institutions, especially business, were shattered. As Harold Evans observed in his 1998 book *The American Century*:

> By 1932, between one quarter and one third of all American workers were unemployed. Only in one year before 1940 would unemployment dip below 8 million. National output was more than cut in half. By 1933 a quarter of all the nation's farmers had lost their land. The American dream seemed to be blowing away with the rich Western soil. And more.[5]

General Motors' employees below the executive level shared the pain and shock, with layoffs imposed at all plants. Under Donaldson Brown's standard volume formula, many factories were completely idled; but the most efficient and critical ones scheduled overtime and increased the assembly-line speed rather than bring people back or add new jobs and costs.

Alfred Sloan was soon vilified by the left and accused of using the Depression as an opportunity to optimize production and profits: a charge that was reinforced by Sloan's own numbers. General Motors was the only automaker that never lost money during the Great Depression. In every year but 1932, it showed a profit margin of at least 10 percent (high by even today's standards), despite slow sales and reduced volume. Indeed, Sloan's team was able to underprice the competition and increase market share in the core automotive business during those dark years, laying the foundation for even more astounding future growth.

When organizers for the United Auto Workers (UAW) appeared

within the workforce in the early 1930s, the Sloan management team's reaction was to supply plant management with tear gas and weapons and deploy Pinkerton guards in the plants as spies: moves that Henry Ford emulated and took to an even higher degree. Push finally came to shove when workers sat down on the job and locked themselves inside General Motors' Fisher Body plant number 2 in Flint on December 29, 1936. The following day, the more critical Fisher Body plant number 1, also in Flint, was shut down.

Violence erupted within two weeks when police tried to stop the locked-in workers' wives and supporters from delivering food. National Guard troops were called in and General Motors sought court injunctions. Because the Flint plants supplied critical components, General Motors' entire U.S. manufacturing network was idled. As tensions mounted, each side printed its own daily newspaper, accusing the other of betrayal and worse.

President Franklin Delano Roosevelt's secretary of labor, Frances Perkins (the first woman ever to hold a cabinet position), intervened directly with Sloan at FDR's behest. In an oral history now stored at Columbia University's Butler Library, Perkins recalled how she met privately with Sloan and got what she thought was a commitment to meet with the UAW. She further recalled Sloan interrupting her dinner that same night with a telephone call and less than gentlemanly language. As she reported the conversation:

> **Perkins:** You are a scoundrel and a skunk, Mr. Sloan. You don't deserve to be counted among decent men.
> **Sloan:** You can't talk like that to me! I'm worth $70 million and I made it all myself! You can't talk to me like that! I'm Alfred Sloan.
> **Perkins:** Haven't you heard what happens to the rich man? It's like the camel trying to go through the eye of the needle. If you've got $70 million it's going to drown you, Mr. Sloan. It's going to sink you. For God's sake, don't say those words to me again. It makes you a worse rotter than I thought you were.[6]

According to Perkins, Sloan then hung up on her.

While there is no other source to verify or disprove her version of the conversation, Sloan did indeed refuse to ever meet with the UAW. He left it to William Knudsen, his head of manufacturing, to settle the strikes. On February 11, 1937, General Motors capitulated and recognized the UAW as the bargaining agent for workers who had already become members of the organization. As *Fortune* magazine observed a year later: "It was the biggest, most significant labor war of the last decade."

As Americans continued to question and even challenge the corporate hands that fed them, Sloan also became obsessed with a one-man crusade against what he saw as the three greatest threats to America itself as well as private industry: Franklin Delano Roosevelt, unions in general, and the United Auto Workers union in particular. He also created the first corporate public relations department in the annals of business for the sole purpose of keeping reporters and their queries away from his desk. In *My Years with General Motors,* there is just one brief reference to Frances Perkins and the sit-down strikes of the 1930s. That reference is in the context of Sloan's analysis of the UAW's next major strike against GM, which occurred in the summer of 1945, right after the end of World War II:

> . . . [I]t appeared that the UAW was able to enlist the support of the government in any great crisis. The government's attitude went back as far as the 1937 sit-down strikes, when we took the view that we would not negotiate with the union while its agents forcibly held possession of our properties. Sit-down strikes were plainly illegal—a judgment later confirmed by the Supreme Court. Yet President Franklin D. Roosevelt, Secretary of Labor Frances Perkins, and Governor Frank Murphy of Michigan exerted steady pressure upon the corporation, and upon me personally, to negotiate with the strikers who had seized our property, until we finally felt obliged to do so.[7]

Sloan would never acknowledge any culpability or responsibility for the strikes and would bitterly oppose everything the unions stood for until his dying day, even as General Motors and the UAW reached ever more generous accommodation with each other in contract negotiations throughout the 1950s and 1960s.

Ironically, a prolonged strike over wage increases at the end of World War II, when General Motors could ill afford production stoppages in the resurging domestic market, led to the institution of health care insurance and pension benefits in lieu of pay hikes. At the time, this was actually viewed by business leaders and Wall Street as an innovative and inexpensive way to buy labor peace. By the first decade of the twenty-first century, however, it had put the

General at a cost disadvantage that Alfred Sloan could never have envisioned in his worst nightmare.

Apart from the contradictions between Sloan's views of the company, its executives, and its hourly plant workers, his business results again speak for themselves. By the end of the 1930s, the General was on what seemed an unstoppable path. Vehicle production had risen from fewer than 10,000 vehicles produced worldwide in 1908 to more than 102,000 in 1915 and exactly 1,597,569 in 1939. General Motors' share of the U.S. car and truck market had climbed from less than 10 percent in 1915 to more than 40 percent in 1939. At the same time, reflecting the General's own relentless march, the number of companies building automobiles in the United States had fallen from more than 200 in 1915 to less than a dozen in 1939.

POLITICIANS AND EXECUTIVES DON'T MIX

Sloan's hatred for FDR was matched by his conviction that his own leaders should never dirty their hands with politics or government: and woe to the GM executive who disagreed.

John Raskob, who had been dispatched by the DuPont company to be chief financial officer of General Motors as DuPont's investments in GM increased, left a lasting mark on corporate accounting and governance in America. However, he incurred Sloan's wrath when Sloan learned he planned to serve as New York Governor (and Democrat) Al Smith's presidential campaign manager in 1928. Sloan abruptly fired Raskob despite the du Pont family's opposition. For his part, Raskob went on to collaborate with Al Smith to build the Empire State Building in response to his friend Walter P. Chrysler's art deco skyscraper in New York City.

William Knudsen, widely considered the man who perfected mass production, had a similar career fate. He was elevated to president of General Motors in 1937, after the Flint sit-down strikes, when Sloan sought to lower his own public profile. Although Sloan retained only the official title of chairman of the board of directors, his power within the company was stronger than ever. When Knudsen was asked by President Franklin Roosevelt to lead the United States' wartime industrial mobilization in 1940, Sloan made it clear that he did not approve of Knudsen's leaving General Motors for the government, regardless of the nature of the position. Knudsen, who had immigrated to the United States from Denmark while in his teens and took great pride in his U.S. citizenship, defied Sloan and left General Motors to lead the war mobilization effort. Rather than take a leave of absence, like most executives tapped for government service, Knudsen was forced to resign from General Motors.

Knudsen was ultimately given the rank of four-star general by FDR. After the war, he asked Sloan in private if he could return to General Motors. Alfred said no, using the excuse that Knudsen had just reached his sixty-fifth birthday in 1945, the official retirement age for General Motors employees. At that time, Alfred was seventy years old.

THE FINEST HOUR: GENERAL MOTORS GOES TO WAR FOR AMERICA

As the United States drew closer to war in 1940, General Motors remained above the public rearmament debate and focused all its U.S. operations on civilian automobiles rather than weaponry and military transport. Yet before Pearl Harbor, the company was already assuming a global war in its business calculations and was actually planning for a postwar expansion in the States as well as overseas. The General even began analyzing wage policies and formulas for cost-of-living increases for an anticipated period of postwar inflation.

Beyond the United States, the General's Adam Opel unit actually made a bid for Adolf Hitler's "people's car" project in the 1930s. Opel lost the bid to Porsche, which eventually created a new company named Volkswagen, but the head of GM Export, James Mooney, was awarded the Merit Cross of the German Eagle First Class by Hitler himself (an award also presented to Henry Ford).

In the United States, Mooney was accused of being one of Hitler's key supporters and was placed under investigation by J. Edgar Hoover's FBI. Henry Ford's blatant anti-Semitism and vocal support of Hitler overrode Mooney's name in the headlines, and Mooney's name was cleared by the time the country entered the war. Some accounts claim that Mooney was actually serving as a secret intermediary between the German people's small anti-Hitler, anti-Nazi movement and the U.S. government. Mooney was an officer in the U.S. Naval Reserve, and in fact, he had two private meetings with the common enemy of Hitler and Sloan, Franklin D. Roosevelt, in 1939 and 1940.

Once the United States officially entered the war, no company converted faster or more comprehensively to wartime production than General Motors. It has been called the greatest industrial transformation in history, with all of the General's 200-plus North American automotive plants shifting to production of airplanes, tanks, machines guns, amphibious transports, and other military vehicles within a matter of months. General Motors alone supplied the U.S. forces with military goods worth more than $12 billion (several hundreds of billions if converted to today's dollars). This was far more than any other company contributed.

General Motors also developed the volume production techniques for manufacturing the top secret and crucial Norden bombsight for the U.S. Army Air Corps, which made high-altitude strategic daylight bombing possible. The Norden bombsight was one of the most complicated and precise instruments ever developed, and the government turned to General Motors' Cadillac division to produce it.

At the same time, the General's Allison division, which had been building aircraft engines as well as transmissions since the 1920s, was tapped to develop the aluminum-block engine that powered the legendary P-38 Lightning, P-40 Flying Tiger, P-51 Mustang, and Wildcat fighter planes. GM diesels also powered the U.S. Navy's submarine fleet as well as its troop landing craft. In Flint alone, GM produced the M-26 Pershing tank and M-18 Hellcat tank destroyer, as well as aircraft-engine cylinder heads, one-and-a-half-ton trucks, armored cars, .50-caliber machine guns, various sizes of artillery shells, and more than 6,000 different engine and truck parts for the armed forces.

The late management theorist Peter Drucker, who spent eighteen months studying GM during the war, went so far as to say General Motors won the war. In the process, as the men who had made unionism a way of life with the Flint sit-down strike entered military service, General Motors trained and retrained a total of 750,000 new employees during the war years. One-fourth of them were women, and nearly all of them had no prior manufacturing experience. The American workplace would never be the same.

At war's end, General Motors was also the fastest and most efficient of all companies in converting back to peacetime production.

Unlike his counterparts at Ford Motor Company and the Chrysler Corporation, Sloan was convinced that the postwar economy would boom and that the automobile market would surge with pent-up demand from Rosie the Riveter and GI Joe alike. Soon, the General had again left all competitors in the dust and was setting the design, engineering, and performance standards for the rest of the industry (and consumers) to follow.

THE SLOAN PHILOSOPHY AND LEGACY OF WINNING

Alfred's record again speaks for itself. After the turf fight that developed over Kettering's engine, he had brought the team together while devising and implementing changes that were unprecedented for any company. Those changes caused internal trauma but quickly transformed Billy's baby into the juggernaut of all corporations.

The legacies from the Sloan years of transformation and domination include a new organizational structure that became the model for all corporations; a new product strategy that redefined the art of marketing; and a unique and revolutionary set of financial controls and measurements that allowed General Motors to maintain production and profitability even during the worst down cycles of the economy. All of his concepts and policy innovations were soon copied in one form or another by companies of all sizes, some more than others (even back then, no other publicly held company's managers were willing to put so much of their own wealth at risk as Sloan's team did with the stock-ownership plan).

Yet the most critical of all of Alfred's changes and legacies is the simplest: namely, the concept of decision making based on facts and open discussion, as opposed to the Durant crew's more mercurial and spontaneous decision-making process. Although it is almost a cliché today, this work philosophy remains as difficult to follow as it is simple to express:

Get the facts. Recognize the equities of all concerned. Realize the necessity of doing a better job every day. Keep an open mind and work hard. The last, gentlemen, is the most important of all. There is no shortcut.[8]

In the end, Alfred Sloan institutionalized a new culture, one never before attempted in a systematic way in any corporation. It came to define the very concept of the corporation throughout most of the twentieth century, until new technologies and new competition forced all kinds of institutions to refocus and restructure. It was what is now called a hierarchical, command-and-control culture, but it also fostered creativity, innovation, and risk taking: the traits all kinds of leaders in all kinds of businesses are trying to instill throughout their organizations in today's era of globalization.

By the time Sloan stepped down as chairman of the board in 1956, after leading the company for thirty-six years, General Motors was America's best-known symbol of not only industrial might and innovation but prosperity and materialism. It employed 800,000 people worldwide, more than any other nongovernmental institution, and sent pension and health-care payments to an additional million people in the United States alone. In his book *The Fifties,* David Halberstam describes General Motors as "a company so powerful that to call it merely a corporation seemed woefully inadequate." It was the country's biggest advertiser as well as its biggest employer (after the federal government). When television host Dinah Shore sang for Americans to "See the USA in your Chevrolet," she struck a chord in every household. And Billy Durant, despite all the snubbing and sniping he had endured, would surely have smiled.

EPILOGUE

WHAT'S GOOD FOR GENERAL MOTORS . . .

While Alfred P. Sloan, Jr., transformed General Motors into the icon of corporate efficiency and success, Billy Durant's new dreams ended hollow. Durant Motors initially drew investors like a magnet, largely on the basis of Billy's personal reputation, but the costs of doing product development, building a new manufacturing and supplier infrastructure, and supporting a new dealer network were soon too daunting for even him. By the time Sloan became president of General Motors in 1923, Durant Motors was already fading and Billy's own interest had shifted back to the stock market rather than the automobile business.

Again through his personal reputation as "the wizard," he settled in on Wall Street and began creating a string of investment pools with several high-profile acquaintances, including Joseph P. Kennedy. The pools were predecessors of today's mutual funds, attracting small investors and then "pooling" contributions to buy shares of companies considered to be highfliers. The pool manager's role (at which charming Billy excelled) was to push the price of the stock up by spreading the word about the companies' track records and growth potential to attract more investors (a practice now illegal, called "hyping" the stock).

The key to success, of course, was gauging when the stock price was peaking and then selling all the shares. Although it was clearly manipulation and speculation (a practice not far from what Billy Durant and his daughter insinuated that the House of Morgan had been doing with General Motors's stock), it was perfectly legal at the time, and no one on the Street was better at it than Billy Durant. At one point, the pools and syndicates that he lent his name to in the 1920s had a total of $4 billion in assets. Durant gained the new unofficial title of "King of the Bulls."

Yet even he knew better than to believe in the euphoria that took hold of the stock market after Herbert Hoover's election in 1928. Shortly before the stock market crash of October 29, 1929, Durant launched a personal campaign to persuade President Hoover and the Federal Reserve to adopt a strong monetary policy to rein in speculation and defend the investments of small investors. He was even granted a private interview with Hoover before the crash, but Hoover did not budge.

Durant was soon proven right and Hoover wrong, of course. That was little comfort, though. Billy never recovered either financially or emotionally from the personal financial losses he suffered in the market. This time, Pierre du Pont and John Jakob Raskob were not there to bail him out.

He avoided bankruptcy until 1936. In September 1938, he stood at the door of the Raymere estate while all of its furnishings were auctioned off and carried away. Still pursuing new dreams and schemes that ranged from mining to toothpaste, razors, and beer, he borrowed $30,000 from C. S. Mott (then the wealthiest man in Flint, Michigan) and $20,000 from Alfred Sloan. Neither loan was repaid.

In January 1940, Sloan finally reestablished personal contact, inviting Billy to attend the Detroit celebration of General Motors' twenty-five-millionth vehicle rolling off the assembly line. Billy sat at Sloan's table, and Sloan led him by the hand to the stage to introduce him to the crowd of executives and dealers.

When portions of Sloan's *Adventures of a White Collar Man* were excerpted in the *Saturday Evening Post* in September of that year, Billy wrote Alfred a letter thanking him for "the handsome compliments" in the article. Fittingly, the letter also included a reminder that there was more to success than the science of management:

> I do wish, Mr. Sloan, that you had known me when we were laying the foundation—when speed and action seemed necessary. You are absolutely right in your statement that General Motors justified an entirely different method of handling after the units had been enlisted, and you with your training and experience surrounded yourself with competent, reliable men of sound judgment, vision, and devotion to the cause, which has enabled you to create the General Motors of today, a truly great institution.
>
> To sum up, the early history [of General Motors] reminds me of the following story: General Wheeler, who came up from the ranks, met Major Bloomfield, a West Pointer, at the Chickamauga battlefield at Chattanooga. In speaking of the engagement, General Wheeler said to Major Bloomfield, "Right up on that hill there is where a company of

infantry captured a troop of cavalry." Major Bloomfield said, "Why, General, you know that couldn't be, infantry cannot capture cavalry," to which General Wheeler replied, "But, you see, this infantry captain didn't have the disadvantage of a West Point education and he didn't know he couldn't do it, so he just went ahead and did it anyway."[1]

Sloan replied in exactly a week with a letter typed on General Motors stationery. It focused on Sloan's own reasons for writing the book and made no direct reference to anything in Durant's letter. That exchange of letters was the last known direct contact between the two former colleagues.

While Catherine Durant remained lovingly at her husband's side through all his triumphs and tragedies, they had no children of their own. After the crash of 1929, they had less and less contact with Billy's daughter Margery and son Cliff. Cliff, who had gained fame as a California playboy and race driver with no steady job and a more than ample girth, died of a heart attack in 1937, ten years before his father. Ironically, Cliff's first ex-wife, Adelaide Frost Rickenbacker (wed to the legendary air ace Eddie Rickenbacker after divorcing Cliff), quietly began sending Billy and Catherine money to help with their living expenses. The money came from a trust fund Billy had set up for her as a wedding gift when she married his ne'er-do-well son.

Margery, who had gone through three divorces and struggled to maintain the image and lifestyle of a debutante, drifted into drugs after her book's publication and her father's fall from Wall Street glory. Just five months after Billy's death in March 1947, Margery was arrested for buying and selling illegal narcotics. As reported in the *New York Daily News* on September 16, 1947, thirty-nine years to the day after Billy incorporated General Motors:

Comdr. Fitzhugh Green, 59, noted author and explorer, and his social-ite wife, Mrs. Margery Durant Green, 60, four-times-wed heiress daughter of the late W. C. Durant, multimillionaire motor magnate, were named in Federal Court today as central figures in a sensational narcotics-peddling case. Accused with them was Frederick P. Deisler, a private detective of 7 E. 44 Street, New York. All three were charged with receiving and concealing narcotics and with knowledge of their unlawful importation. The Greens, both named as drug addicts, had paid more than $100,000 for narcotics in the last two years, the indictments charged.

Mercifully, Margery's story faded from the press after that one headline, along with her father's legacy.

Billy Durant's final venture, before his stroke in 1942, was to open a bowling alley and one of the country's first drive-in hamburger restaurants in Flint. Ever the dreamer, his new vision was that bowling would become a national family pastime and that bowling families would prefer not to squander time on formal sit-down dinners. His North Flint Recreation Center, opened in 1940, had eighteen lanes. He also talked of plans for a national chain of fifty such centers, each to be strategically located in a growing community and promoted as a local enterprise.

Bowling and fast food would both become popular and profitable. However, Billy was not destined to cash in. After suffering the stroke in 1942, at the age of eighty, he moved back to New York and was soon confined to the Gramercy Park apartment, where his speech and physical capabilities steadily degenerated.

Learning of Billy's condition and his need for nursing care, Alfred Sloan again intervened. In 1944, Sloan asked three other colleagues on the General Motors board of directors (all of whom owed much of their success to Durant) to join him in coming to Billy and Catherine's financial aid. The three directors were C. S. Mott, who had moved his axle operations to Flint at Billy's suggestion in 1907; Sam McLaughlin, who had brought the Buick to Canada and led the creation of GM-Canada; and John Thomas Smith, the lawyer who had been Billy's adviser and was now General Motors' general counsel. Every three months, a different one of the four associates sent Catherine a check for $2,500. The checks continued until Durant's death, which came peacefully the morning of March 18, 1947.

Not until August 1958, during General Motors' fiftieth anniversary year, did Billy Durant receive formal public recognition for the greatest and most improbable of all his gambles and achievements: the founding of what had become the world's largest industrial enterprise. Rather than a plaque or statue, Billy's marker is an inconspicuous ten-foot-square slab of granite, big enough to use for a stage, rising just two feet off the ground, in a park in Flint, Michigan. The one-time protégé and employee who had taken over the leadership of Billy's baby, Alfred P. Sloan, Jr., was still alive, retired, and sitting on General Motors' board of directors at the time. Sloan did not attend the ceremonial inauguration of Durant's platform, however. The marble slab was laid by the city of Flint rather than General Motors.

Durant's memorial sits in the center of the Flint Cultural Center, opposite the entrance to the Alfred P. Sloan Museum, which was also built by the city rather than General Motors. Today, despite the high-sounding name, the Flint Cultural Center is dominated by empty parking lots and the weeds surrounding them. There are two flagpoles atop the Durant platform, but on most days, no flags fly. The aluminum poles are scratched with graffiti and the grass is pocked with weeds. Billy's final epitaph is carved in the granite on the side facing the museum:

> William Crapo Durant, 1861–1947, Founder of General Motors, 1908:
> In the golden milestone year of the corporation its proud birthplace
> dedicates this plaza in lasting appreciation of what his vision, genius,
> and courage contributed to his home city and to the renown of
> American industry.

Most passersby do not seem to notice the inscription or the platform itself. They are mainly schoolchildren on bus excursions rather than curious pilgrims eager to soak in Flint's culture.

In the end, Billy Durant's life played out the way the American Dream itself plays out in today's media culture: a life in three acts, perfectly scripted for fifteen minutes of fame. Alfred Sloan's life, in contrast, remained shrouded beneath the veil of the unrivaled success of both men's true passion, General Motors. As Durant's name disappeared from the business world, Sloan's General Motors continued to set the standard and raise the benchmark for the rest of the automobile industry until his death in 1966.

In 1952, following Dwight Eisenhower's election to the White House, General Motors' then president, Charles "Engine Charlie" Wilson, was nominated to serve as Eisenhower's secretary of defense. This time, Sloan did not protest the defection from the company because he disagreed with Wilson's more cooperative stance with the UAW. During his Senate confirmation hearing, Wilson issued his famous one-liner: "What is good for our country is good for General Motors, and vice versa." Those words were immediately misquoted in the press as "What's good for General Motors is good for America," a phrase that soon became a catchall to describe much of the public's perception of corporate America's power and arrogance during the 1950s.

What happened thereafter to Sloan's General Motors and America's auto industry has been the subject of dozens of books and hundreds of articles. As the General approaches its hundredth birthday, a new generation of leaders and executives young enough to be Billy and Alfred's great-grandchildren continues to grapple with the same issues the young company confronted in the crisis of 1920, as do their counterparts in large companies in all kinds of businesses. They find themselves in a market that has turned uncertain and has defied many of their most basic assumptions, thanks to changing technology, customer demands, competition, and cost pressures.

The difference is that today, the changes are faster and more drastic, and they keep on coming as all markets and manufacturing bases become more globally linked. It is an environment far more intense and demanding than even Alfred Sloan could have foreseen. The structure, controls, and culture that he built were the paradigm for success during most of the twentieth century, but it has been difficult, to say the least, to adapt them to the more brutal twenty-first century.

Alfred Sloan's final observations on the process of change were again prescient:

No company ever stops changing. Change will come for better or worse. I hope I have not left the impression that the organization runs itself automatically. An organization does not make decisions; its function is to provide a framework, based upon established criteria, within which decisions can be fashioned in an orderly manner. . . . The task of management is not to apply a formula but to decide issues on a case-by-case basis. No fixed, inflexible rule can ever be substituted for the exercise of sound business judgment in the decision-making process.[2]

The debate continues about whether many large companies, including General Motors, stuck with Sloan's own organizational and management paradigms too long in the face of competition from beyond the United States.

Will the lessons learned from how Alfred Sloan adapted the General to a rapidly changing environment, especially in the aftermath of the crisis of 1920, be heeded by a different generation of managers and executives?

Will it ever be possible for any large enterprise to achieve the kind of turnaround that Sloan accomplished and then continued to grow for so many years?

As technology makes manufacturing techniques and logistics simpler and more global, is the day of the large plant and the independent dealership nearing an end?

Will the automobile itself be assembled and sold in a radically different way, with modules assembled at different locations and shipped directly to the retail outlet for final assembly?

Will traditional manufacturers like Ford Motor, General Motors, and even Toyota be relegated to the far smaller (but perhaps more profitable) roles of design, marketing, and finance?

Although the answers to such questions grow more tenuous as the pace of change and reaction accelerates, the legacies and lessons of what Billy Durant and Alfred Sloan wrought grow all the more relevant to those who would be players.

1861 Billy Durant is born on December 8 in Boston, Massachusetts.

1863 Henry Ford is born on July 30 in Dearborn, Michigan.

1870 Pierre S. du Pont is born on January 15 in Brandywine, Delaware.

1875 Alfred P. Sloan, Jr., is born on May 23 in New Haven, Connecticut.

1886 Billy Durant creates the Flint Road Cart Company with $2,000 in borrowed capital.

1899 Ransom E. Olds opens the first factory built exclusively for automobile production in Detroit.

1901 The "Curved Dash" Oldsmobile becomes the first mass-produced American car.

1902 Cadillac Automobile Company is created in Detroit by Henry M. Leland (renamed Cadillar Motor Car Company in 1904).

1903 Buick Motor Company is created by David Dunbar Buick. Henry Ford establishes the Ford Motor Company.

1904 Billy Durant takes charge of Buick Motor Company.

1908 General Motors is incorporated. Ford Motor launches its Model T.

1910 Bankers assume management control of General Motors and remove Billy Durant from power.

1911 Charles "Boss" Kettering's electric self-starter is demonstrated in a Cadillac. Billy Durant establishes the Chevrolet Motor Company.

1914 Ford Motor institutes the moving assembly line and the $5-a-day minimum wage at its Highland Park plant in Detroit.

1915   On November 16, Pierre S. du Pont is elected chairman of the General Motors board of directors.
Billy Durant begins purchasing shares of General Motors common stock with shares of Chevrolet stock in a campaign to regain control of GM.

1916   Durant creates United Motors Corporation.
Durant announces that Chevrolet owns 54.5 percent of GM's outstanding shares and takes over the GM presidency from his former protégé Charles W. Nash.

1917   E. I. du Pont de Nemours & Company (DuPont) makes its initial investment in General Motors, purchasing 25 percent of GM's outstanding common shares.

1919   General Motors Acceptance Corporation (GMAC) is established to finance the sale of General Motors cars and trucks.
Construction of the General Motors Building begins in Detroit.
GM purchases all outstanding stock of the Frigidaire Corporation from Billy Durant.

1920   Billy Durant resigns as president of General Motors in November and Pierre S. du Pont, then chairman of the board, succeeds him.

1921   Pierre du Pont proceeds with commercial application of Kettering's "copper-cooled" engine, intended to replace the traditional water-cooled piston engine.

1923   The copper-cooled engine program dies, and Alfred Sloan is elected president of GM.
GM's first European assembly plant is established in Copenhagen, Denmark.

1924   Alfred Sloan articulates his product strategy of "a car for every purse and purpose."

1927   The milestone Cadillac LaSalle, the first production car designed by a professionally trained designer, is introduced.
Chevrolet overtakes Ford as the sales leader in the U.S. automobile market.

1929   Germany's largest auto manufacturer, Adam Opel, is acquired by GM.

1934 GM introduces the first diesel-powered locomotive.

1936 Billy Durant files for personal bankruptcy.
Workers in Flint, Michigan, go on sit-down strike during the last week of December.

1937 On February 11, the sit-down strikes end with GM's recognition of the United Auto Workers (UAW) union.

1940 GM produces its 25 millionth car on January 1. Billy Durant is invited by Alfred Sloan to attend the celebration.

1942 GM converts 100 percent of its production to war materiel for the Allied forces.

1947 Billy Durant dies in New York City on March 18.

1954 GM produces its 50 millionth U.S.-made car on November 23.

1956 Alfred Sloan retires on April 2.

1962 GM produces its 75 millionth U.S.-made vehicle on March 14.
The number of GM shareholders passes the one-million mark.

1963 Alfred Sloan's *My Years with General Motors* is published and becomes an immediate bestseller.

1966 Sloan dies in New York City on February 17.

NOTES

Introduction

1. Letter from W. C. Durant to Margery Durant-Fitzhugh Green, December 15, 1941, Durant Collection, Scharchburg Archives, Kettering University.
2. Alfred P. Sloan, Jr., with John McDonald, *My Years with General Motors* (New York: Doubleday, 1963), p. xx.

Chapter 1

1. Peter Gavrilovich and Bill McGraw, eds., *The Detroit Almanac* (Detroit: Detroit Free Press, 2000), p. 289.
2. General Motors annual report, 1919.
3. Arthur Pound, *The Turning Wheel* (New York: Doubleday, Doran & Company, 1934), pp. 177–178.
4. Walter P. Chrysler, with Boyden Sparkes, *Life of an American Workman* (New York: Curtis Publishing, 1938), p. 143.
5. Chrysler, *Life of an American Workman,* pp. 156–157.
6. Alfred P. Sloan, Jr., with Boyden Sparkes, *Adventures of a White Collar Man* (New York: Doubleday, Doran & Company, 1941), pp. 116–117.
7. Letter from Alfred P. Sloan, Jr. to W. C. Durant, August 22, 1919, Durant Collection, Scharchburg Archives, Kettering University.
8. Ibid.
9. Sloan, *Adventures of a White Collar Man*, pp. 119–120.

Chapter 2

1. Margery Durant, *My Father* (New York: Knickerbocker Press, 1929), p. vii.
2. Durant, *My Father,* pp. 23–24.
3. Ibid, pp. 24–25.
4. Ibid, pp. 30–31.
5. Letter to William W. Crapo, August 13, 1863, Henry Howland Crapo Collection, Michigan Historical Collections, University of Michigan, Ann Arbor, as quoted by Richard Scharchburg in his self-published

book, *W. C. Durant: The Boss,* 1979, now on file at the Scharchburg Archives, Kettering University.

6. Letter to William W. Crapo, July 30, 1868, Henry Howland Crapo Collection.

7. Durant, *My Father,* p. 18.

8. Untitled narrative and notes, Durant Collection, Scharchburg Archive, Kettering University.

9. Ibid.

10. Ibid.

11. Ibid.

12. Ibid.

Chapter 3

1. Some of these documents are also preserved in the trial record of the federal government's antitrust case against the E. I. du Pont Corporation (known simply as DuPont), alleging that the company had an unfair advantage in selling paint to General Motors because it also happened to be the largest holder of General Motors stock. The case originated in 1949 and was not settled until 1954, when the U.S. Supreme Court finally ruled against DuPont and the company liquidated its equity in General Motors.

2. John A. McDonald, *A Ghost's Memoir* (Cambridge, MA: MIT Press, 2002), pp. 41–42, includes a discussion of Alfred Chandler and the research team's role in Sloan's book.

3. McDonald, *A Ghost's Memoir,* p. 4.

4. Ibid, pp. 25–26.

5. Alfred P. Sloan, Jr., with John McDonald, *My Years with General Motors* (New York: Doubleday, 1963), p. 17.

6. Alfred P. Sloan Jr., with Boyden Sparkes, *Adventures of a White Collar Man* (New York: Doubleday, Doran & Company, 1941), p. 5.

7. Sloan, *Adventures of a White Collar Man,* pp. 7–8.

8. Ibid, pp. 13–14.

9. Ibid, p. 21.

10. Ibid, pp. 21–22.

11. Letter from Alfred Sloan to L. G. Kaufman, May 16, 1916, Durant Collection, Scharchburg Archives, Kettering University.

12. *An Introduction to the Accessory Companies,* Pierre S. du Pont, General Motors Corporation, February 1, 1922.

13. Sloan, *Adventures of a White Collar Man,* p. 25.

14. Ibid, pp. 26–27.

15. Ibid, p. 31.

Chapter 4

1. Richard Crabb, *Birth of a Giant* (Philadelphia: Chilton, 1969), p. 28.

2. Crabb, *Birth of a Giant,* p. 31.

3. Ibid, p. 46.

4. As quoted in Arthur Pound, *The Turning Wheel* (New York: Doubleday, Doran & Company, 1934), pp. 52–53.

5. *New York Tribune,* November 7, 1901, as quoted in Crabb, *Birth of a Giant,* pp. 66–67.

6. Oldsmobile ad copy reprinted in Pound, *The Turning Wheel,* pp. 61–62.

7. Alfred P. Sloan, Jr., with Boyden Sparkes, *Adventures of a White Collar Man* (New York: Doubleday, Doran & Company, 1941), p. 33.

8. See especially Robert Lacey, *Ford: The Men and the Machine* (Boston: Little Brown, 1986); Peter Collier and David Horowitz, *The Fords: An American Epic* (New York: Summit Books, 1987); and Douglas Brinkley, *Wheels for the World* (New York: Viking Press, 2003).

9. Lacey, *Ford: The Men and the Machine,* p. 11.

10. Henry Ford, with Samuel Crowther, *My Life and Work* (New York: Doubleday, Doran, 1923), pp. 23–24.

11. Lacey, *Ford: The Men and the Machine,* p. 40.

12. Ford, *My Life and Work,* p. 36.

13. Lacey, *Ford: The Men and the Machine,* p. 49.

14. Collier and Horowitz, *The Fords: An American Epic,* pp. 37–38.

15. Lacey, *Ford: The Men and the Machine,* p. 60.

16. Sloan, *Adventures of a White Collar Man,* pp. 37–39.

17. Alfred P. Sloan, Jr., with John McDonald, *My Years with General Motors* (New York: Doubleday, 1963), p. 20.

18. Sloan, *My Years with General Motors,* pp. 41–42.

Chapter 5

1. Margery Durant, *My Father* (New York: Knickerbocker Press, 1929), pp. 3–9.

2. Letters between William C. Durant and Charles Nash, January 17, 1942,

and March 5, 1942, Durant Collection, Scharchburg Archives, Kettering University.

3. Durant, *My Father,* pp. 64–65.

4. Ibid, pp. 54–55.

5. Bernard A. Weisberger, *The Dream Maker* (Boston: Little, Brown, 1979), p. 51.

6. Axel Madsen, *The Deal Maker* (New York: Wiley, New York, 1999), p. 40.

7. Billy Durant saved many of his mother's handwritten letters and his responses, some of which were on Durant-Dort Securities Company stationary, but nothing remains pertaining to his wife Clara, except for documentation related to their eventual divorce proceedings, parts of which are now on file, along with the personal correspondence, in the Durant Collection, Scharchburg Archives, Kettering University.

Chapter 6

1. Arthur Pound, *The Turning Wheel* (New York: Doubleday, Doran & Company, 1934), pp. 79–80.

2. Margery Durant, *My Father* (New York: Knickerbocker Press, 1929), pp. 57–58.

3. Durant, *My Father,* p. 59.

4. William C. Durant, "The Chevrolet," p. 8, manuscript in the Durant Collection, Scharchburg Archives, Kettering University.

5. Alfred P. Sloan Jr., with Boyden Sparkes, *Adventures of a White Collar Man* (New York: Doubleday, Doran & Company, 1941), pp. 48–49.

6. Sloan, *Adventures of a White Collar Man,* pp. 49–50.

7. Durant, *My Father,* pp. 57–59.

8. Bernard A. Weisberger, *The Dream Maker* (Boston: Little, Brown, 1979), p. 115.

9. William C. Durant autobiographical notes, Durant Collection, Scharchburg Archive, Kettering University.

10. Ibid.

11. Ibid.

12. Alfred P. Sloan, Jr., with John McDonald, *My Years with General Motors* (New York: Doubleday, 1963), p. 3.

13. Letter from William C. Durant to John Carton, March 14, 1906, as quoted in George S. May, *A Most Unique Machine* (Grand Rapids, MI: W. E. Eerdmans, 1975), p. 202.

14. Historical data from *100 Year Almanac* (Detroit: Automotive News, 1996), p.105, and the Antique Automobile Club of America Automotive chronology website (www.aaca.org), as well as various industry sources cited in Robert Lacey, *Ford: The Men and the Machine* (Boston: Little Brown, 1986), p. 62; Pound, *The Turning Wheel,* pp. 86–90; May, *A Most Unique Machine,* p. 279; and Weisberger, *The Dream Maker,* pp. 119–120.

Chapter 7

1. Alfred P. Sloan, Jr., with Boyden Sparkes, *Adventures of a White Collar Man* (New York: Doubleday, Doran & Company, 1941), p. 68.

2. Sloan, *Adventures of a White Collar Man,* p. 68.

3. Ibid, pp. 78–79.

4. Ibid, pp. 79–80.

5. Ibid, pp. 71–72.

6. George S. May, *A Most Unique Machine* (Grand Rapids, MI: W. E. Eerdmans, 1975), p. 272.

7. Douglas Brinkley, *Wheels for the World* (New York: Viking Press, 2003), p. 54.

8. Sloan, *Adventures of a White Collar Man,* pp. 69–71.

9. William C. Durant, "The True Story of General Motors," p. 1, unfinished manuscript, Durant Collection, Scharchburg Archives, Kettering University.

10. Ibid, p. 2.

11. Bernard A. Weisberger, *The Dream Maker* (Boston: Little, Brown, 1979), p. 128.

12. Durant, "True Story of General Motors," p. 2.

13. Ibid, p. 2.

14. Ibid, p. 3.

15. Ibid.

16. Ibid, p. 4.

17. Ibid, p. 5.

18. See Arthur Pound, *The Turning Wheel* (New York: Doubleday, Doran & Company, 1934), pp. 111–118; May, *A Most Unique Machine,* pp. 300–303; and Weisberger, *The Dream Maker,* pp. 123–128.

19. Durant, "True Story of General Motors," p. 5.

20. Sidney Olson, *Young Henry Ford* (Detroit: Wayne State University Press, 1963), p. 147.

21. May, *A Most Unique Machine,* pp. 311–312, and Weisberger, *The Dream Maker,* pp. 129–30.

22. Durant, "True Story of General Motors," p. 8.

23. Ibid, p. 9.

24. Ibid.

25. Ibid.

26. Ibid, p. 10.

27. *Flint Journal,* July 3, 1908, as quoted in May, *A Most Unique Machine,* pp. 310–311.

28. *The New York Times,* July 31, 1908; see also May, *A Most Unique Machine,* p. 314.

29. May, *A Most Unique Machine,* p. 312.

30. This version of how the name General Motors came into being is corroborated in Billy Durant's own manuscript. One of the many urban legends of the auto industry is that Durant himself came up with the name during his talks with Ben Briscoe.

31. Pound, *The Turning Wheel,* p. 118.

32. Durant, "True Story of General Motors," p. 16.

Chapter 8

1. William C. Durant, "The Cadillac," manuscript in Durant Collection, Scharchburg Archives, Kettering University.

2. Arthur Pound, *The Turning Wheel* (New York: Doubleday, Doran & Company, 1934), p. 121.

3. William C. Durant, "The True Story of General Motors," pp. 13–15, unfinished manuscript, Durant Collection, Scharchburg Archives, Kettering University.

4. Alfred P. Sloan, Jr., with Boyden Sparkes, *Adventures of a White Collar Man* (New York: Doubleday, Doran & Company, 1941), pp. 83–85.

5. Pound, *The Turning Wheel,* p. 107.

6. Ed Cray, *Chrome Colossus* (New York: McGraw-Hill, 1980), p. 81.

7. Durant, "The Cadillac," p. 22.

8. William C. Durant, "The Ford Motor Company Incident," unpublished manuscript, Durant Collection, Scharchburg Archives, Kettering University.

9. Ibid.

10. George S. May, *A Most Unique Machine* (Grand Rapids, MI: W. E. Eerdmans, 1975), p. 327.

11. Durant, "Ford Motor Company Incident."

12. Ibid.

13. Ibid.

14. William C. Durant, "The A. C. Spark Plug," Durant Collection, Scharchburg Archives, Kettering University.

15. Ibid.

16. Ibid

17. *Motor World* as quoted in Bernard A. Weisberger, *The Dream Maker* (Boston: Little, Brown, 1979), p. 143.

18. Weisberger, *The Dream Maker,* pp. 140–142.

19. Pound, *The Turning Wheel,* p. 95.

Chapter 9

1. Arthur Pound, *The Turning Wheel* (New York: Doubleday, Doran & Company, 1934), p. 126.

2. Ibid, p. 126.

3. William C. Durant, "The Chevrolet," manuscript in the Durant Collection, Scharchburg Archives, Kettering University.

4. Margery Durant, *My Father* (New York: Knickerbocker Press, 1929), pp. 121–122.

5. Durant, *My Father,* pp. 126–133.

6. Alfred P. Sloan Jr., with Boyden Sparkes, *Adventures of a White Collar Man* (New York: Doubleday, Doran & Company, 1941), pp. 83–85.

7. Historic sales numbers are from the *100 Year Almanac* (Detroit: Automotive News), pp. 105–106. While all statistics from this period are subject to some question, the general growth pattern shown in the *Automotive News* numbers is in line with that of all the other published sources.

8. Ibid.

9. Sloan, *Adventures of a White Collar Man,* p. 85.

10. Ibid, p. 87.

11. Ibid, pp. 75–76.

12. Arthur Pound, *The Turning Wheel* (New York: Doubleday, Doran & Company, 1934), p. 129.

13. Henry G. Pearson, *Son of New England: James Jackson Storrow* (Boston: Little, Brown, 1932), p. 144.

14. Pound, *The Turning Wheel,* p, 133.

15. Walter P. Chrysler, with Boyden Sparkes, *Life of an American Workman* (New York: Curtis Publishing, 1938), p. 120.

16. Chrysler, *Life of an American Workman,* pp. 123–124.

17. Ibid, p. 126.

18. Ibid.

19. Ibid, p. 127.

20. Ibid, pp. 139–140.

21. Pound, *The Turning Wheel,* p. 139. Pound does not cite his source, but a division of total net sales by number of employees as reported in company annual reports gives the same productivity numbers.

22. Durant, "The Chevrolet."

Chapter 10

1. While William Durant's exact wealth at this time cannot be determined, both he and daughter Margery noted that he still held every share of General Motors stock that he had personally acquired, which amounted to several thousand shares trading in a range of $100 a share in 1910. He also had his Durant-Dort fortune and continued to buy more shares of GM over the next five years. During this period, GM's common stock price soared, reaching $558 by the fall of 1915.

2. Arthur Pound, *The Turning Wheel* (New York: Doubleday, Doran & Company, 1934), p. 154.

3. *Flint Journal,* July 11, 1912, as quoted by Bernard A. Weisberger, *The Dream Maker* (Boston: Little, Brown, 1979), pp. 164–165.

4. Weisberger, *The Dream Maker,* pp. 146–147.

5. William C. Durant "The Chevrolet" pp. 9–10, manuscript in the Durant Collection, Scharchburg Archives, Kettering University.

6. Durant, "The Chevrolet," pp. 11–12.

7. Margery Durant, *My Father* (New York: Knickerbocker Press, 1929), p. 152.

8. Henry Ford, with Samuel Crowther, *My Life and Work* (New York: Doubleday, Doran, 1923), p. 83.

9. Ibid.

10. Ibid.

11. Alfred P. Sloan, Jr., with Boyden Sparkes, *Adventures of a White Collar Man* (New York: Doubleday, Doran & Company, 1941), pp. 77–78.

12. Alfred D. Chandler and Stephen Salsbury, *Pierre S. du Pont and the*

Making of the Modern Corporation (New York: Harper & Row, 1971), p. 144.

Chapter 11

1. Bernard A. Weisberger, *The Dream Maker* (Boston: Little, Brown, 1979), p. 188.
2. *Flint Journal,* September 29, 1915, as quoted by Margery Durant, *My Father* (New York: Knickerbocker Press, 1929), p. 184.
3. William C. Durant's notes referring to the *Detroit Times*, Durant Collection, Scharchburg Archives, Kettering University.
4. Ibid.
5. Durant, *My Father,* pp. 171–172.
6. Letter from Pierre du Pont to J. A. Haskell, dated September 17, 1915, as quoted in Alfred D. Chandler and Stephen Salsbury, *Pierre S. du Pont and the Making of the Modern Corporation* (New York: Harper & Row, 1971), p. 437.
7. Chandler and Salsbury, *Pierre S. du Pont and the Making of the Modern Corporation,* p. 443.
8. Durant, *My Father,* p. 169.
9. Chandler and Salsbury, *Pierre S. du Pont,* p. 444.
10. Nash Motors ended up being merged into American Motors in 1954. American Motors in turn was bought by the French automaker Renault in 1979 and then sold to the Chrysler Corporation in 1987, where its product lines (including the Jeep line) were folded into Chrysler's other brands.
11. "Memorandum: The Chrysler Incident," Durant Collection, Scharchburg Archives, Kettering University.
12. Walter P. Chrysler, with Boyden Sparkes, *Life of an American Workman* (New York: Curtis Publishing, 1938), p. 145.
13. Alfred P. Sloan, Jr., with Boyden Sparkes, *Adventures of a White Collar Man* (New York: Doubleday, Doran & Company, 1941), pp. 93–94.
14. Alfred P. Sloan, Jr., with John McDonald, *My Years with General Motors* (New York: Doubleday, 1963), p. 22.
15. Sloan, *Adventures of a White Collar Man,* p. 94.
16. Ibid, pp. 95–96.
17. Ibid, p. 97.
18. Ibid, p. 99.
19. Ibid, pp. 99–100.

20. Ibid, p. 101.

21. Sloan, *My Years with General Motors,* p. 47.

Chapter 12

1. Robert Lacey, *Ford: The Man and the Machine* (Boston: Little, Brown, 1986), p. 198.

2. Trial transcript, as quoted in Lacey, *Ford: The Man and the Machine,* pp. 200–201.

3. *100 Year Almanac* (Detroit: Automotive News, 1996), pp. 107–108.

4. Arthur Pound, *The Turning Wheel* (New York: Doubleday, Doran & Company, 1934), p. 169.

5. Ibid.

6. Billy Durant clipped this article and one other regarding the Lelands' charges and kept them with his personal papers, now in the Durant Collection, Scharchburg Archives, Kettering University.

7. All four telegrams from William C. Durant to Henry and Wilfred Leland, as well as the text of Durant's public response, are on file with Durant's personal papers, Durant Collection, Scharchburg Archive, Kettering University.

8. Walter P. Chrysler, with Boyden Sparkes, *Life of an American Workman* (New York: Curtis Publishing, 1938), p. 143.

9. William C. Durant, "The True Story of General Motors," p. 33, unfinished manuscript, Durant Collection, Scharchburg Archive, Kettering University.

10. Ibid.

11. DuPont Company 1918 annual report, as quoted in Bernard A. Weisberger, *The Dream Maker* (Boston: Little, Brown, 1979), pp. 239–240.

Chapter 13

1. General Motors 1919 annual report to stockholders. This list does not include companies in which General Motors held less than 100 percent equity.

2. Alfred P. Sloan, Jr., with John McDonald, *My Years with General Motors* (New York: Doubleday, 1963), p. 31.

3. Report drafted by E. L. Bergland, as quoted in Alfred D. Chandler and Stephen Salsbury, *Pierre S. du Pont and the Making of the Modern Corporation* (New York: Harper & Row, 1971), pp. 468–469.

4. Maury Klein, *Rainbow's End: The Crash of 1929* (New York: Oxford University Press, 2001), p. 28.

5. Sloan, *My Years with General Motors,* p. 30.

6. Pierre S. du Pont's letter to stockholders, General Motors 1922 annual report, p. 13.

7. Letter from William Durant to John Raskob, January 28, 1920, Durant Collection, Scharchburg Archives, Kettering University.

8. These letters, dated February 17, 1921, are on file in the Durant Collection, Scharchburg Archives, Kettering University.

9. Alfred P. Sloan, Jr., with Boyden Sparkes, *Adventures of a White Collar Man* (New York: Doubleday, Doran & Company, 1941), pp. 113–115.

10. W. A. P. John, "That Man Durant," *Motor* magazine (January 1923), p.250.

11. Margery Durant, *My Father* (New York: Knickerbocker Press, 1929), p. 259.

12. John, "That Man Durant," p. 251.

13. Letter from Pierre S. du Pont to Irénée du Pont, president of E. I. du Pont de Nemours & Company, November 26, 1920, presented for the DuPont General Motors' antitrust case as Defendants' Trial Exhibit No. DP50 and reprinted in its entirety in Alfred D. Chandler, *Giant Enterprise* (New York: Harcourt, Brace, 1964), pp. 81–86.

14. Ibid.

15. John, "That Man Durant," p. 252.

16. Arthur Pound, *The Turning Wheel* (New York: Doubleday, Doran & Company, 1934), p. 194.

17. Pound, *The Turning Wheel,* pp. 188–189.

18. Sloan, *My Years with General Motors,* p. 4.

19. Pound, pp. 190–191.

Chapter 14

1. Arthur Pound, *The Turning Wheel* (New York: Doubleday, Doran & Company, 1934), p. 196.

2. Alfred P. Sloan, Jr., with John McDonald, *My Years with General Motors* (New York: Doubleday, 1963), p. 72.

3. Undated letter, as quoted by Sloan, *My Years with General Motors,* p. 77.

4. Ibid, p. 78, quoting letter from George Hannum, Oakland general manager, to Pierre du Pont, November 8, 1921.

5. Ibid, p. 93.

6. Alfred P. Sloan, Jr., with Boyden Sparkes, *Adventures of a White Collar Man* (New York: Doubleday, Doran & Company, 1941), pp. 139–140.

7. Sloan, *Adventures of a White Collar Man,* p. 134.

8. Ibid, pp. 134–135.

9. Ibid, pp. 135–136.

10. Norman Beasley, *Knudsen: A Biography* (New York: Whittlesey House/McGraw-Hill, 1947), pp. 93–94 and 107–108.

11. Beasley, *Knudsen: A Biography,* p. 108.

12. All historic sales numbers are from the *100 Year Almanac* (Detroit: Automotive News), p. 109.

Chapter 15

1. Alfred P. Sloan, Jr., with John McDonald, *My Years with General Motors* (New York: Doubleday, 1963), p. 167.

2. Sloan, *My Years with General Motors,* pp. 282–283.

3. *How Members of the General Motors Family Are Made Partners in General Motors,* p. 6, General Motors pamphlet from Alfred Sloan, March 12, 1927.

4. Speech by William Knudsen to General Motors Executive Conference, October 19, 1934, as quoted in Norman Beasley, *Knudsen: A Biography* (New York: Whittlesey House/McGraw-Hill, 1947), p. 126.

5. Harold Evans, *The American Century* (New York: Knopf, 1998), p. 218.

6. Perkins-Sloan conversation as quoted in David Farber, *Sloan Rules* (Chicago: University of Chicago Press, 2002), p. 205.

7. Sloan, *My Years with General Motors,* p. 393.

8. Interview with the author at Drucker's residence, Claremont, CA, August 9, 1999.

9. Speech by Alfred Sloan to U.S. newspaper editors invited to tour the Milford Proving Ground, September 28, 1927, as quoted in Arthur Pound, *The Turning Wheel* (New York: Doubleday, Doran & Company, 1934), p. 347.

Epilogue

1. Letter from William C. Durant to Alfred Sloan, September 13, 1940, Durant Collection, Scharchburg Archives, Kettering University.

2. Alfred P. Sloan, Jr., *My Years with General Motors* (New York: Doubleday, 1963), p. 443.

SELECTED BIBLIOGRAPHY

Books

Adams, James Truslow. *Big Business in a Democracy*. New York: Charles Scribner's Sons, 1946.

Allen, Frederick Lewis. *Only Yesterday: An Informal History of the 1920s*. New York: Harper & Row, 1931.

Bailey, L. Scott, ed. *General Motors: The First Seventy-five Years of Transportation Products*. Princeton, NJ: Automobile Quarterly, 1983.

Beasley, Norman. *Knudsen: A Biography*. New York: Whittlesey House/McGraw-Hill, 1947.

Brinkley, Douglas. *Wheels for the World: Henry Ford, His Company and a Century of Progress*. New York: Viking Press, 2003.

Brown, Peter, ed. *American Automobile Centennial 100 Year Almanac*. Detroit: Automotive News, 1996.

Chandler, Alfred D. *Giant Enterprise: Ford, General Motors and the Automobile Industry, Sources and Readings*. New York: Harcourt, Brace, 1964.

Chandler, Alfred D., and Stephen Salsbury. *Pierre S. du Pont and the Making of the Modern Corporation*. New York: Harper & Row, 1971.

Chrysler, Walter P., with Boyden Sparkes. *Life of an American Workman*. New York: Curtis Publishing, 1938.

Collier, Peter, and David Horowitz. *The Fords: An American Epic*. New York: Summit Books, 1987.

Cormier, Frank, and William J. Eaton. *Reuther*. Princeton, NJ: Prentice Hall, 1970.

Crabb, Richard. *Birth of a Giant: The Men and Incidents That Gave America the Motorcar*. Philadelphia: Chilton, 1969.

Cray, Ed. *Chrome Colossus*. New York: McGraw-Hill, 1980.

Curcio, Vincent. *Chrysler: The Life and Times of an Automotive Genius*. New York: Oxford University Press, 2000.

Dale, Ernest. *Readings in Management: Landmarks and New Frontiers*. New York: McGraw-Hill, 1965.

Donner, Frederick. *The Worldwide Industrial Enterprise*. New York: McGraw-Hill, 1967.

Drucker, Peter. *Adventures of a Bystander.* New York: Harper & Row, 1978.

———. *Concept of the Corporation.* New York: Transaction Publishers, 1995.

Dunham, Terry, and Lawrence Gustin. *The Buick: A Complete History.* Princeton, NJ: Automobile Quarterly, 1997.

Durant, Margery. *My Father.* New York: Knickerbocker Press, 1929.

Earley, Helen, and James Walkinshaw. *Setting the Pace: Oldsmobile's First Hundred Years.* Lansing, MI: Oldsmobile Division, General Motors Corporation, 1996.

Evans, Harold. *The American Century.* New York: Knopf, 1998.

———. *They Made America.* New York: Little, Brown and Company, 2004.

Farber, David. *Sloan Rules: Alfred P. Sloan and the Triumph of General Motors.* Chicago: University of Chicago Press, 2002.

Fine, Sidney. *Sit-Down: The General Motors Strike of 1936–1937.* Ann Arbor, MI: University of Michigan Press, 1969.

Folsom, Burton. *Empire Builders: How Michigan Entrepreneurs Helped Make America Great.* Traverse City, MI: Rhodes and Easton, 1998.

Ford, Henry, with Samuel Crowther. *My Life and Work.* New York: Doubleday, Doran, 1923.

Galbraith, John Kenneth. *The Great Crash.* Boston: Houghton Mifflin, 1954.

Gavrilovich, Peter, and Bill McGraw, eds. *The Detroit Almanac: 300 Years of Life in the Motor City.* Detroit: Detroit Free Press, 2000.

Gould, Jean, and Lorena Hickock. *Walter Reuther: Labor's Rugged Individualist.* Boston: Dodd, Mead & Company, 1972.

Gustin, Lawrence. *Billy Durant: Creator of General Motors.* Flushing, MI: Craneshaw Publishers, 1984.

Halberstam, David. *The Fifties.* New York: Villard Books, 1993.

———. *The Reckoning.* New York: Morrow, 1986.

Jenkins, Alan. *The Twenties.* New York: Universe Books, 1974.

Ketchum, Richard. *The Borrowed Years, 1938–1941: America on the Way to War.* New York: Random House, 1989.

Klein, Maury. *Rainbow's End: The Crash of 1929.* New York: Oxford University Press, 2001.

Klingaman, William A. *The Year of the Great Crash, 1929.* New York: Harper & Row, 1989.

Kuhn, Arthur. *GM Passes Ford, 1918–1938.* University Park, PA: The Pennsylvania State University Press, 1986.

Lacey, Robert. *Ford: The Men and the Machine.* Boston: Little, Brown, 1986.

Lichtenstein, Nelson. *Walter Reuther: The Most Dangerous Man in Detroit.* Urbana, IL: University of Illinois Press, 1995.

Lochner, Louis. *Always Expect the Unexpected.* New York: Macmillan Company, 1956.

———. *Tycoons and Tyrants: German Industry from Hitler to Adenauer.* New York: Henry Regnery Co., 1954.

Madsen, Axel. *The Deal Maker: How William C. Durant Made General Motors.* New York: Wiley, 1999.

May, George S. *A Most Unique Machine: The Michigan Origins of the American Automobile Industry.* Grand Rapids, MI: W. E Eerdmans, 1975.

McDonald, John A. *A Ghost's Memoir: The Making of Alfred P. Sloan's "My Years with General Motors."* Cambridge, MA: MIT Press, 2002.

McManus, Theodore, and Norman Beasley. *Man, Money, and Motors.* New York: Macmillan Company, 1929.

Mortimer, Wyndham. *Organize! My Life as a Union Man.* Boston: Beacon Press, 1971.

Nitschke, Robert. *The General Motors Legal Staff, 1920–1947.* Self-published, 1989.

Olson, Sidney. *Young Henry Ford: A Picture History of the First Forty Years.* Detroit: Wayne State University Press, 1963.

Pearson, Henry G. *Son of New England: James Jackson Storrow.* Boston: Little, Brown, 1932.

Pound, Arthur. *The Turning Wheel.* New York: Doubleday, Doran & Company, 1934.

Rae, John. *The American Automobile, a Brief History.* Chicago: University of Chicago Press, 1965.

Scharchburg, Richard. *W. C. Durant: The Boss.* Flint, MI: [Self-published] Scharchburg Archives, Kettering University, 1979.

Sloan, Alfred P., Jr., with Boyden Sparkes. *Adventures of a White Collar Man.* New York: Doubleday, Doran & Company, 1941.

Sloan, Alfred P. Jr., with John McDonald. *My Years with General Motors.* New York: Doubleday, 1963.

Thomas, Gordon, and Max Morgan-Witts. *The Day the Bubble Burst: A Social History of the Wall Street Crash of 1929.* New York: Doubleday, 1979.

Walker, Charles, and Robert Guest. *The Man on the Assembly Line.* Cambridge, MA: Harvard University Press, 1952.

Weisberger, Bernard A. *The Dream Maker: William C. Durant, Founder of General Motors.* Boston: Little, Brown, 1979.

Newspaper and Magazine Articles

"Alfred P. Sloan, Jr., the Chairman." *Fortune,* April 1938.

Allen, Frederick Lewis. "Morgan the Great." *Life,* April 25, 1949.

Ashdown, William. "Confessions of an Automobilist." *The Atlantic Monthly,* June 1925.

Atwood, Albert. "The Great Bull Market." *The Saturday Evening Post,* January 12, 1929.

Barton, Bruce. "The Future of American Business." *The American Magazine,* June 1929.

Brewster, Mike. "Billy Durant: Greasing Detroit's Wheels." *BusinessWeek,* April 27, 2004.

Child, Richard. "Hoover, or Some Other?" *The Saturday Evening Post,* March 16, 1929.

Crowther, Samuel. "Everybody Ought to Be Rich: Interview with John Jacob Raskob." *Ladies' Home Journal,* August 1929.

Garsten, Ed. "Ford Shapes the Work Place." *Detroit News,* May 5, 2003.

"General Motors." *Fortune,* December 1938.

"General Motors II: Chevrolet." *Fortune,* January 1939.

"General Motors III: How to Sell Automobiles." *Fortune,* February 1939.

"General Motors IV: A Unit in Society." *Fortune,* March 1939.

Howes, Daniel. "20th Century Life Shaped by Ford's Vision." *Detroit News,* June 9, 2003.

Iacocca, Lee. "Builders and Titans, Henry Ford." *Time,* December 7, 1998.

John, W. A. P. "That Man Durant." *Motor,* January 1923.

Marchand, Roland. "The Corporation Nobody Knew: Bruce Barton, Alfred Sloan, and the Founding of the General Motors Family." *Business History Review,* Winter 1991.

"Mr. Raskob's Poor Man's Investment Trust." *The Literary Digest,* June 1, 1929.

Noyes, Alexander D. "The Stock Market Panic." *Current History,* December 1929.

Raff, Donald M. "Making Cars and Making Money in the Interwar Automobile Industry." *Business History Review,* Winter 1991.

Rothenberg, Al. "The Skinflint of Flint: C. S. Mott Gave Away Millions . . . but He Watched his Pennies." *Ward's Auto World,* May 1, 1996.

————. "Witness to Automotive History: Up Close and Personal with Those Who Lived It." *Ward's Auto World,* May 1, 1996.

Sparkes, Boyden. "A Career in Wall Street." *The Saturday Evening Post,* March 8, 1930.

"What American Labor Wants." *American Mercury,* February 1944.

"Will We Succumb to Collective Begging?" *The Bomber,* UAW-CIO Local 731, May 4, 1945.

Other Documents

Annual Reports, 1919–1947, General Motors Corporation.

Development of Installment Purchasing. Pamphlet, John J. Raskob, Chairman, General Motors Finance Committee, General Motors Corporation, December 1926.

GM World, General Motors' in-house monthly magazine for non-U.S. employees, 1922–1946.

General Motors and Its Labor Policy. Pamphlet, Alfred P. Sloan, Jr., General Motors Corporation, January 5, 1937.

The General Motors Institute of Technology. Pamphlet, Alfred P. Sloan, Jr., General Motors Corporation, March 1929.

The General Motors Strike: The Facts and Their Implications. Pamphlet, Alfred P. Sloan, Jr., April 18, 1946.

General Motors and the Strike Conference. Pamphlet, February 8, 1937.

General Motors Is Not in Politics. Pamphlet, Alfred P. Sloan, Jr., General Motors Corporation, August 1928.

How Members of the General Motors Family Are Made Partners in General Motors. Pamphlet, General Motors Corporation, March 12, 1927.

Installment Selling: A Study in Consumers' Credit with Special Reference to the Automobile. Pamphlet, John J. Raskob, Chairman, General Motors Finance Committee, General Motors Corporation, November 1927.

An Introduction to the Accessory Companies. Pamphlet, Pierre S. du Pont, General Motors Corporation, February 1, 1922.

A Message to Our Employees on Progress of the Strike Situation. Pamphlet, Alfred P. Sloan, Jr., General Motors Corporation, January 27, 1937.

North American Vehicle Sales History, 1910–2000 Calendar Years. Global Market Data Management Staff, General Motors Corporation, 2000.

Pricing Policy in Relation to Financial Control. Pamphlet, Donaldson Brown, General Motors Corporation, 1924.

"Report on the Motor Vehicle Industry." Federal Trade Commission, U.S. Government Printing Office, 1939.

The Story of General Motors. Pamphlet, General Motors Corporation, 1948.

The Story of the General Motors Strike. Pamphlet, Alfred P. Sloan, Jr., General Motors Corporation, April 1937.

"A Study of the Antitrust Laws." Hearings before the Subcommittee on Antitrust and Monopoly of the Committee on the Judiciary, U. S. Senate, S. Res. 61, Parts 1-8, General Motors, December 9, 1955.

To All Employees in General Motors Factories. Pamphlet letter, Alfred P. Sloan, Jr., General Motors Corporation, October 15, 1934.

The Trained Man Wins. Pamphlet, General Motors Corporation, 1926.

Trial Proceedings and Exhibits, DuPont-General Motors Antitrust Case, U.S. Supreme Court, 1954.

The Worker in General Motors. Pamphlet, Alfred P. Sloan, Jr., December 1937.

We Sat Down with the Strikers and General Motors. Pamphlet, Hartley W. Barclay, United Automobile Workers of America, 1956.

INDEX

AC Spark Plug, 143–144, 236
Adam Opel, 258, 269
Adventures of a White Collar Man
   (Sloan), 12–13, 43, 60, 71–72,
   246, 274–275
advertising, xvii, 60, 272
air-cooled engine, 239–245, 254,
   255
Aldrich, Fred, 81, 93–94
Alexander Manufacturing Com-
   pany, 88
Alfred P. Sloan Foundation, 39
Alger, John, 28, 31, 93
Allison division, General Motors,
   270
aluminum-block engine, 270
Amalgamated Copper Company,
   139
American Century, The (Evans),
   265
American Federation of Labor
   (AFL), 80
American Locomotive Company,
   160–162
American Motors, 59
American Sugar Refining Company, 43–45
Anderson, Robert, 52
annual model change, 255–257
annual performance bonuses, 263,
   264
Apperson, Edgar, 58
Arrow (racer), 73–74
assembly lines, 34, 59, 72, 154,
   174, 179–182, 214
Association of Licensed Automobile Manufacturers (ALAM),
   52–53, 85, 138, 140

Austin Healey, 257
automatic transmissions, 254
automobile industry
   advertising by, xvii, 60, 272
   automobile shows, 51, 59–60,
      70, 72–73, 85, 97–99, 161,
      243
   car races, 54–57, 69, 73–74,
      104, 112, 134, 141–142, 167,
      169–170, 174–175, 178
   development of, 52–56
   rise of, 47–49, 51–52
   World War I and, 4, 210–214
   World War II and, 39, 268–271

Baby Grand (Chevrolet), 176–177
Bank One, 159
Barthel, Oliver, 68
Bedford Motors, Ltd., 144
Belin, Lammot, 190
Bennett, F. S., 135
Benz, Karl, 53–55
Blout Carriage and Buggy, 36
bonus plans, 184, 263, 264
bowling, 276
Brinkley, Douglas, 113, 138
Briscoe, Benjamin, 90–91, 116–
   120, 123–125, 127
Briscoe, Walter, 90–91, 127
Brown, Donaldson, 260–261, 265
Brown & Sharpe, 61–62
Budd, Ralph, 259
Buick, David Dunbar, 88–92, 96,
   106–107, 116, 127, 175, 213
Buick/Buick Motor division, Gen-
   eral Motors, 3, 78, 87–99,
   101–108, 112–113, 116, 118,
   119, 122–125, 127, 147–148,

General Motors (*continued*)
  bid to purchase Ford Motor
    Company, 137–141
  capitalization at $1 billion, 13
  creation in 1908, xviii, 124–
    128, 152, 235
  crisis of 1910, 147–168,
    170–171
  crisis of 1920, 1–15, 19, 46–47,
    120, 221–236, 260, 278–279
  dividend of 1915, 189–190
  divisions in 1949, 222
  employee benefits and, 5–6,
    9–11, 38–39
  employee relations, 38–39, 81
  end of voting-trust agreement,
    187–190
  headquarters in Detroit, 4, 38,
    172, 221–222, 227–228
  incorporation in New Jersey,
    126–127
  innovations of, 253–254
  product design, 131–133,
    254–255
  proxy battle of 1915, 190–193,
    196
  public relations department, 40
  recapitalization of 1919, 219
  sales trends, 2, 13, 185, 224–
    227, 252, 268
  stock issuance to executives,
    262–263
  unions and, 38–39, 181, 264,
    265–268, 270
  voting-trust agreement, 147–
    168, 178, 185, 187–190
  wartime mobilizations, 4, 39,
    210–214, 268–271
General Motors Acceptance Corporation (GMAC), 6, 222, 251
General Motors Europe, Ltd., 222
General Motors Export Company,
  165–166, 222, 257–258,
  269–270

General Motors Institute (GMI),
  40, 262
General Motors Japan, 257–258
General Motors of Canada (GM-
  Canada), 144, 177, 222, 276
General Motors Research,
  239–242
Gilded Age, 36, 81
GMAC (General Motors Accep-
  tance Corporation), 6, 222,
  251
GMC Truck division, General Mo-
  tors, 144, 166, 222
golden parachutes, 234
Goss, Arnold, 148
Great Depression, 5–6, 12, 38,
  159, 174–175, 237, 253, 265
Green, Fitzhugh, 19, 231, 275–276
Guardian Frigerator, 6

Halberstam, David, 272
Harding, Warren G., 3–4, 209
Hardy, A. B. C., 81, 83–86, 90–91,
  148, 173
Harrison Radiator, 203–204
Haskell, J. A., 5–6, 9, 190, 194
Haynes, Elwood, 47–48, 54, 55, 58
health insurance, 38, 267–268,
  272
Heany, John A., 145
Heany Lamp, 145
hierarchical command-and-con-
  trol culture, 271–272
Hills, Herbert H., 94
Hitler, Adolf, 209, 269–270
holding company status, 119–
  120, 125–127, 133, 136, 147–
  148, 150, 199–200, 222
Hoover, Herbert, 273–274
Hoover, J. Edgar, 269
Horowitz, David, 68
Howard, Charles S., 46, 98–99
Hudson Motor Company, 59

Hyatt, John, 44
Hyatt Roller Bearing Company, 43–49, 56, 60, 70–73, 99–101, 108, 109–112, 114, 155–157, 182, 198–200, 202, 219, 249–250
Hygienic Refrigerator, 44

incremental design and engineering, 132–133
independent front-wheel suspension, 254
installment buying, 6, 222, 251
integrated supplier networks, 202–204
interchangeable parts, 72–73, 134–135, 180, 214
internal combustion engine, 77, 154, 254
International Motor Company, 125, 126
interstate highway system, 154–155

J. P. Morgan and Company, 116–127, 137, 139–140, 147–148, 189, 229–231, 273
Jazz Age, 4
Jefferson, Thomas, 59
John, W. A. P., 229–231, 233
Johnson Company, 183–184

kanban, 100
Kaufman, Louis G., 46, 188–190, 201
keiretsu, 202
Kennedy, Joseph P., 273
Kettering, Charles "Boss," 166–167, 198, 201–202, 239–243, 254, 255, 259
Kettering University, 40
King, Charles, 54, 56
Klaxon Company, 203–204

Klingensmith, Frank, 207
Knudsen, William K., 242–243, 245, 249, 264, 266, 268–269
Ku Klux Klan, 3–4

Lacey, Robert, 66, 69
LaSalle, 254–255
leaded gasoline, 253–254
Lee, Higginson and Company, 12, 149–150, 157–159, 162, 189
Leland, Falconer & Norton, 62–63, 135, 165
Leland, Henry Martyn, 61–63, 69–72, 77, 78, 89, 94, 103, 104, 106, 112, 134–137, 159–160, 165–167, 180, 194, 203, 210–214
Leland, Wilfred, 134–137, 148, 150, 159–160, 165, 210–214
Lenoir, Jean-Joseph-Etienne, 52
Liberty aircraft engines, 211, 213
Life of an American Workman (Chrysler), 7, 12
Lincoln (model), 61
Lincoln, Abraham, 61, 213
Lincoln Motor Company, 213–214
Lindberg, Charles, 19, 231
Little, "Big" Bill, 172, 173
Little Motor Car Company, 171–172

Malcomson, Alexander, 74–75, 112–113, 114–115
market segmentation, 35–36, 104, 154, 249, 251–252
Marr, Walter, 89, 91–92, 103
Martini, Francesco di Giorgio, 52
Mason, Arthur, 103–104, 171
Mason engine, 103–104
Mason Motor Company, 171, 173
Massachusetts Institute of Technology (MIT), Sloan School of Management, 39–40

ABOUT THE AUTHOR

WILLIAM PELFREY is a veteran U.S. Foreign Service Officer (FSO) and former director of executive communications for General Motors Corporation, where he was also speechwriter and public relations counselor for the CEO and chairman of the board. Before entering public service and then the corporate world, he reported from Vietnam, Appalachia, and Pakistan for *The New York Times, The Atlantic Monthly,* and *The New Republic.* His first book, *The Big V,* was the first Vietnam war novel written by a combat infantryman. It was nominated for the National Book Award and won him a National Endowment for the Arts fellowship.